FROM FATWA TO JIHAD

FROM FATWA TO JIHAD

The Rushdie Affair and Its Aftermath

Kenan Malik

MELVILLE HOUSE PUBLISHING
BROOKLYN, NEW YORK

FROM FATWA TO JIHAD

First published in hardcover in Great Britain in 2009
by Atlantic Books, an imprint of Grove Atlantic Ltd.

Copyright © Kenan Malik, 2009

First Melville House Printing: June 2010

Melville House Publishing
145 Plymouth Street
Brooklyn, New York 11201
mhpbooks.com

ISBN: 978-1-935554-00-4

Library of Congress Control Number: 2010923402

For Carmen
(who seems to have little trouble with
the concept of free expression)

Contents

How Salman Rushdie changed my life

'A poet's work,' he answers. 'To name the unnamable, to point at frauds, to take sides, start arguments, shape the world and stop it from going to sleep.' And if rivers of blood flow from the cuts his verses inflict, then they will nourish him.

Salman Rushdie, *The Satanic Verses*, p.97.

1

It was February 1989. I was in Bradford, a grey town in northern England. Nestled in the hills of West Yorkshire, it was a place dominated by its woollen mills, huge Victorian structures that seemed to reach up into the clouds, though by the late eighties few were still producing any wool. Surrounding the now derelict mills were row upon row of dreary back-to-back houses that had become as decayed as the textile industry itself. The mood of the town was not improved by a climate grey like its brickwork.

It was a town of which few people outside of Britain would have heard. Until, that is, a thousand Muslim protestors had, the previous month, paraded with a copy of Salman Rushdie's *The Satanic Verses*, before ceremoniously burning the book. The novel was tied to a stake before being set alight in front of the police station. It was an act calculated to shock and offend. It did more than that. The burning book became an icon of the rage of Islam. Sent around the world by a multitude of photographers and TV cameras, the image proclaimed, 'I am a portent of a new kind of conflict and of a new kind of world.'

Ten months after that January demonstration an even more arresting image captured the world's imagination: protestors on top of the Berlin Wall hacking away at their imprisonment. These two images – the burning book in Bradford, the crumbling wall in Berlin – came in the following years to be inextricably linked in many people's minds. As the Cold War ended, so the clash of ideologies that had defined the world since the Second World War seemed to give way to what the American political scientist Samuel Huntington would later make famous as 'the clash of civilizations' (a phrase he had borrowed from the historian Bernard Lewis). The conflicts that had convulsed Europe over the past centuries, Huntington wrote, from the wars of religion between Protestants and Catholics to the Cold War, were all 'conflicts within Western civilization'. The 'battle lines of the future' would be between civilizations. Huntington identified a number of civilizations, including Confucian, Japanese, Hindu, Orthodox, Latin American and African. The primary struggle, however, would be, he believed, between the Christian West and the Islamic East. Such a struggle would be 'far more fundamental' than any war unleashed by 'differences among political ideologies and political regimes'. The 'people of different civilizations have different views on the relations between God and man, the individual and the group, the citizen and the state, parents and children, husband and wife, as well as differing views of the relative importance of rights and responsibilities, liberty and authority, equality and hierarchy'.

Huntington did not write those words until 1993. But already, four years earlier, many had seen in the battle over *The Satanic Verses* just such a civilizational struggle. On one side of the fault line stood the West, with its liberal democratic traditions, a scientific worldview and a secular, rationalist culture drawn from the Enlightenment; on the other was Islam, rooted in a pre-medieval theology, with its seeming disrespect for democracy, disdain for scientific rationalism and deeply illiberal attitudes on everything from crime to women's rights. 'All over again,' the novelist Martin Amis would later write, 'the West confronts an irrationalist, agonistic, theocratic/ideocratic system which is essentially and unappeasably opposed to its existence.' Amis wrote that while still in shock over 9/11. The germ of the sentiment was planted much earlier, in the Rushdie affair.

Shocked by the sight of British Muslims threatening a British author and publicly burning his book, many people started asking a question that in 1989 was startlingly new: are Islamic values compatible with those of a modern, Western, liberal democracy? The Bible, the novelist, feminist and secularist Fay Weldon wrote in her pamphlet *Sacred Cows*, provides 'food for thought' out of which 'You can build a decent society'. The Qur'an offers 'food for no thought. It is not a poem on which a society can be safely or sensibly based. It forbids change, interpretation, self-knowledge, even art, for fear of treading on Allah's creative toes.' Or as the daytime TV chat-show host and one-time Labour MP Robert Kilroy-Silk put it, 'If Britain's resident ayatollahs cannot accept British values and laws then there is no reason at all why the British should feel any need, still less compulsion, to accommodate theirs.'

Even those who had originally welcomed Muslims into Britain were having second thoughts. As one of Britain's most liberal Home Secretaries, Roy Jenkins had, in 1966, announced an end to this country's policy of assimilation and launched instead a new era of 'cultural diversity, coupled with equal opportunity in an atmosphere of mutual tolerance' – one of the first expressions of what came to be known as 'multiculturalism'. Nearly a quarter of a century later, the now ennobled Lord Jenkins mused in the wake of the burning book that 'in retrospect we might have been more cautious about allowing the creation in the 1950s of substantial Muslim communities here'.

I had watched the burning of *The Satanic Verses* with more than a passing interest. Like Salman Rushdie, I was born in India, in Secunderabad, not far from Rushdie's own birthplace of Mumbai (or Bombay, as it was then), but brought up in Britain. Like Rushdie, I was of a generation that did not think of itself as 'Muslim' or 'Hindu' or 'Sikh', or even as 'Asian', but rather as 'black'. 'Black' was for us not an ethnic label but a political badge (although we never defined who exactly could wear that badge). Unlike our parents' generation, who had largely put up with discrimination, we were fierce in our opposition to racism. But we were equally hostile to the traditions that often marked immigrant communities, especially religious ones. Today, when people use the word 'radical' in an Islamic context, they usually have in mind a religious fundamentalist. Twenty years ago 'radical' meant the very opposite: someone who was militantly secular, self-consciously Western and avowedly left-wing. Someone like me.

I had grown up in communities in which Islam, while deeply embedded, was never all-consuming – indeed, communities that had never thought of themselves as 'Muslim', and for which religion expressed a relationship with God, not a sacrosanct public identity. 'Officially, as it were,' observes Jamal Khan, the narrator of Hanif Kureishi's novel *Something to Tell You*, 'we were called immigrants, I think. Later for political reasons we were "blacks" . . . In Britain we were still called Asians, though we're no more Asian than the English are European. It was a long time before we became known as Muslims, a new imprimatur, and then for political reasons.' So what, I wanted to know, as I watched the pictures of that demonstration, had changed? Why, I wondered, were people now proclaiming themselves to be Muslims and taking to the streets to burn books – especially the books of a writer celebrated for giving voice to the migrant experience? And was the dividing line really between a medieval theology and a modern Western society?

My day job then was as a research psychologist. But I also wrote the occasional article for the *Voice*, Britain's leading black newspaper. When the editor asked me to write something about the Rushdie affair, I jumped at the chance. I already knew Bradford, and many of the players in the Rushdie drama, having organized anti-racist protests in the town, including a march against racist attacks in 1986. And so I arrived that February to talk to Sher Azam, president of the Bradford Council of Mosques, the man who had helped torch the book. I came also to try to answer my own questions. It was a journey that would transform my own views about myself, my politics and my faith – and continues to do so. Little did I know that those questions would return to haunt me again and again over the next twenty years, or that the issues raised by the Rushdie affair – the nature of Islam, its relationship to the West, the meaning of multiculturalism, the limits of tolerance in a liberal society – would become some of the defining problems of the age, linking the burning book in Bradford to the burning towers in Manhattan on 9/11 and the burning bus in London on 7/7.

2

When *The Satanic Verses* was published in September 1988, it had been expected to set the world alight, though not quite in the way that it did. Salman Rushdie was then perhaps the most celebrated British novelist of his generation. Not that he saw himself as British. He was, he said, someone inhabiting a world 'in between' three cultures: those of India, Pakistan and England. *Midnight's Children*, his sprawling, panoramic, humorous mock-epic of post-independence India, was a literary sensation when it came out in 1981. It interlaced reality, myth, dream and fantasy, turned history into fable, and yet directly addressed highly charged contemporary political issues. The swagger of its historical sweep, the panache of its confident, modernist prose, the knowingness of its infectious humour, the confidence with which it drew upon European classics, Hindu myths, Persian fables, Islamic history, as well as popular cultures from Bollywood to Bob Dylan, and its insistence that the creative imagination was also a political imagination – all announced the arrival of not just a new literary voice but also a new kind of novel, the aim of which was to unlock the untold tales of those who, like Rushdie, inhabited the worlds 'in between'. Politicians, Rushdie once remarked, 'have got very good at inventing fictions which they tell us as the truth. It then becomes the job of the makers of fiction to start telling the real truth.' *Midnight's Children* won the Booker Prize in 1981, and went on to win in 1993 the Booker of Bookers, as the greatest of all Booker Prize winners. Fifteen years later, when Man Booker reran the competition to celebrate the fortieth anniversary of the prize, it again returned triumphant, having by now established itself as perhaps the most important British novel of the post-war years.

Two years after *Midnight's Children* came *Shame*, which retold the history of Pakistan as a satirical fairy tale. Many saw it as a certainty to win the Booker Prize again, but it lost out to J.M. Coetzee's *Life and Times of Michael K*. Nevertheless, *Shame* consolidated Rushdie's reputation both as a novelist and as a controversialist. *Midnight's Children* had been banned in India for its acid portrayal of the Nehru dynasty. Indira Gandhi sued for libel in a London court and won, which was not surprising, given that Britain's libel laws were – and remain – as archaic as the regime that Rushdie was satirizing. *Shame* caused similar outrage among Pakistan's political elite (the late Benazir Bhutto reputedly took particular exception to Rushdie's mocking of her as the Virgin Ironpants) and was again banned.

And then came *The Satanic Verses*. Almost five years in the making, supported by a then virtually unheard-of $850,000 advance from his new publishers, Penguin, and published in the wake of a much talked-about split between Rushdie and his long-time friend and publisher, Liz Calder of Bloomsbury, the novel had become myth even before the public had read a word of it. Rushdie could undoubtedly have written an acidly baroque tale about its gestation.

In an interview in the Australian literary magazine *Scripsi* in 1985, Rushdie mentioned that he was working on two novels. One was 'about God . . . that was not just a secular sneer'; the other was 'a much larger project . . . a novel set in the West that deals with the idea of migration'. Over the next three years, the two became stitched together into a not altogether coherent whole: one a fantastic tale about the migrant experience in Britain, the other a fable about the origins of Islam. Rushdie himself seemed somewhat uncertain about the character of the novel, both describing it as 'a serious attempt to write about religion and revelation from the point of view of a secular person', and insisting that 'the book isn't actually about Islam, but about migration, metamorphosis, divided selves, love, death'.

The Satanic Verses opens with a hijacked jumbo jet exploding above the Sussex coast. There are only two survivors. Gibreel Farishta is a Bollywood superstar who depicts gods and is revered as one by his fans. Saladin Chamcha is an Anglophile – 'more-loyal-than-the-Queen' – so fanatically British that he wears a bowler hat even when tumbling from 29,002 feet (the height of Mount Everest and the very height at which the aircraft was blown up). As they fall, Saladin and Gibreel metamorphose. Saladin becomes hairy and goat-like, his feet turn to hoofs and he sprouts horns. Gibreel acquires a halo that he has to hide under a hat. The two men become the unwitting, and unwilling, protagonists in an eternal battle between good and evil, the divine and the satanic.

The progress of Saladin and Gibreel through the dark, surreal landscape of Vilayet (the Hindi word for 'foreign place', which Rushdie uses as a label for Britain) acts as the holding frame for the novel. Into this frame Rushdie inserts a number of novellas, each arising out of Gibreel's dreams, and each of which confronts the nature of religion. The first tells the story of God's revelation to the Prophet Mahound and how the new religion of Submission swept through Jahilia, a city built entirely of sand. This is a fictionalized, satirical account of the creation of Islam. Mahound is an ancient Christian derogatory name for Muhammad, Submission is the literal translation of 'Islam', and *jahiliyyah* is an Arabic word for 'ignorance', used by Muslims to describe the condition in which Arabs found themselves before the revelation of the Qur'an to Muhammad. The second novella concerns an imam in London (who, as Rushdie would put it, both is and is not Ayatollah Khomeini exiled in Paris) and his uncompromising struggle against the ruler of contemporary Jahilia. A third tells of Ayesha, a visionary peasant girl shrouded in butterflies, who leads her entire Indian village on a pilgrimage to Mecca during which they all walk into the sea and drown, a story based on a real event. Rushdie weaves into this tapestry the threads of other stories, of love and passion, betrayal and faith, reconciliation and death.

The Satanic Verses is held together not by a conventional narrative structure but by a cat's cradle of cross-referenced names, images and allusions. Mount Cone is the mountain on which Mahound receives his revelation; Allie Cone is the mountaineer whom Gibreel loves. Allie

Cone's dream is a solo ascent of Everest; in Bombay, Gibreel lives at the very top of the Everest Apartments. Hind was the wife of the Grandee of Jahilia and Mahound's mortal enemy; she is also the wife of Muhammed Sufyanin, in whose café Saladin finds refuge. Ayesha is the visionary who leads the suicidal pilgrimage to Mecca; she is also the empress of present-day Jahilia, against whom the exiled imam wages war. The imam's henchmen are avatars of those in the service of Mahound. And so it goes on. The result is a complex, chaotic novel, the sheer bravura of which sweeps the reader along.

A work as boisterous, allusive and transgressive as *The Satanic Verses* would never give itself up to a single reading. Yet it was also, as Rushdie's previous novels had been, a politically engaged work which, through its imaginative reworkings of modern Vilayet and ancient Jahilia, confronted many of the most charged questions of our time, religious and secular. Inevitably, many readers overlooked the unruliness of the novel and took instead a one-eyed view of Rushdie's words. Western critics rarely saw beyond a migrant's tale. Many Muslims were blind to anything aside from what they perceived as a gratuitously blasphemous assault on their faith. *The Satanic Verses*, the novelist Angela Carter observed in a review in the *Guardian*, was 'an epic hung about with ragbag scraps of many different cultures'. It was peopled 'mostly by displaced persons of one kind or another. Expatriates, immigrants, refugees.' Not once in her review did she mention Islam. For the Muslim philosopher Shabbir Akhtar, on the other hand, Rushdie's novel was an 'inferior piece of hate literature' which 'falsified historical records' in 'a calculated attempt to vilify and slander Muhammad'. From the space between these two readings emerged the Rushdie affair.

3

The Rushdie affair was the moment at which a new Islam dramatically announced itself as a major political issue in Western society. It was also the moment when Britain realized it was facing a new kind of social conflict. From the very beginnings of post-war immigration, blacks and Asians had been involved in bitter conflicts with authority. In 1958 the Notting Hill race riots in west London led the local Labour MP George Rogers to declare that 'the tremendous influx of coloured people from the Commonwealth' had helped 'foster vice, drugs, prostitution and the use of knives'. He added that 'For years white people have been tolerant. Now their tempers are up.' Two decades later, Notting Hill had become home to the largest carnival outside the Caribbean – and to explosive confrontations between police and black youth. In 1976, as reggae star Junior Murvin's 'Police and Thieves' pumped out of the sound systems – 'Police and thieves in the streets / Fighting the nation with their guns and ammunition' – the carnival degenerated into bitter street battles. The following year came the Grunwick dispute, in which the struggle of a group of low-paid Asian women to form a union led to violent confrontation and became a national cause célèbre, with mass pickets outside the factory gates and miners and postal workers taking industrial action in support of the women. And, of course, there were the inner-city riots of the 1980s, culminating in the Broadwater Farm confrontation in 1985.

All these conflicts raised tensions and generated widespread and often fractious debates about the desirability of mass immigration. But these were also in the main political struggles, or issues of law and order. Confrontations over unionization or discrimination or police harassment were of a kind that was familiar even prior to mass immigration.

The Rushdie affair was different. It was the first major cultural conflict, a controversy quite unlike anything that Britain had previously experienced. Muslim fury seemed to be driven not by questions of harassment or discrimination or poverty, but by a sense of hurt that Salman Rushdie's words had offended their deepest beliefs. Where did such hurt come from, and why was it being expressed now? How could a novel create such outrage? Could Muslim anguish be assuaged, and should it be? How did the anger on the streets of Bradford relate to traditional political questions about rights, duties and entitlements? Britain had never asked itself such questions before. Twenty years on, it is still groping for the answers.

4

The Rushdie affair was a turning point in the relationship between British society and its Muslim communities. It was a turning point for me too.

I was born in India, but came to Britain in the sixties as a five-year-old. My mother came from Tamil Nadu in southern India. She was Hindu. My father's family had moved to India from Burma when the Japanese invaded in 1942. It is through him that I trace my Muslim heritage. Mine was not, however, a particularly religious upbringing. My parents forbade me (and my sisters) from attending religious education classes at school, because they did not want us to be force-fed Christianity. But we were not force-fed Islam or Hinduism either. I still barely know the Hindu scriptures, and while I read the Qur'an in my youth, it was only after the Rushdie affair that I took a serious interest in it.

What shaped my early experiences was not religion but racism. I arrived in Britain just as 'Paki-bashing' was becoming a national sport. 'Paki' was the abusive name for any Asian, and 'Paki-bashing' was what racists called their pastime of hunting out and beating up Asians. My main memory of growing up in the 1970s was of being involved almost daily in fights with racists, and of how normal it seemed to come home with a bloody nose or a black eye. (A few years ago I was making a TV documentary on which the runner was a young, hip, street-wise Asian, just out of university. During a conversation I happened to mention 'Paki-bashing'. 'What's Paki-bashing?' he asked, genuinely puzzled, never having heard the phrase, still less having experienced its effects – an indication of how much Britain has changed in the past thirty years.)

Like many Asians of my generation, I was drawn towards politics by my experience of racism. I was left-wing, and, indeed, joined a number of far-left organizations in my twenties. But if it was racism that drew me to politics, it was politics that made me see beyond the narrow confines of racism. I came to learn that there was more to social justice than the injustices done to me, and that a person's skin color, ethnicity or culture was no guide to the validity of his or her political beliefs. Through politics, I was introduced to the ideas of the Enlightenment, and to concepts of a common humanity and universal rights. Through politics, too, I discovered the writings of Marx and Mill, Kant and Locke, Paine and Condorcet, Frantz Fanon and C.L.R. James.

By the end of the 1980s, however, many of my friends had come to see such Enlightenment notions as dangerously naive. The Rushdie affair gave notice not just of a new Islam but also of a new left. Radicals slowly lost faith in secular universalism and began talking instead about multiculturalism and group rights. They became disenchanted with Enlightenment ideas of rationalism and humanism, and many began to decry the Enlightenment as a 'Eurocentric' project. Where once the left had argued that everyone should be treated equally, despite their racial, ethnic, religious or cultural differences, now it pushed the idea that different people should be treated differently *because* of such differences. Lee Jasper, who became the Mayor of London's race advisor in 2000, cut his teeth in anti-racist campaigning in the late 1980s, being a founder member of such organizations as the National Black Caucus and the National Assembly Against Racism. 'You have to treat people differently to treat them equally,' he told me when I interviewed him for a Channel 4 TV documentary in 2003.

Over the past two decades many of the ideas of the so-called 'politics of difference' have become mainstream through the policies of multiculturalism. *We're All Multiculturalists Now*, observed Nathan Glazer, the

American sociologist and former critic of pluralism, in the title of a book. And indeed we are. The celebration of difference, respect for pluralism, avowal of identity politics – these have come to be regarded as the hallmarks of a progressive, anti-racist outlook and as the foundation stones of modern liberal democracies. Yet there is a much darker side to multiculturalism, as the Rushdie affair demonstrated. Multiculturalism has helped foster a more tribal England and, within Muslim communities, has undermined progressive trends while strengthening the hand of conservative religious leaders. While it did not create militant Islam, it helped, as we shall see in this book, create for it a space within British Muslim communities that had not existed before.

5

I was in the drab Victorian semi near the university that housed the Bradford Council of Mosques, waiting to speak to the Council's chairman, Sher Azam. Suddenly, I heard a familiar voice.

'Hello, Kenan, what are you doing here?'

It was Hassan, a friend from London, whom I had not seen for over a year. 'I'm doing some interviews about Rushdie,' I told him. 'But what are you doing in this God-forsaken place?'

Hassan laughed. 'Trying to make it less God-forsaken,' he said. 'I've been up here a few months, helping in the campaign against Rushdie.' And then he laughed again when he saw my face. 'No need to look so shocked,' he said. He had had it with the 'white left'. He had got tired of all those dreary political meetings and the hours spent on street corners selling newspapers that no one wanted. But it had also become something more than simply disaffection with radical politics. He had, he said, lost his sense of who he was and where he'd come from. So he had returned to Bradford to try to rediscover it. And what he had found was a sense of community and a 'need to defend our dignity as Muslims, to defend our values and beliefs'. He was not going to allow anyone – 'racist or Rushdie' – to trample over them.

The Hassan I had known in London had been a member of the far-left Socialist Workers Party (as I had been for a while). Apart from Trotskyism, his other indulgences were Southern Comfort, sex and the Arsenal football club. We had watched the Specials and the Clash together, smoked dope together, argued together about football. We had marched together, chucked bricks together at the National Front, together been arrested.

There was nothing unusual about any of this. This was what it was like for many an Asian growing up in Britain in the 1980s. Hassan had been born, as I had, on the subcontinent (in Pakistan, not India) but brought up in Britain. His parents were observant Muslims, but, like many of their generation, were of the kind that only visited the mosque whenever the 'Friday feeling' gripped them. Hassan had attended mosque as a child, and learnt the Qur'an. But by the time he left school God had left him. 'There's a hole inside me where God used to be,' Salman Rushdie once told an interviewer. I had never detected any such hole in Hassan. He seemed to have been hewn from secular rock. A football fanatic, the only God he worshipped was Liam Brady, Arsenal's magical midfielder. But now here he was in Bradford, an errand boy to the mullahs, inspired by book-burners, willing to shed blood for a thousand-year-old fable that he had never believed in.

Unlike Gibreel Farishta and Saladin Chamcha, Hassan sported neither horns nor a halo. But his metamorphosis from left-wing wide boy to Islamic militant was no less extraordinary than that of the anti-heroes of *The Satanic Verses*. In that metamorphosis lies the story of the wider changes that were taking place both in Britain and in other Western nations, changes that made possible not just the Rushdie affair but eventually 9/11 and 7/7 too. This book is the story of that metamorphosis. It is a guidebook to the road from fatwa to jihad.

CHAPTER ONE

Satanic delusions

> 'Chamcha,' Mishal said excitedly, 'you're a hero. I mean, people can
> really identify with you. It's an image white society has rejected for
> so long that we can really take it, you know, occupy it, inhabit it,
> reclaim it and make it our own. It's time you considered action.'
>
> 'Go away,' cried Saladin, in his bewilderment. 'That isn't what I
> wanted. This is not what I meant, at all.'
>
> Salman Rushdie, *The Satanic Verses*, pp.286–7.

1

'It would be absurd to think that a book can cause riots,' Salman
Rushdie told the Indian journalist Shrabani Basu shortly before publication of *The Satanic Verses*. 'That's a strange sort of view of the world.'
It is in retrospect a comment either extraordinarily naive or piquantly
ironic.

It was in India that the campaign against *The Satanic Verses* began.
Even before it was published in Britain, Kushwant Singh, a distinguished novelist and journalist who acted as an editorial advisor for
Penguin Books India, had raised concerns. He had read the book in
typescript and 'was positive it would cause a lot of trouble'. 'There are,'
he told Chitrita Banerji of *Sunday* magazine, 'several derogatory refer-
ences to the Prophet and the Qur'an. Muhammad is made out to be a
small-time impostor.' Penguin decided to publish the novel in India –
but not under its own imprint.

On 5 October, barely a week after it had been published in Britain, the Indian ministry of finance placed *The Satanic Verses* on its list of proscribed books. The ban, the ministry proclaimed, 'did not detract from the literary and artistic merit of Rushdie's work'. To which Rushdie sardonically replied, 'Thanks for the good review' – while also wondering what the world might make of the fact 'that it is the finance ministry that gets to decide what Indian readers may or may not read'. The ministry was in fact acting on orders from prime minister Rajiv Gandhi, who had been alerted to the issue by a letter from the MP Syed Shahabuddin, a member of the opposition Janata Party and a self-proclaimed champion of India's 150 million-strong Muslim community.

'The very title' of Rushdie's book, Shahabuddin complained in an article in the *Times of India*, was 'suggestively derogatory'. In Islamic theology, the Qur'an is the word of God given to the Prophet Muhammad by the Archangel Gabriel. Muhammad excised two of the original verses believing them to have been inspired by Satan masquerading as Gabriel. These are the Satanic Verses. Rushdie presents the whole of the Qur'an as the work of Muhammad masquerading as the Prophet of God. Mahound, as Rushdie calls Muhammad, is an archaic name for the Prophet used as an insult by the crusaders. And most insultingly, Shahabuddin observed, Rushdie depicts the Prophet's wives as prostitutes in a brothel called the Curtain, the literal translation of *al-hijab*, the Arabic word for the veil. In fact, as Rushdie himself has pointed out, Muhammad's wives do not work in the brothel. Rather, the twelve prostitutes take on the names of the Prophet's wives. For Shahabuddin, however, that amounted to the same.

Like virtually all of Rushdie's opponents, Shahabuddin had not actually read *The Satanic Verses*. 'I do not have to wade through a filthy drain to know what filth is,' he retorted. He had been alerted to the novel's significance by Jamaat-e-Islami activists. Jamaat-e-Islami is an Islamist organization founded in India in 1941 by Sayyid Abul A'la Maududi, one of the heroes of the modern jihadist movement. Rushdie had already taken aim at the Jamaat in *Shame*. Its response was the campaign against *The Satanic Verses*. It organized protests and petitioned Indian MPs. With a general election due in November, the result of which was too close to call, no politician was willing to alienate an important Islamic organization. A ban on *The Satanic Verses* was inevitable, whether or not anyone had read the book, and whatever its 'literary and artistic merit'.

The Jamaat had a network of organizations in Britain, funded by the Saudi government, at the heart of which was the Islamic Foundation, based in Leicester. According to the *Illustrated Weekly of India*, Aslam Ejaz of the Islamic Foundation in Madras wrote to his friend Syed Faiyazuddin Ahmed, who had recently arrived at the Leicester center, about the furor in India over *The Satanic Verses* and urged him to do God's work in Britain. Ahmed bought the book, photocopied extracts, and mailed them to other Islamic groups in Britain and to the London embassies of Muslim countries. Soon afterwards, the Saudi-backed weekly Islamic magazine *Impact International* published a selection of the most controversial passages from *The Satanic Verses*, and Ahmed was invited to Saudi Arabia, where he briefed officials about the novel and mobilized Saudi support for a campaign against it.

The Saudis encouraged a number of Jamaat-influenced organizations in Britain to set up the United Kingdom Action Committee on Islamic Affairs (UKACIA) to coordinate the campaign against what one UKACIA circular described as 'the most offensive, filthy and abusive book ever written by any hostile enemy of Islam'. But however overwrought the language, the Jamaat and the Saudis wanted to keep the anti-Rushdie campaign low-key. The Saudis' style was that of back-room manoeuvrings rather than street protests. They hoped that a combination of diplomatic pressure and financial muscle could suppress *The Satanic Verses*, just as it had managed to ensure that *Death of a Princess*, a 1980 TV documentary hostile to the Saudis, was never reshown on British TV. This time the campaign had little success. Penguin refused to withdraw the book and the British government refused to ban it. Even Muslim states seemed barely interested. Few responded to the Saudi campaign or banned the novel. In November, Pakistan and South Africa followed India's lead in proscribing the book, and soon afterwards Saudi Arabia, Egypt, Bangladesh, Malaysia and Sudan did so too. But in the majority of Muslim countries, including virtually all Arab states, *The Satanic Verses* continued to be freely available, even after the Organization of the Islamic Conference had called for a ban.

In December – almost three months after the publication of the novel – came the first major street protest in Britain. Almost seven thousand Muslims marched through Bolton, another northern mill town, across the Pennines from Bradford. The demonstration was organized not by the Jamaat but by a rival Islamic faction, the Deobandis. The Jamaat possessed money and political influence, thanks to the Saudi connection, but little support on the ground. The majority of British Muslims were Barelwis, a Sufi-influenced tradition founded in India by Ahmad Raza Khan. Most mosques were run by the Deobandis, another movement founded in nineteenth-century British India with the aim of cleansing Islam, which placed particular stress on Qur'anic study and law. They created a network of madrasas throughout India (and subsequently Pakistan), the aim of which was to create a cadre of *ulema*, or religious leaders, capable of issuing fatwas on all aspects of everyday life based on a strict interpretation of the Qur'an. Most leaders of the Taliban, who came to power in Afghanistan in 1996, were trained in the Deobandi tradition. Conflict between Jamaatis, Barelwis and Deobandis was a feature of British Islam, and helped fuel the Rushdie controversy.

The Bolton protest was an impressive call to arms. Almost seven thousand protestors from across Britain marched through a town with a total Muslim population of around ten thousand. As in Bradford, they carried a copy of *The Satanic Verses* which they torched – the first time it had been burnt in anger in Britain. Yet almost no one took any notice. Whatever the grievances of British Muslims about *The Satanic Verses*, they had not yet registered on the national radar.

The Bradford protest the following month was different, partly because Bradford itself was different. In 1985 a Sufi mystic, Pir Maroof Hussain Shah, died. A poster in Urdu displayed in corner-shop windows throughout Britain urged his followers to attend a celebration of his life in Britain's 'Islamabad' – the 'city of Islam'. 'Islamabad' was Bradford. By the 1980s, this small northern town had become the heartbeat of Britain's Muslim communities. The creation of the Bradford Council of

Mosques in 1981, and the close relationship between the mosques, around half of which were controlled by the Deobandis, and Bradford City Council, provided the town's imams with considerable political clout. Bradford's heart also beat strongly to a secular pulse. The Asian Youth Movement, which gave voice to young radical Asians, and was as critical of the mosques as it was of racists, organized strongly in the town. More than a decade of militancy and protest had made Bradford's Muslim leaders – religious and secular – politically astute and media savvy. They understood the gospel of Marshall McLuhan as well as the teachings of the Prophet Muhammad. The demonstrators videoed the protest and dispatched the images to media outlets across the world. The flames that incinerated *The Satanic Verses* were fanned into an international controversy.

In response to the Deobandi demonstrations the Jamaat organized its own street protests – not in Britain but in Pakistan, a country that had already banned the novel. But the Islamic Democratic Alliance, of which Jamaat-e-Islami was an influential part, had recently lost an election to Benazir Bhutto's Pakistan People's Party. 'Was the agitation really against the book which has not been read in Pakistan, is not for sale in Pakistan,' Bhutto wondered, or 'was it a protest by those people who lost the election . . . to try and destabilize the process of democracy'? The Jamaat organized an anti-Rushdie demonstration on 12 February, targeting neither the British embassy nor the offices of Penguin Books, but the American Cultural Centre in Islamabad. An angry Jamaat-led mob, 2000-strong according to some reports, 10,000-strong according to others, tried to storm the center, shouting 'Allahu Akhbar' and 'American Dogs'. They pulled down the Stars and Stripes flying on top of the building and burnt it, along with an effigy of Salman Rushdie. Eyewitnesses described the police repeatedly firing into the crowd with semi-automatic rifles and pump-action shotguns. By the end of the day at least five people had been killed and more than a hundred injured – the first fatalities of the Rushdie affair.

Yet even now fury about *The Satanic Verses* was largely confined to Muslims in the Indian subcontinent and in Britain. Critics of Rushdie

5

have consistently argued that the blasphemies in his novel caused mortal offence to all Muslims. 'The life of the Prophet Muhammad', the liberal Muslim writer Ziauddin Sardar has observed, 'is the source of Muslim identity.' Because 'the Prophet and his personality define Islam', so 'every Muslim relates to him directly and personally'. That is why Sardar 'felt that every word, every jibe, every obscenity in *The Satanic Verses* was directed at me – personally'. Every Muslim would have felt the same, Sardar insisted. 'Just as people threatened with physical genocide react to defend themselves, Muslims en masse would protest against this annihilation of their cultural identity.'

Leaving aside the question of whether the blasphemies in *The Satanic Verses* are really any more offensive than, say, the attempt to compare the publication of a novel with the Final Solution, Sardar's claim that all Muslims would see such blasphemies as the 'annihilation of their cultural identity' was not borne out by events. The novel had little impact on Muslims in other European countries. There is no evidence that on reading the book French or German Muslims imagined, as Sardar did, that 'this is how . . . it must feel to be raped'. There was barely a squeak of protest in either country when the novel was published there. In America there was an organized letter campaign aimed at Viking Penguin, and bomb threats against its offices, but no mass protests as in Britain, India or Pakistan. Arabs and Turks, too, seemed as unmoved by Rushdie's blasphemies as did their European and American brethren.

Even within the Islamic Republic of Iran there appeared to be little concern. Unlike the governments of India, Pakistan, Saudi Arabia and South Africa, Tehran's revolutionary mullahs felt no need to ban the book. In December 1988, *Kayhan Farangi*, a leading Iranian literary journal, published a review. *The Satanic Verses*, it suggested, 'contains a number of false interpretations about Islam and gives wrong portrayals of the Qur'an and the Prophet Muhammad. It also draws a caricature-like and distorted image of Islamic principles which lacks even the slightest artistic credentials.' Though highly critical of the novel, there was no intimation that the 'distorted images' amounted to blasphemy or that Rushdie's 'moral degradation' constituted apostasy. Nor was there any suggestion that *The Satanic Verses* was, as the Jamaat-inspired United Kingdom Action Committee put it, 'the most offensive, filthy and abusive book ever written by any hostile enemy of Islam'. *Kayhan Farangi* acknowledged Rushdie's insistence 'that his book is nothing more than a work of imagination which tries to investigate the birth of a major religion from the point of view of a secular individual'. It acknowledged, too, Rushdie's fear that the campaign against the novel in the subcontinent was driven by politics rather than theology. As Indian politicians attempted to 'win the hearts and minds of 100 million Muslims', so *The Satanic Verses* had 'become a ball in this political game'.

Today, Ghayasuddin Siddiqui is a founding trustee of British Muslims for Secular Democracy. Twenty years ago his views about Islam and secularism were very different. He was a great admirer of the Iranian revolution and, in 1974, one of the founders, together with the scholar Kalim Siddiqui and the writer Ziauddin Sardar, of the Muslim Institute, a London-based organization that was eventually entirely funded by Tehran. Sardar, who soon became disenchanted with the revolution, describes the Institute as 'an extension of the Iranian embassy in London'. 'Being the first Sunni organization to support the revolution, we had privileged access to the revolutionaries,' says Ghayasuddin Siddiqui. He was frequently in Tehran and in the autumn of 1988 had plenty of discussions about *The Satanic Verses*, in street cafés and government ministries. 'There was little hostility to the novel,' he recalls. 'It was widely discussed. There were even some good reviews in the press.'

2

It was the evening of 13 February 1989. Ghayasuddin Siddiqui and Kalim Siddiqui were in Tehran attending a conference. On the way home they were, as usual, ushered into the VIP lounge at the airport. Waiting for them was Mohammad Khatami. Almost a decade later Khatami would become the most liberal of Iran's post-revolutionary presidents. In 1989 he was in charge of the Ministry of Religious Guidance. 'He took Kalim aside,' remembers Siddiqui, 'and they were engaged in earnest discussion. When he came back, I asked him what that was about. "He wanted to know about Rushdie's book," Kalim said. "What did you tell him?" I asked. And Kalim said with a laugh, "I told him it was obnoxious."'

At the same time as Kalim Siddiqui was conferring with Mohammad Khatami, on the other side of the city, in his modest house, Ayatollah Khomeini was summoning a secretary. He dictated a simple four-paragraph message:

In the name of Him, the Highest. There is only one God, to whom we shall all return. I inform all zealous Muslims of the world that the author of the book entitled *The Satanic Verses* – which has been compiled, printed and published in opposition to Islam, the Prophet and the Qur'an – and all those involved in its publication who were aware of its contents, are sentenced to death.

I call on all zealous Muslims to execute them quickly, wherever they may be found, so that no one else will dare to insult the Muslim sanctities. God willing, whoever is killed on this path is a martyr.

In addition, anyone who has access to the author of this book, but does not possess the power to execute him, should report him to the people so that he may be punished for his actions.

May peace and the mercy of God and His blessings be with you. Ruhollah al-Musavi al-Khomeini, 25 Bahman 1367

The following day – 14 February, Valentine's Day – the sheet of paper was hand-delivered to Tehran Radio just before the 2 p.m. news, at the start of which it was read out. It was a message that was to transform the Rushdie affair.

At the very moment that Khomeini was dictating his death sentence, Salman Rushdie was attending a book party for his American wife Marianne Wiggins's new novel *John Dollar* in the elegant art deco atrium of Michelin House on the Fulham Road in west London. They were plan-

ning a joint book tour of America. Apprehensive about the consequences of the riots in Pakistan, they spent that night with friends
rather than in their Islington home. It was early next morning that a
telephone call from the BBC World Service alerted Rushdie to the fatwa.
Within hours he was in the BBC studios at Broadcasting House in
central London responding to Khomeini's edict. 'I am very sad it should
have happened,' he said. 'It is not true this book is a blasphemy against
Islam. I doubt very much Khomeini or anyone else in Iran has read the
book, or anything more than selected extracts taken out of context.'
Later, interviewed for the CBS *This Morning* television show, Rushdie
added, 'Frankly, I wish I had written a more critical book. A religion
that claims it is able to behave like this, religious leaders who are able
to behave like this, and then say this is a religion that must be above
any kind of whisper of criticism: that doesn't add up.'

'By the time I came off the air,' Rushdie recalled a year later, 'Marianne
had rung the studio and said, "Don't come home, because everybody and
his mother is parked on the pavement."' Rushdie was smuggled instead
into his agent's office, where 'of course every telephone in the building
was ringing non-stop and everybody was being told I wasn't there'.

He was due that evening to attend a memorial service for the writer
Bruce Chatwin, who had been 'probably my closest writer friend'. Should
he go? 'It was very important for me to go to that service,' Rushdie
recalled, 'but I had no way of knowing what I should or shouldn't do.
In the end I just said, "The hell with it, let's go."' It was to be Rushdie's
last public appearance for years. 'Your turn next,' the travel writer Paul
Theroux whispered to him on leaving the church. 'I suppose we'll be
back here for you next week.' 'It wasn't the funniest joke I ever heard,'
Rushdie later remarked, 'but I did write him a letter subsequently
saying that I was glad he's a less good prophet than he's a novelist.'

By the following morning there was not just a fatwa against Rushdie
but a price on his head. Hossain San'ei, leader of the 15 Khordad, a
Tehran-based charitable foundation set up to uphold Islamic principles
in Iran, offered $3 million for the murder of Rushdie (or $1 million if
the assassin happened to be non-Muslim). Rushdie was immediately

given 'grade one' protection by Scotland Yard's Special Branch and removed to a safe house. 'I remember Salman as a hunted man,' says the novelist Hanif Kureishi. 'He was always on the move. It was very difficult to keep in touch, but he was desperate to see people. Sometimes he just popped up at a friend's house, but always with his Special Branch minders. It was a harried existence.'

For a decade Rushdie was compelled to live like a fugitive, constantly moving from house to house – he was supposed to have slept in fifty-seven beds during the first five months of hiding – and forced into cloak and dagger operations in order to meet friends or journalists. He made the occasional surprise public appearance, such as joining Bono on stage at a U2 gig at Wembley in 1993. But it was not till 1998, when the Iranian government publicly declared that it would 'neither support nor hinder assassination operations on Rushdie' – the closest it would ever get to disowning the fatwa, which still stands – that he felt safe enough to return to the public glare.

3

Peter Mayer, Penguin's CEO, was in New York on Valentine's Day 1989. Early in the morning he received a call from Patrick Wright, the head of sales in London. 'Have you seen the headlines?' Wright asked. 'What headlines?' Mayer wanted to know. 'The Ayatollah Khomeini', Wright said, 'has issued a fatwa against Salman Rushdie and his publisher.' 'What's a fatwa?' asked a bemused Mayer.

Mayer went out to get a paper. The news was splashed on the front page of the *New York Times*. 'I was astonished', he says, 'to see the headlines. The *New York Times* dealt with world stories. I was just a publisher of a novel. I still did not see it as a world event.'

As Penguin CEO, Mayer was at the heart of the mayhem unleashed by the fatwa. He has never talked about it before, but it is an issue that twenty years on still causes him both pain and bafflement.

'If you're a publisher, you will always find people offended by books you publish,' he observes. 'That's the fate of being a publisher. I have published books that have offended Jews and Christians. Five or six of them. People wrote to Penguin trying to suppress those books. I wrote back, explaining that as a publisher I cannot just publish books that offend no one. It was generally a civilized dialogue. We originally put *The Satanic Verses* controversy in the same category. We thought we were dealing with the same kind of thing, the same kind of offence. Our view was that it would soon be sorted out by dialogue, as these things always were. What we wanted to say to Muslims who were upset was that this was a novel, by a serious writer, and the right to publish included the right to publish such books. It's what we said in all these cases. One relied on the sanity of secular democracy – that people met together, discussed their differences and sorted them out. It never occurred to us that this time it might be different or that it would become such a huge worldwide event.'

As a liberal, Mayer says, he 'accepted that Muslims needed protection from discrimination and hatred. But the idea that non-Muslims should be prevented from reading a novel never entered my head. I never saw "rights" as meaning the right of the minority to impose on the majority. I saw it as meaning that the majority rules, but that minorities must have their rights protected. Those rights had to be based on the law of the land; they could not be rights that the minority simply arrogates to itself.'

When Mayer first read the manuscript of *The Satanic Verses*, he saw it quite straightforwardly as 'a serious novel by a serious writer. I still don't think that Penguin did anything extraordinary in publishing it. We never set out to incite or to inflame or to offend. We did not see the novel as blasphemous or anti-Islamic. The question never came up. Neither Salman Rushdie nor his agent alerted us to it being a controversial book. And a publisher should not have to be an authority on the Qur'an.'

The first intimation of trouble came with Kushwant Singh's report on the possible reaction in India. 'He opined that it might cause "communal violence",' says Mayer. 'But Penguin only had a tiny office in India. We might have sold perhaps 150 hardcover copies. So we did not see it as a big issue.'

11

Even the protests in Britain barely registered. In hindsight the activities of the UKACIA and of the Bolton protestors, the intervention of Jamaat-e-Islami and the backroom manoeuvrings of the Saudi authorities all seem highly significant. In 1988, however, they caused hardly a ripple. 'I cannot recall the protests here in the UK before the fatwa,' Mayer admits. He cannot remember receiving any letter of complaint from the protestors, nor any request for a meeting. 'If I had I would have responded as I did to all the other letters I received.'

The fatwa transformed the affair, an event both terrifying and confusing. 'My immediate thought', Mayer recalls, 'was to be frightened for Salman. And frightened for Penguin staff. I didn't know what the reach was of a fatwa, whether it could travel beyond Tehran.'

The day following the fatwa, armed police started patrolling the street outside Penguin offices. Special X-ray machines were installed to check packages for explosives. 'My fear', says Mayer, 'was that a member of Penguin staff would be shot or stabbed to death and a note pinned on them, "This is what happens to people who work for Penguin". I felt a terrible responsibility for all the staff. If anyone had been killed because of the decision to continue publishing *The Satanic Verses* I would have carried a sense of responsibilty to the end of my life.'

Mayer himself was subject to a vicious campaign of hatred and intimidation. 'I had letters written in blood pushed under the door of my house. I had telephone calls in the middle of the night, saying not just that they would kill me but that they would take my daughter and smash her head against a concrete wall. Vile stuff.' To this day he does not know from whom the letters and calls came.

The Special Branch offered Mayer armed protection and a bulletproof vest. 'I said no. Of course I was scared. In New York I remember thinking, "I could come out of my apartment block, there might be a car waiting outside, engine revving, and I could get sprayed by a couple of machine guns. As easy as that." But my view was that if my number's up, my number's up. And I did not want to live like a victim. I did not see myself as a victim.'

Mayer still seethes with rage not simply at the intimidation he faced but also at what he sees as the callousness of others towards his predicament. 'My daughter was nearly expelled from her school,' he recalls. 'A group of parents said, "What would happen if the Iranians sent a hit squad and got the wrong girl?" And I was thinking, "What, you think my daughter is the right girl?"'

In New York he applied for a co-op apartment. 'There were objections that the Iranians could send a hit squad and target the wrong apartment,' he says. 'As if I had done something wrong.'

Despite the constant threat of violence, Mayer never wavered in his commitment to *The Satanic Verses*. And Penguin never wavered in its backing of his judgement. 'An emergency meeting of the Penguin board unanimously supported the continued publication of the novel,' Mayer recalls. 'I told the board, "You have to take the long view. Any climbdown now will only encourage future terrorist attacks by individuals or groups offended for whatever reason by other books that we or any publisher might publish. If we capitulate, there will be no publishing as we know it."'

The board supported Mayer, as did Pearson, Penguin's parent company. But there was considerable unease within the organization. 'People would take me aside in the corridor and say, "I have Muslim friends who are very upset, it's an anti-Muslim book." Or, "It's not right to offend Muslims, you should withdraw the book." And I would say, "That would be the thin end of the wedge. Next year we publish another book. And another group says you can't do that, it's offensive." My view was, and still remains, that rights you possess that are not used are not rights at all.'

There was, as Mayer recalls it, almost a frontier mentality within Penguin. 'We had never had to have this kind of discussion before,' he observes. 'Today there is a constant stream of discussion about multiculturalism and minority rights and sharia law. Not then. We had never had to think about free speech, or about why we were publishers.'

Out of countless discussions, both in formal board meetings and in ad hoc chats with colleagues, Mayer and his colleagues 'developed the argument that what we did now affected much more than simply the fate of this one book. How we responded to the controversy over *The Satanic Verses* would affect the future of free inquiry, without which there would be no publishing as we knew it, but also, by extension, no civil society as we knew it. We all came to agree that all we could do, as individuals or as a company, was to uphold the principles that underlay our profession and which, since the invention of movable type, have brought it respect. We were publishers. I thought that meant something. We all did.'

Mayer feels a debt of gratitude not just to the management of Penguin who backed him, but also to the staff. 'We had to fight intellectual battles throughout Penguin. Everyone came to understand the issues. Not just the editors or the executives, but the secretaries and the people moving boxes, too. All of them deserve praise.'

The only point at which Penguin wobbled was over the publication of the paperback. 'Salman Rushdie thought that only the publication of the paperback would bring an end to the terror and death threats. I did not agree. I feared that it might inflame, like a poker in the eye of the critics. I told Rushdie, "We will publish it but only when we think it safe to do so."'

There was a time in the middle of 1990 when the furor seemed to have died down. Mayer decided that the time had arrived for a paperback edition and picked a date. There was, he says, 'a huge debate within Penguin. It was the most dramatic board meeting I've ever been in. But we finally agreed to go ahead with the paperback. The idea was to print the paperback quickly and to release it out of the blue without the normal two to three months' publicity that would normally attend such a publication to head off any protests or demonstrations that might have taken place.'

Mayer was due to fly to America straight after the board meeting. Just as he arrived at Heathrow he received an urgent phone call. One of Penguin's bookstores in London had been firebombed, thankfully with no casualties. Mayer returned immediately to his London office. The paperback was postponed. 'We still had every intention of publishing it,' Mayer says. 'But we just could not publish it at that time. Salman Rushdie wanted to publish it straight away. Eventually he bought back the rights to the paperback edition and set up a consortium of publishers to bring it out.'

Twenty years on, Mayer remains defiantly proud of Penguin's stance. 'Neither our decision to publish *The Satanic Verses*, nor the subsequent decision to continue publishing it despite the violence and death threats, was taken to put us on the side of the angels. We were just doing our job – publishing a novel we wanted to publish by a well-known author. Yet I am not sure any other company would have done what we did. It was not in our corporate interest to continue publishing *The Satanic Verses*. We faced an enormous financial burden because of the security measures we were forced to take. Every Penguin employee was a potential target for terrorists and the whole affair disrupted the rest of our publishing business for years. But politically it was important not to give in to terror. It was important to defend the right to publish freely. And I am not the sort of person who easily backs down.'

4

Peter Mayer was spared his worst nightmare. No Penguin employee was killed as a consequence of *The Satanic Verses*. Other publishers and translators were not so fortunate.

William Nygaard was Rushdie's publisher in Norway. He has never spoken publicly before about the day he was shot outside his house on Dagaliveien in Oslo, but the memory is clearly etched into his mind. 'It was the 11th of October 1993,' he recalls. 'I had just returned from the Frankfurt Book Fair. I left my house around about 8.30. My car was parked around the corner. As soon as I got to the car I noticed that the front tyre had been punctured. "Damn it," I thought, "I've got no time for this." I opened the car door and reached in to get the phone numbers for the garage and to get a taxi. Suddenly I got what felt like an electric shock in my back and my arm. It's like nothing you can imagine.'

He had been shot by an assailant hiding in some bushes on the other side of the road. A second shot hit him in the shoulder. 'I started screaming. I threw myself down a little hill by the side of the road. That's when I got shot a third time, in the hip. It was about half an hour before one of my neighbours found me and called an ambulance. I still did not realize I had been shot by a gunman.'

Nygaard was rushed off to hospital to undergo an emergency operation, followed by months of rehabilitation. It was two years before he could fully use his arms and legs again. 'Journalists kept asking me, "Will you stop publishing *The Satanic Verses*?" I said, "Absolutely not."' The assailant was never caught.

Two years earlier, in July 1991, Hitoshi Igarashi, a Japanese professor of literature and translator of *The Satanic Verses*, had been knifed to death on the campus of Tsukuba University. That same month another translator of Rushdie's novel, the Italian Ettore Capriolo, was beaten up and stabbed in his Milan apartment. In neither case were the assailants caught or even identified.

The greatest tragedy of the Rushdie affair happened in Turkey. In July 1993 hundreds of artists, writers and musicians had gathered in the town of Sivas, in the central Anatolian region, to celebrate the life of Pir Sultan Abdal, a legendary sixteenth-century Alevi poet. The Alevis are a Turkish Muslim sect, closely related to the Sufis, whose theology has been deeply influenced by humanism (in the same way as, say, Quaker ideas have been in Christian cultures). Alevis are broadly supportive of secularism and have faced considerable hostility from more traditional Muslims. One of the speakers at the Sivas gathering was Aziz Nesin, the Turkish translator of *The Satanic Verses* and a prominent secularist. After Friday prayers, a mob of anti-Rushdie protestors, fired up by local imams, surrounded the hotel in which the conference was taking place and demanded that Nesin be handed over for summary execution. They then razed the hotel to the ground. Thirty-seven people were killed, though Nesin himself escaped. In 1997, thirty-three people were sentenced to death – later commuted to life imprisonment – for their part in the massacre. The government also tried unsuccessfully to charge Nesin with inciting the violence by 'criticizing Islam'. As the Turkish journalist Yalman Onaran put it, the Ankara regime was charging Nesin with 'inciting the crowd to kill him'.

5

The fatwa transformed the Rushdie affair from a dispute largely confined to Britain and the subcontinent (albeit with considerable Saudi involvement) into a global conflict with historic repercussions, from a quarrel about blasphemy and free speech into a matter of terror and geopolitics.

According to one story, Ayatollah Khomeini was watching the evening news on TV when he saw the Islamabad demonstrations and the killing of the protestors. So moved was he by the deaths that he immediately called for his secretary and dictated the fatwa. In reality, the fatwa was less an emotional response to the Islamabad killings than a political tactic to respond to inter-Islamic strife both inside and outside Iran. Kalim Siddiqui's conversation with Mohammad Khatami at Tehran airport suggests that the regime was already discussing taking action against Rushdie's book and that the liberals may have been worried about the consequences.

The 1979 revolution, which had overthrown the Shah and established an Islamic republic, had made Tehran the capital of Muslim radicalism, and Ayatollah Khomeini its spiritual leader. Yet Tehran's attempts, in the following decade, to broaden the Islamic revolution had made little headway. It had failed to destabilize the deeply conservative Saudi regime or to loosen the Saudi grip on the direction of Islam worldwide. It had also been forced, in 1988, to abandon ingloriously its bitter and bloody eight-year war against Iraq, and with it its hopes of bringing down Saddam Hussein. Up to a million Iranians, many of them barely teenagers, had been sacrificed in killing fields reminiscent of Ypres and Passchendaele, as wave after wave of 'martyrs' charged through bullets and barbed wire in vain attempts to take enemy trenches on the other side of no-man's-land. Inside Iran, Khomeini was facing increased opposition from reformers such as the speaker of the parliament, Ali Akbar Hashemi Rafsanjani, who had condemned the 'short-sightedness' of Iranian foreign policy for 'making enemies without reason', and was pushing for improved relations with the West.

The fatwa turned the tables on Khomeini's Islamic enemies. His bold action seemed to contrast with the spinelessness of the Saudis and allowed him to appeal over the heads of his opponents to the disappointed and deprived multitudes, offering them a new moral and religious struggle to restore their pride. Today Inayat Bunglawala is a prominent British Muslim leader. In 1989 he was a student at London's Queen Mary College. He was distressed by *The Satanic Verses* and frustrated by the Saudi campaign, which 'did not seem to be getting anywhere'. Then came the fatwa. 'I felt a thrill', he remembers. 'It was incredibly uplifting. The fatwa meant that as British Muslims we did not have to regard ourselves just as a small, vulnerable minority; we were part of a truly global and powerful movement. After the fatwa we could say, "If we are not treated with respect, then we have friends capable of forcing you to respect us."'

The fatwa sowed confusion and division among supporters of the Saudi regime. A number of militants who had taken part in the Afghan jihad against the Soviet Union and who had been within Riyadh's orbit now pledged allegiance to Tehran – among them the Egyptian Sheik Omar Abdel-Rahman, who is currently serving a life sentence in America for planning to bomb the World Trade Center in New York in 1993. Inside Iran, the fatwa stopped in its tracks attempts to improve relations with the West. The reformers were forced to denounce Rushdie, Rafsanjani describing the publication of *The Satanic Verses* as 'an organized and planned' plot involving the intelligence services of Britain, France, Germany, the United States, and certain 'Zionist publishers'.

The fatwa helped transform the very geography of Islam. Under traditional Islamic law, a fatwa was only valid within those areas in which sharia law applied. Muslims may have emigrated to Britain or converted in India, but a fatwa could have no validity there because those states were not under Islamic authority. With his four-paragraph pronounce-ment, the ayatollah had transcended the traditional frontiers of Islam and brought the whole world under his jurisdiction. At the same time, he helped relocate the confrontation between Islam and the West, which until then had been played out largely in the Middle East and south Asia, into the heart of western Europe. For the West, Islam was now a domestic issue.

6

In May 1989 the British Muslim Action Front, an ad hoc group of which the UKACIA was a member, called for a national demonstration against *The Satanic Verses* in London. It was the second such protest. The first, on 29 January, had drawn some eight thousand protestors. More than twice as many attended the second, on 27 May, marching from Parliament Square to Hyde Park, on the way burning copies of the novel and Rushdie's effigy. Tehran reportedly contributed about $1 million to the organization of the May demonstration, and the Iranian Revolutionary News Agency described Hyde Park as having been turned into 'a vast open-air mosque'.

The writer and former professor of Islamic studies Malise Ruthven opens *A Satanic Affair*, one of the first accounts of the Rushdie contro-versy, with a vivid description of the Hyde Park demonstration:

They came in their thousands from Bradford and Dewsbury, Bolton and Macclesfield, the old industrial centers; from outer suburbs like Southall and Woking; from Stepney and Whitechapel in London's East End; from the cities of Wolverhampton, Birmingham, Manchester and Liverpool. They wore white hats and long baggy trousers with flapping shirt tails. Most of them were bearded; the older men looked wild and craggy with curly grey-flecked beards – they were moun-tain men from the Punjab, farmers from the Ganges delta, peas-ants from the hills of Mirpur and Campbellpur. After decades of living in Britain they still seemed so utterly foreign: even in Hyde Park, a most cosmopolitan part of a very cosmopolitan city, where Arab families foregather in summer, where French, Spanish and Dutch are spoken sooner than English, they were aliens. They were not sophisticated, suave metropolitans like the blacks – the Afro-Caribbeans – with whom the racists and anti-racists banded them; they seemed like men from the sticks, irredeemably provincial.

Anyone with memories of Britain in the 1980s might find a little irony in the description of Afro-Caribbeans as 'sophisticated, suave metro-politans'. This, after all, was the decade of the urban riot, when confrontations between young blacks and the police set alight many of Britain's inner cities – from St Paul's in Bristol in 1980, through Brixton and Toxteth in 1981, to Handsworth in Birmingham in 1985, and, most notoriously, Broadwater Farm in north London that same year, where PC Keith Blakelock was hacked to death with a machete. West Indians, the Metropolitan Police commissioner, Kenneth Newman, told a journalist in 1982, are 'constitutionally disorderly . . . It's simply in their make up.' The perception of Afro-Caribbeans in the 1980s was as anything but sophisticated and suave.

Ruthven's view of Muslim protestors, on the other hand, would probably strike a chord with many people. For this is the popular image of the anti-Rushdie campaigners: male, middle-aged, poorly educated, badly integrated, devout to the point of blindness. Many were indeed like that. But equally, many were like Hassan: young, left-wing, articulate, educated, integrated. Few of these were religious, let alone fundamentalist. They were more familiar with the pub than with the mosque, had probably read *Midnight's Children* with more interest than they had the Qur'an, and were more likely to be clutching a packet of Durex than the Holy Book. Many had, like me, been involved in anti-racist campaigning in the 1980s. And for many Salman Rushdie was a hero. In the early 1980s Rushdie was better known for his brutal battering of racism than for his incendiary assaults on Islam.

'Four hundred years of conquest and looting, four centuries of being told that you are superior to the fuzzy-wuzzies and the wogs, leave their stain,' Rushdie told viewers in a TV documentary for the newly established Channel 4 in 1982. 'This stain has seeped into every part of the culture, the language and daily life; and nothing much has been done to wash it out . . . British thought, British society, has never been cleansed of the filth of imperialism. It's still there, breeding lice and vermin, waiting for unscrupulous people to exploit it for their own ends.'

Rushdie's talk was entitled 'The New Empire within Britain'. At a time when race on British TV meant execrable sitcoms such as *Love Thy Neighbour* and *It Ain't Half Hot, Mum* (programmes that made America's *The Cosby Show* seem like a manifesto for Black Power), Rushdie's provocative language was clearly intended to discomfit and offend. At the very end of the documentary Rushdie looked his viewers straight in the eye. 'The members of the new colony', he told them, 'have only one real problem, and that problem is white people . . . And until you, the whites, see the issue is not integration, or harmony, or multiculturalism, or immigration, but simply the business of facing up to and eradicating the prejudices within almost all of you, the citizens of your new, and last, Empire will be obliged to struggle against you. You could say that we are required to embark on a new freedom movement.'

There was, of course, something cartoonish about Rushdie's analysis. Even back then I never believed that the 'problem is white people', or that the issue was 'simply the business of facing up to and eradicating the prejudices within almost all of you'. Yet his was a voice that conjured up all the anger, bitterness and bravado that fired up so many young blacks and Asians then.

By the end of the 1980s much of that anger, bitterness and bravado was looking for a new home. A decade and more of secular anti-racist campaigning seemed to have done little to dislodge skinheads from the streets, to prevent deportations, or to lessen the pain of beatings in police cells. Racism appeared as firmly entrenched as ever. Disaffection with secular politics was deepened by a sense that many left-wing organizations seemed more interested in class issues than in tackling racial discrimination. At the same time, the idea that all non-whites had a common goal began to break down. Instead, people started increasingly to see themselves in narrower, ethnic terms: Afro-Caribbean, Sikh, Muslim. Every group began to insist that it had its own specific culture, rooted in its own particular history and experiences. Every group had to be true to its own culture, to pursue faithfully the traditions that marked out that culture as unique, and to rebuff the advances of other cultures. Such ideas seeped, as we shall see, into public policy in the 1980s through the pursuit of multiculturalism.

These changes created new opportunities for Islamic fundamentalists. There were many young Asians, like my friend Hassan, who had begun as secularists but had come by the end of the 1980s to form the pool of discontents in which radical Islamic organizations started fishing for recruits. It was in the late 1980s and early 1990s that militant Islamic groups like Hizb ut-Tahrir began organizing in Britain, particularly on university campuses. Formed in 1953 in Jerusalem by Taqiuddin al-Nabhani, Hizb ut-Tahrir is a radical Islamic party whose goal is to unite all Muslim lands into a global Islamic state, or caliphate. Banned in many Muslim countries, it has in recent years gained influence among British Muslims, especially the young and the educated. Like Hassan, many of Hizb ut-Tahrir's recruits came from the ranks of former secularists and, indeed, from the ranks of former left-wing activists. Farid Kassim, for instance, who, with Omar Bakri Muhammad, set up the British arm of Hizb ut-Tahrir and has been its most charismatic leader, was as a student in Sheffield a member of the Socialist Workers Party. Anjem Choudary, a spokesman for Al-Mouhajiroun, which Bakri Muhammad set up as a radical alternative to Hizb ut-Tahrir, was another SWP activist, at Southampton University.

Why should the background of someone like Hassan matter to us now? Because, two decades on, commentators often view today's radical Islamists as Malise Ruthven saw the anti-Rushdie demonstrators. Newspapers are peopled by caricatures of mad mullahs, bearded fanatics and foreign zealots. TV cameras are transfixed by figures such as Abu Hamza, the hook-handed imam from the Finsbury Park mosque, or Omar Bakri Muhammad himself, who won fame as the rent-a-quote

'Tottenham Ayatollah' before eventually exiling himself to the Lebanon in order to escape detention in Britain.

The real face of radical Islam is, however, often very different. Marc Sageman is a former CIA case officer who worked with the mujahideen in Afghanistan in the late 1980s. He is now a forensic psychologist and political sociologist who teaches at the University of Pennsylvania and is a counter-terrorism consultant to the US government. For the past six years he has been poring over the available data on terrorists known to be associated with al-Qaeda. These include direct members of what Sageman calls 'al-Qaeda Central', people like Osama bin Laden and his second-in-command Ayman Muhammad Rabaie al-Zawahiri; members of other groups known to share al-Qaeda's goals, including Egyptian Islamic Jihad and Jemaah Islamiyah, responsible for the Bali bombing in 2002; terrorists from the Maghreb; and European- and American-based terrorists, such as many of those involved in the 9/11, 7/7 and Madrid train bombings – more than five hundred case studies in all. Sageman's data come from government documents, police wiretaps, news reports, academic publications and transcripts from trials in America, France, Germany, Egypt, Indonesia and Morocco, as well as from face-to-face interviews. It is the most detailed study yet of al-Qaeda supporters and the results are laid out in two books, *Understanding Terror Networks* (2004) and *Leaderless Jihad* (2008). The conclusion to be drawn from all this is the unsettling thought that, in the words of a review of Sageman's work in *The Economist*, 'Terrorists are a bit like you and me.'

'Most people', Sagemen says, 'think that terrorism comes from poverty, broken families, ignorance, immaturity, lack of family or occupational responsibilities, weak minds susceptible to brainwashing – the sociopath, the criminal, the religious fanatic.' In fact, terrorists are among the 'best and brightest', from 'caring, middle-class families', who usually came to the West to study, and 'who can speak, four, five, six languages'. According to Sageman, 'Al-Qaeda's members are not the Palestinian fourteen-year-olds we see on the news, but join the jihad at the average age of 26. Three-quarters are professionals or semi-professionals. They are engineers, architects, and civil engineers, mostly scientists.' Few had grown up religious or had been to a religious school. 'At the time they joined the jihad', Sageman observes, 'the terrorists were not very religious. They only became religious once they joined the jihad.' Nor were they sociopaths. Only 1 percent had any detectable mental illness – well below the worldwide norm. 'It's comforting to believe these guys are different from us, because what they do is so evil,' says Sageman. 'Unfortunately, they aren't that different.'

Of course, terrorists are different. They are not simply like you and me. They are, after all, terrorists. Yet there is an important truth in Sageman's analysis. When I first came across his work I was struck immediately by the similarities between the people who populate his study and the people I used to know: the anti-Rushdie campaigners I met in Bradford, the Hizb ut-Tahrir members I argued with at the Polytechnic of North London, the young radicals who wanted to shove leaflets in my hand outside Brixton Tube station. Commentators often view Islamic radicals now as they did the Rushdie demonstrators then, in almost the same way as the government agents view the extraterrestrials in the cult TV series *Torchwood*. They are seen as the demonic 'Other', an alien force threatening Western societies, values and ways of life. And once it is viewed in this fashion, the 'Muslim problem' becomes a clash of civilizations or a war of the worlds. The ideas of radical Islam certainly challenge basic tenets of Western liberal democracy, and the actions of Islamic terrorists are undoubtedly demonic. Yet the fault lines run not between civilizations but deep within Western societies themselves. Many of the ideas and arguments of Islamic radicals have, as we shall see, wide purchase within Western societies. And many of the individuals who espouse such ideas and arguments are 'Westernized'.

Shiraz Maher is a former Islamic radical who now campaigns against Islamism. He joined Hizb ut-Tahrir shortly after 9/11, not because it seemed theologically right, but because it gave him a sense of political identity and allowed him to 'defend Islam' from the 'humiliation' being heaped upon it. 'I wasn't too concerned with religious practice,' he writes, 'I wouldn't go to the mosque all too often, but I'd tick the box that said "Muslim" when filling out the census form.' His first contact with Hizb ut-Tahrir was through someone who had just graduated from Durham University. 'I was struck by the fact that he was an intellectual and had obviously worked hard to better himself . . . He didn't look like the typical "mad mullah" – and wore normal clothes and sported only a short, trimmed beard.' It is not mosques but universities that provide the real recruiting ground for Islamists, because 'for young people eager for new ideas they provide an environment far removed from the deadening conservatism of the mosques'.

Twenty years ago, the anti-Rushdie demonstrators were often as integrated as I was; they were the children of multicultural Britain. Today's radical Islamists are equally so. Many of the young men who flew the planes into the Twin Towers, or blew themselves up on a London Tube, were educated in the West, joined the jihad in the West, and expressed an anger and a nihilism nurtured in the West. In July 2007 Islamic terrorists attacked Glasgow airport and attempted, unsuccessfully, to set off two car bombs in the center of London. Commentators were astonished that at least six of the alleged plotters were doctors working for the National Health Service, including a neurosurgeon. They should not have been surprised – for the plotters' CVs fitted perfectly with the profiles of many radical Islamists and, indeed, of many Islamic terrorists.

It is true that radical Islam is irrationally hostile to the West. But it has also been deeply shaped by the West. 'The illusion held by Islamic radicals', the French sociologist Olivier Roy has written, 'is that they represent tradition when in fact they express a negative form of Westernization.' What he means is that contemporary Islamic radicalism, far from being an expression of ancient theological beliefs, is really a reaction to new political and social changes: the loss of a sense of belonging in a fragmented society, the blurring of traditional moral lines, the increasing disenchantment with politics and politicians, the growing erosion of the distinction between our private lives and our public lives. Radical Islamists have responded to the political crisis created by these changes by returning to the Qur'an and taking literally its strictures. In *The Satanic Verses* the Archangel Gibreel 'found himself spouting rules, rules, rules' to Mahound, from 'which sexual positions have received divine sanction' to 'the manner in which a man should be buried, and how a property should be divided'. 'It was as if', says Salman (as Rushdie, with delicious conceit, calls Muhammad's scribe), 'no aspect of human existence was . . . left unregulated, free.'

For radical Islamists the Qur'an has truly left no aspect of human life unregulated. According to Hizb ut-Tahrir, Islam 'is able to deal with all the modern-day issues due to the nature of the Islamic texts'. The Qur'an 'addresses the Islamic response to in vitro fertilization (IVF) in its rules on kinship and the permissibility of seeking medical treatment'. The right attitudes to 'genetically modified foods were addressed by using the evidence for the improvement of the quality of plants and food'. The Qur'an 'permits nanotechnology', but 'prohibits intellectual property and its results such as patents and copyrights'. It 'allows the cloning of plants and animals', but 'forbids the cloning of humans'. Indeed, everything from 'the double-helix structure of DNA' to 'E-commerce' is addressed by the Qur'an.

Yet despite this fixation with divine 'rules, rules, rules', the belief that the political vision of radical Islamists is a throwback to a theological past is as illusory, Olivier Roy suggests, as the belief that the Qur'an is the word of God. Radical Islamists may seem obsessed by the strictures of the Holy Book, but their political ideas draw upon distinctly modern sentiments. The very literalism of fundamentalist Islam is a modern phenomenon and little found in traditional Islam.

Islam, like all religions, comprises both a set of beliefs and a complex of social institutions, traditions and cultures that bind people in a unique relationship to a particular conception of the sacred. What is striking about religion today – and not just Islam – is that religious belief has been wrenched apart from religious institutions, traditions and cultures. Faith, as the philosopher Charles Taylor observes, has become disembedded from its historical culture, and reconstituted instead as part of the culture of 'expressive individualism', forms of spirituality grounded in the primacy of individual experience and rooted in the social values of what the writer Tom Wolfe has called the 'me generation'.

In *The Spiritual Revolution*, their study of religious practices in a small town in northern England, the sociologists Paul Heelas and Linda Woodhead show that while traditional religious congregations are in decline, 'New Age' forms of spirituality are beginning to fill the gap. But more than this, many once-traditional believers are beginning to adopt New Age attitudes and rituals, developing forms of faith that celebrate the emotional aspects of spirituality and seek to fulfil the believer's inner needs. Such congregations often combine a literal reading of the holy book, and an insistence on the unchanging character of religious truths, with a God who speaks to their individual, subjective needs. 'We don't go to Mass because we feel like it, or not go because we don't feel like it, we go because the Church gave us an obligation to go to Mass,' an elderly Roman Catholic lady explained to Heelas and Woodhead. For all the literalism of the new forms of faith, such obligation is alien to them. Instead, they provide 'more space for each individual participant to explore and express his emotions in his own way, and to let those emotions set the agenda of the religion rather than vice versa'. 'A one-hour service on a Sunday morning?' one of Heelas and Woodhead's interviewees snorted; 'It's not enough to explore your self-esteem issues, is it?' The new religions are crafted to help people feel good rather than do good. They are faiths fit for the age of Oprah. Such 'congregations of experiential difference' are burgeoning, Heelas and Woodhead suggest, while traditional 'congregations of humanity', which feel a religious duty to serve wider society, face a struggle for existence.

The growth of many contemporary forms of faith, then, whether radical Islam or the Pentecostal Church, marks not a return to traditional religion but a break with it. A traditional Muslim would be as appalled by the rituals of radical Islam as that Catholic worshipper was by the New Age-ishness of charismatic Christianity. Contemporary radical

Islam, the Turkish academic Nilufer Gole, professor of sociology at the École des Hautes Études in Paris, observes, is a 'religious experience of a new kind; it is not directly handed over by community, religious or state institutions'. Rather, it presents 'an affirmative reconstruction of identity'.

Take, for instance, the changing face of Islamic religious texts. For centuries, such works were written by *ulema*, or religious scholars, and carried titles such as *The Explanations of Secrets* and *The Pearls of Knowledge*. Contemporary texts are without precedent in Islamic history, penned as they are by laypeople and addressing issues such as *What Does it Mean to Be Muslim?* and *How to Experience Islam* – questions the answers to which would have seemed self-evident in the past. Today, though, the answers are far from clear, because Islam, like all religions, is being reinvented and redefined in order to meet secular, not religious, needs. Islam 'today is constructed, reinterpreted and carried into public life', Nilufer Gole writes, 'not through religious institutions, but through political agency and cultural movements'.

As broader political, cultural and national identities have eroded, and as traditional social networks, institutions of authority and moral codes have weakened, so the resultant atomization of society has created both an intensely individual relationship to the world and a yearning for the restoration of strong identities and moral lines. Radical Islam, like many new forms of fundamentalist faiths, addresses both these needs. It is very much a child of modern plural societies with its celebration of 'difference' and 'authenticity'.

7

'Salman Rushdie has been good for us Muslims.' Tall, stiff-backed and with an Abraham Lincoln beard, Sher Azam, chairman of the Bradford Council of Mosques, was a patriarch from central casting. I had gone to Bradford in February 1989 to talk to him about the Rushdie affair, and it was difficult not to be impressed by his quiet self-assurance and unwavering commitment to defending what he saw as the dignity of the Muslim community. But why would the man who had helped torch *The Satanic Verses* seemingly approve of Salman Rushdie? 'You've just burnt his book,' I said in puzzlement. 'You've denounced him as a blasphemer. So why is he good for Muslims?'

'We used to have questions about who we are and where we were going,' Azam replied. 'Now we know. We've found ourselves as Muslims. There are action committees in every city up and down the country. It's bringing us together. Muslims are becoming much more united.'

There were echoes here of what Hassan had said to me. So I told him about meeting Hassan outside his office, and about how he had 'found himself' in the anti-Rushdie campaign. 'For a long time we thought we had lost our children,' Azam replied. 'They were growing up hating our culture. They were angry, withdrawn, we could not reach them. Now they're coming back to us.'

Perhaps what they hated was not Sher Azam's culture but the restrictions that subcontinental traditions placed upon them? Perhaps what they wanted were the freedoms of Western culture? 'Freedom always comes at a price. And that price has been crime, drugs and being lost. Now they're coming back to us. Finding themselves as Muslims has made them more British, not less. They're calling themselves Muslims. Not Pakistanis, not Indians, but Muslims. They are British. But they are also Muslim.'

He looked at me. 'So what about you? When are you coming back to us?' I laughed. I was not a Muslim, I told him. I was an unbeliever. And I was very happy without God.

'Only time,' he said. 'We will wait for you.'

Had he read *The Satanic Verses*, I asked him. He had not. So how had he found out about the novel?

'We received some letters from the Hizb ul Ulama in Blackburn which had some articles from two Indian magazines which said what kind of book it was. So I asked some colleagues who were interested in books to read it. They almost fainted, it was so filthy.'

The Council of Mosques had portions of the book translated into

Urdu so that *ulema* could rule on it. The religious scholars unanimously declared the novel blasphemous. 'So we held some meetings to see what we could do. And we decided to write a letter to the prime minister.' It was Sher Azam himself who took on the task. 'Honourable Madam,' he wrote to Mrs Thatcher; 'The Muslims of Bradford and all over the world are shocked to hear about the Novel called "SATANIC VERSES" in which the writer Salman Rushdi [*sic*] has attacked our beloved Prophet Muhammad PBUH and his wives using such dirty language which no Muslim can tolerate.' 'As citizens of this great country,' he pleaded, 'we have expressed our very ill feelings about such harmful novel and its publishers and state that the novel should be banned immediately.'

He received no reply. 'So we held a meeting. But no one reported it. We weren't being heard. Someone suggested that we hold a bigger meeting at the university. And then someone said that we should hold a meeting outside because it would be bigger and we could have a march. And then one of the imams – I can't remember who – suggested that we should burn the book. Because that might attract attention. And it did.'

Didn't Salman Rushdie have the right to criticize Islam, even to abuse it?

'Criticize yes, abuse no. Islam is the religion of free speech. But there are limits. There are limits in England. Look at how the government banned *Spycatcher*. Why can't they ban this filthy novel?'

Spycatcher was the autobiography of the one-time MI5 agent Peter Wright which the British government had tried to suppress in 1985. It was co-written with Paul Greengrass, the director who is probably best known for his *United 93*, the film of the hijacking on 11 September of United Airlines flight 93, the plane destined for Capitol Hill but which, thanks to the courage of the passengers in fighting the hijackers, eventually crashed in an empty field in Pennsylvania. As well as detailing Wright's attempt to catch a Soviet mole in MI5, *Spycatcher* told of the MI6 plot to assassinate President Nasser during the Suez Crisis in the 1950s, and of joint MI5–CIA plotting against the Labour prime minister Harold Wilson in the 1960s. In America the book was, ironically, published by Viking, whose parent company was Penguin. As with *The Satanic Verses*, Peter Mayer had to face down calls for its suppression. 'There was huge pressure from the British government to stop publication of *Spycatcher* not just in Britain but in America and elsewhere too,' Mayer remembers. 'I refused to cave in. I heard later that government ministers had even contacted Michael Blakenham, who was at the time the CEO of Pearson, and suggested to him, "You can sack Mr Mayer." To his immense credit he didn't.'

After the book was banned in England (bizarrely, it continued to be sold in Scotland, thanks to a loophole in the law), a number of English newspapers attempted to cover *Spycatcher*'s principal allegations. They were served with gagging orders and subsequently tried for contempt of court. Again, Scottish newspapers were free to publish. Eventually, in 1988, the book was cleared for sale in England, when the Law Lords acknowledged that, given its publication in Scotland and overseas, there was no point in trying to keep its contents secret. In November 1991 the European Court of Human Rights ruled that the government gag on the newspapers had breached the European Convention on Human Rights.

Was not the moral of the *Spycatcher* story, I asked Sher Azam, that there needed to be fewer, not greater, restrictions on free speech? No, he said, because the eventual publication of *Spycatcher* demonstrated this society's weakness, not its strength. It revealed its inability to stand up for what was necessary to protect social order. The willingness of many people, including many Christians, to let blasphemy laws perish was another sign of such weakness. Islam, Sher Azam insisted, would not go the way of Christianity. 'Christians don't mind what people say about their God, because they no longer believe in Him. But look at what it means. It means a country where the values have gone. People drink, take drugs, have sex like dogs. If people believed in God, most of these problems would disappear. Many people in this country think that Islam is against them. With Rushdie, all those sleeping demons about Muslims have come awake. But what they don't realize is that it is Islam that is saving this country's morals.'

8

Immediately after the fatwa, the British government withdrew all its personnel from Tehran and demanded that Iranian representatives leave London. It did not, however, break off diplomatic relations. Instead Britain insisted on what it called 'reciprocity at zero' – the unprecedented act of maintaining diplomatic relations but without any personnel. The British government's intention was clearly to signal both displeasure and regret at the same time, to take a stand against the fatwa without seeming to be intransigent about it. In Tehran's eyes it signalled only weakness. In the end it was not Britain but Iran that, three weeks after the fatwa, broke off all diplomatic ties, claiming that 'in the past two centuries Britain has been in the front line of plots and treachery against Islam and Muslims'. This collision of Western moral evasion and Islamist political intransigence became a characteristic not just of the Rushdie affair but of the whole road from fatwa to jihad.

A few days before Iran broke off diplomatic relations, the British foreign secretary Geoffrey Howe went on the BBC World Service to distance himself from Salman Rushdie. 'We can understand why it could be criticized,' he said of The Satanic Verses. Not only had the book 'been found deeply offensive by people of the Muslim faith', but it was 'offensive in many other ways as well'. According to Howe, 'The British government, the British people have no affection for the book.' The Satanic Verses, he pointed out, 'is extremely critical, rude about us. It compares Britain with Hitler's Germany. We do not like that any more than the people of Muslim faith like the attacks on their faith contained in the book.'

Two weeks later, another Foreign Office minister, William Waldegrave, went on the BBC's Arabic service to 'put on record that the British government well recognizes the hurt and distress that this book has caused, and we want to emphasize that because it was published in Britain, the British government had nothing to do with it and is not associated with it in any way'. The 'best way forward', Waldegrave concluded, 'is to say that the book is offensive to Islam, that Islam is far stronger than a book by a writer of this kind'.

Prime minister Margaret Thatcher joined her ministers in criticizing the novel. 'We have known in our own religion people doing things which are deeply offensive to some of us,' she said. 'We feel it very much. And that is what has happened to Islam.' Norman Tebbit, one of Margaret Thatcher's chief lieutenants, went even further, calling Rushdie 'an outstanding villain', a man whose 'public life has been a record of despicable acts of betrayal of his upbringing, religion, adopted home and nationality. Now he betrays even his own sneers at the British establishment.' 'How many societies,' Tebbit wondered, 'having been so treated by a foreigner accepted in their midst, could go so far to protect him from the consequences of his egotistical and self-opinionated attack on the religion into which he was born?'

In his original World Service statement at the beginning of March, Geoffrey Howe had pointed out that the British government was 'not co-sponsoring the book', but was 'sponsoring . . . the right of people to speak freely'. By the end of the month, he seemed to have given up on even such a half-hearted defence of the virtues of free speech. During a visit to Pakistan, the foreign secretary not only expressed, according to Radio Islamabad, his 'deep sympathy with the Muslims over the publication of the book', but also promised to 'explore the possibility of taking necessary steps under British law to resolve the problem created by the publication of the book'. The Foreign Office, an *Economist* editorial observed, seemed 'more irritated by Mr Rushdie and his band of supporters than it is shocked by the Iranians'.

European Union countries withdrew their ambassadors from Tehran after the fatwa. Within a month all but those of Britain, France and West Germany had returned. The Europeans, Khomeini taunted, had come back 'humiliated, disgraced and shame-faced'. The French foreign ministry called Khomeini's description an 'exaggeration'.

The American government was equally limp. After riots in Islamabad, the U.S. embassy there expressed its 'wish to emphasize that the US government in no way associates itself with any activity that is in any sense offensive or insulting to Islam or any other religion'. When Ayatollah Khomeini issued his fatwa the worst that the Secretary of State, James Baker, could say of it was that it was 'regrettable'. President George Bush senior would go no further than to suggest that however offensive *The Satanic Verses* may have been, inciting murder was also 'deeply offensive to the norms of civilized behaviour'. There have been times in history, the writer Susan Sontag told the Senate foreign relations subcommittee on terrorism in March 1989, when 'the promise or presence of federal law enforcement officials has been vital to the meaningful exercise of a constitutional right – to vote, or register in school or march on a public street. This time, when First Amendment freedoms are at risk, the message has been: you're on your own.'

For a decade the West had looked upon Iran as a mortal enemy, and portrayed Ayatollah Khomeini as Lucifer in black robes. It had backed Saddam Hussein in his bloody eight-year war with the ayatollah, piled him high with arms and the means to make chemical weapons, and all but turned a blind eye to his gassing of the Kurds, because it perceived Tehran as posing an unacceptable menace to Western interests. Yet, when faced with the fatwa, Western politicians seemed incapable of taking a united, unequivocal stand in defence of free speech and against the threat to Salman Rushdie's life.

Politicians were willing to lecture Muslims at home about the importance of democracy and freedom. In July 1989, the new British home secretary, John Patten, wrote a letter to Iqbal Sacranie of the UKACIA 'to set forth in full some of our recent thinking' about the Rushdie controversy and to demand that influential Muslim figures 'think deeply . . . about what it means to be British and particularly what it means to be a British Muslim'. 'Putting down roots in a new community', the minister explained, 'does not mean severing the old. No one would expect or indeed want British Muslims, or any other group, to lay aside their faith, traditions or heritage. But the new roots must be put down and must go deep, too.' Muslims were expected to possess 'knowledge of [Britain's] institutions, history and traditions'. They also had to recognize that 'The same freedom which has enabled Muslims to meet, march and protest against the book, also preserves the author's right to freedom of expression for so long as no law is broken. To rule otherwise would be to chip away at the fundamental freedom on which our democracy is built.' British ministers were willing to take on minor ayatollahs like Iqbal Sacranie. But when faced with the real thing in Tehran, they suddenly became timorous, equivocating on the very values about which they were lecturing British Muslims.

The American writer Daniel Pipes is an unabashed proponent of the clash of civilizations thesis. Western European societies, he wrote in the wake of the fatwa, 'are unprepared for the massive immigration of brown-skinned peoples cooking strange foods and maintaining different standards of hygiene', adding that while 'All immigrants bring exotic customs and attitudes . . . Muslim customs are more troublesome than most.' Despite such visceral distaste for Islam, Pipes's summary of the consequences of British policy in the Rushdie affair was to the point. 'The prime minister and foreign secretary of Britain humiliated themselves by officially attacking a novel, something unheard of in British public life', he wrote. 'Rather than gain goodwill in Tehran, their weakness stimulated yet more demands, ones they could not possibly fulfil.'

It was a lesson unlearnt. In the twenty years since the fatwa, Western politicians have continued to show greater willingness to lecture Muslims about the importance of liberty, freedom and democracy than to defend such values in practice. Indeed, the responses of Western nations first to the fatwa and subsequently to jihad have helped undermine civil liberties, erode freedom of speech and weaken democracy.

CHAPTER TWO

From street-fighters to book-burners

'It's incredible,' Saeed cried. 'Mishal, Mishu, is this you? All of a sudden you've turned into this God-bothered type from ancient history?'

Salman Rushdie, *The Satanic Verses*, p.238.

1

'When the trouble started', Nasreen Saddique wrote in her diary on 25 January 1982, 'we phoned the police, but they never came. Then my father went to the police station to get the police, we had a witness. The police said they didn't need a witness.'

The 'trouble' was a gang of forty white youths attacking Nasreen's home in the East End of London. They threw stones, smashing the windows and narrowly missing the family crouched in the darkness inside. They daubed swastikas, gave Nazi salutes and chanted 'Fucking Pakis out'. Nasreen wrote her diary by candlelight as the family huddled in an upstairs room. She was fourteen. She would be twenty by the time the trouble finally ended.

The Saddiques had moved into a new house in the West Ham area of east London in January 1982. It was an unprepossessing three-storey building in the middle of a small semicircle of houses which enclosed a little strip of green and a church. On one side of the house stood a minicab office, on the other a pub. Opposite was a newsagent's. The house had a shopfront which the Saddiques had hoped to turn into a family business. Within days of moving in, however, the entire ground-floor window had to be boarded up. Dozens of skinheads would gather daily on the strip of green. Sometimes they threw stones. Sometimes they pushed excrement through the door. Sometimes they just stood and taunted.

26 *January*: Trouble. Got no sleep. Three or four of them throw stones at our window.

27 *January*: Trouble. Got no sleep.

28 *January*: Every night we have to call the police but the police don't do anything. Two youths kick our front door and went in the minicab office.

29 *January*: My uncle came round and before he came there was trouble. My uncle came in and the youths were swearing. Three or four youths were standing in the church and threw stones at our house and broke windows (three times). The police came four times and did nothing but told the youths to go away. When the windows were being broken, the glass just missed my father's head.

And so the diary went on in the same vein, for days, weeks, months, years.

The Saddiques were not willing to be passive victims. First Nasreen wrote to Arthur Lewis, the local Labour MP, asking for help. He wrote back that while he 'sympathized', there was little he could do because 'this is a police matter'. Nasreen tried again. 'Things have got worse,' she told him. 'One evening a group of youths painted NF [National Front] slogans all over our door. Lots of youths on motorbikes drive past the house all the time, shouting and making lots of noise. Our door is always being kicked and stones are still being thrown at the windows and at the doors. The police have not done anything at all and we are frightened that the attacks will get worse until finally we will have petrol bombs thrown.' She concluded the letter by pleading with Lewis,

'You are our last hope.' Again, Lewis wrote that there was nothing he could do as it was a police matter.

The police blamed the Saddiques themselves for their predicament. 'The arrival of a demonstrative Asian family in a predominantly whites' playground area had unpleasant effects,' Chief Superintendent Barratt wrote to Tony Banks, who, in 1983, had replaced Lewis as the local MP. 'The cul-de-sac environment is unsuitable for peaceful residential purposes . . . Police do feel there is a case for rehousing this family.' As anti-racist activist Keith Tompson wrote in his book *Under Seige*, 'Barratt only stated more boldly what everybody else had hinted at – that the Saddiques were to blame for their choice of a "whites' playground" and that the solution to their problem was not for the racists to be made to desist but for the family to be uprooted.'

Nasreen had written a sheaf of letters to her local MPs, to the council, to the police. She had even written to the prime minister, Margaret Thatcher. All sympathized with her plight. None did anything about it. So she turned to an organization called East London Workers Against Racism (ELWAR), of which Tompson was the organizer. ELWAR was a radical anti-racist movement, which had been set up by a small Trotskyist group called the Revolutionary Communist Party, but which had become something of an institution in east London because of its willingness to take direct action against racists. It set up street patrols, ensured the physical protection of families under attack, and organized local meetings, often in people's front rooms, to win support for those facing harassment or worse. In the case of the Saddiques, 'direct action' meant staying in the house, physically confronting the youths whenever they gathered, and canvassing the local area, house by house, shop by shop, both to win support for the family's plight and to find out more about their tormentors. All of which explains why I spent much of 1984 not at university but camped out in a house in London's East End. Almost two years on from when the trouble had started, it still had not abated. It was in Nasreen's front room that I first met Hassan. He, too, was skipping college to find an education on the streets, and hoping to hand out a lesson to the racists.

There were a thousand tales just like Nasreen's – and many far worse. In the recession-hit Britain of the seventies and eighties, hostility to blacks and Asians was as much an everyday fact of life as public sector strikes and double-digit inflation. Racism then was vicious, visceral and often fatal. Stabbings were common, firebombings almost weekly events. In May 1978, the same month as the far-right National Front won a quarter of the votes in local elections in London, ten thousand Bengalis marched from Whitechapel to Whitehall to protest at the murder of garment worker Altab Ali near Brick Lane – one of eight racist murders that year. In the decade that followed there were another forty-nine such killings. A few months before the Saddiques' troubles began, in July 1981 an Asian mother, Parveen Khan, and her three children were murdered in a firebomb attack on their house in Walthamstow, in north-east London. In 1985 a pregnant woman, Shamira Kassam, died with her three small sons in another firebomb attack a few miles away in Ilford.

If Nasreen's encounter with the racists was depressingly familiar, so was her experience of police attitudes. Even more than the unofficial racists, the ones in uniform caused consternation within minority communities. In 1982 cadets at the national police academy in Hendon in north-east London were asked to write essays about immigrants. 'Wogs, nignogs and Pakis', wrote one, 'come into Britain, take up our homes, our jobs and our resources and contribute relatively less to our once glorious country. They are, by nature, unintelligent. And can't at all be educated sufficiently to live in a civilised society of the Western world. It is my opinion that they themselves would be better off living in their native lands, so send them packing, carpet bags, funky music, curries, all their relatives and stereo transistor radios.' Another wrote that 'all blacks are pains and should be ejected from society'.

Such sentiments were not confined to cadets. In the early 1980s, Superintendent John Ellis was in charge of the predominantly Afro-Caribbean Chapeltown district of Leeds. 'There are 15,000 West Indians in this locality,' he told an audience, 'and I can tell you that 15,000 West Indians are very difficult to police. They create all sorts of problems. Drugs is one, prostitution, brothels and vice are others.'

With attitudes such as these it is not surprising that blacks and Asians rarely bothered reporting racist attacks to the police. Not only were they unlikely to be taken seriously, but the victims of such attacks all too often found themselves locked up. It was common practice in those days for the police to ignore the racist violence and instead to investigate the immigration status of those beaten up. And when the police did take the violence seriously, they were often more concerned with the violence of the victim than that of the perpetrator. It was not uncommon for blacks to fight back against their attackers – only for the attackers to walk free while the victims were arrested for causing affray or grievous bodily harm.

Worse still were the deaths in police custody. In the twenty years between the deaths of David Oluwale in Leeds in 1969 (his body was found floating in the River Aire; two policemen were subsequently convicted of assaulting him) and of Edwin Carr in London in 1989 (he ended up on a life-support machine after having been arrested and taken to Carter Street police station in Southwark for possession of cannabis; what happened at the police station is still unknown), no fewer than thirty-seven blacks and Asians were killed in police custody – almost one every six months. The same number again died in prisons or in hospital custody. 'It sometimes seems', Salman Rushdie observed in his TV lecture, 'The New Empire within Britain', 'that the British authorities, no longer capable of exporting governments, have chosen instead to import a new Empire, a new community of subject peoples of whom they think, and with whom they can deal, in very much the same way as their predecessors thought of and dealt with "the fluttering folk and wild", the "new-caught, sullen peoples, half-devil and half-child", who made up, for Rudyard Kipling, the White Man's burden.' And 'for the citizens of the new imported Empire' the police force represented a 'colonizing army, those regiments of occupation and control'.

The first generation of post-war immigrants had largely accepted racism as a fact of life. They had kept their heads down and got on with the job of survival. Their children refused to do so. They saw themselves as British, insisted on being treated as such, and challenged racism head-on. The confrontations outside Nasreen's house were just one expression of the changing relationship between Britain's black and Asian communities and wider British society. 'Self-defence is no offence' rang out the slogan.

It was against this background of a nation increasingly polarized on the issue of race, a nation in which a new intensity of racism was matched by the fierceness of the response from a new generation of blacks and Asians, that the multicultural policies of the 1980s developed. One of the myths of recent years is that Britain became a multicultural nation because minorities demanded that their differences be recognized. Multicultural policies were, in fact, imposed from the top, part of a government strategy to defuse the anger created by racism. To unpick this tale, I want to begin at the beginning with the story of Asian immigration into Britain.

2

Anwar was born in a small village near Rawalpindi in what was then British India. 'Our village was very small,' he says, 'there were around one hundred houses . . . The worst thing was there was no school there, so we had to walk every day four miles for a middle-school education.' In 1958, aged twenty-one, Anwar made his way to Britain and stayed with a cousin in Bradford. 'I was welcomed [by my clan] . . . They never took my rent or food bill.'

Anwar's first job was in a woollen mill. Then he got a job on the buses. With a bigger wage packet he was able to pay his own way, put money aside for his family back home, and eventually help them to come to Britain too. 'I felt my first job was to bring the people here. First I brought my brother-in-law. Then another brother-in-law. Then my own brothers and my uncles . . . Whenever I called anyone, we became two, and two became four.' It was, he says, 'like a chain'.

These days, Anwar is no run-of-the-mill Pakistani immigrant. He is Sir Anwar Parvez, owner of the Best Way Asian supermarket chain and one of the richest men in Britain. Yet his early history was typical of Pakistani migrants.

The first migrants were single men who came simply to work. Britain needed labour for its post-war reconstruction and the migrants could earn wages some thirty times higher than back home. They came not from the poorest areas of the subcontinent, but from poor areas with a tradition of emigration. Most Pakistanis in Britain hail from Mirpur in Azad Kashmir, and Campbellpur on the borders of the North-West Frontier and the Punjab, a corner of the world so remote that it does not even show up in the *Times Atlas*. (It was said that after independence Campbellpur was not renamed more appropriately because officials in Islamabad simply forgot that it existed.) Ninety-five percent of Britain's Bangladeshis come from Sylhet, in the north-east of the country. These areas had long provided recruits for the merchant navy and the British army. There were Sylheti workers in London as early as 1873. Many had come as galley hands and cooks on British ships. There were twenty Indian restaurants in the capital by 1940, the majority run by Sylhetis.

The first Muslims to settle in Bradford were former seamen who, in the early 1940s, were directed from seaports such as Liverpool and Hull to munitions factories and essential wartime services in the Bradford and Leeds region. The success of these pioneers led others to follow in the 1950s. They clubbed together to buy run-down back-to-back or terraced houses in the city center that no one else wanted, mainly in Manningham and Little Horton. You could buy a beat-up back-to-back for £45 in those days; a spacious Victorian terrace might cost £250. Put down a £10 deposit, pay £1 a week to the seller, and the house was yours. This allowed the new immigrants to buy property without the need for a mortgage (which the pervasive racism of the time would probably have denied them). It was not uncommon for ten or twelve men to live in one house, and in some cases as many as forty.

Mohammed Manzoor arrived in Britain from Karachi in 1963. Like many migrants he was drawn along a chain. 'Mohammed made his way out of Heathrow', his son, the writer and broadcaster Sarfraz Manzoor recalls, 'and hailed a taxi. In his trouser pocket he had a piece of paper with the name and address of his childhood friend Shuja whose brother worked with him in Pakistan. When Shuja had learnt Mohammed was coming to England he had told him he was welcome to live with him.' Shuja lived in a seven-bedroom house which was already home to thirty-one Pakistanis. 'It was soon explained to my father', Manzoor writes, 'that they slept in shifts; some of the men worked nights and others during the day. It was important that the beds were free by the morning as another group of men would be sleeping in them during the daytime.'

Communal living allowed a new arrival to be fed and looked after until he found a job. It also helped minimize expenditure, leaving men to remit to their families up to a quarter of their earnings, or to save up to buy their own house. That was how Anwar Parvez first lived in Bradford, and how he managed to get his kinsmen there.

Most of the original migrants thought they would work in Britain for a few years before returning home. So why did they end up staying? The answer, ironically, was the legislation that the British government introduced to keep them out. The arrival of large numbers of blacks and Asians led to a panic among policy-makers about the changing color of Britishness. 'A large coloured community as a noticeable feature of our social life', a 1955 Colonial Office report observed, 'would weaken . . . the concept of England or Britain to which people of British stock throughout the Commonwealth are attached.' The solution was the Immigration Act of 1962, which closed the door on automatic entry for Commonwealth citizens. In the months leading up to the Act there was a determined effort to use the 'chain' system that Anwar Parvez talked about to beat the closing door. A total of 17,120 Pakistanis came to Britain between 1955 and 1960. In the eighteen months preceding the 1962 Act, some 50,170 more came. 'Proudly, I can say I helped my whole area to come here,' Parvez recalls.

Not only was there a surge of migrants, but most now had little choice but to settle in Britain. Had they left, it was unlikely that they would have been allowed to return. So the men now brought over from the subcontinent their wives and children, and established communities in Britain. The 1961 census records just eighty-one women among the 3376 Pakistani men in Bradford. Ten years later there were 9090 men – and 3160 women. The attempt to keep Britain white had tinted many of its inner cities a little bit browner.

The character of chain migration, with each individual from a family or a village helping another to come to Britain and to settle there, tended to recreate the village and kin networks, or *biradari* system, that existed back home, reinforcing mutual ties of obligation, especially to the more powerful figures within a community. As the British documentary maker Navid Akhtar has put it, the *biradari* system ensures that 'Good times, bad times, there is always someone there for you. If you need money, someone in the *biradari* will always help you. When there is a dispute, the *biradari* sorts it out. When you die the *biradari* savings account pays to send your body back to Pakistan.' The importance of the *biradari*, and its power, was reinforced by the climate of hostility that the newcomers faced in Britain. 'Everything was alien to us,' recalled the chairman of the Bradford Council of Mosques, Sher Azam, when I talked to him in the wake of the Rushdie controversy, 'the people, the language, the culture, even the weather.' Racism meant that it was difficult to find jobs, accommodation or even food without the help of fellow clansmen.

The *biradari* system helped provide shelter in an alien and hostile land. But it also helped insulate many subcontinental communities from wider British society, reinforced links with Pakistan and Bangladesh, and subordinated the interests of the individual to the honour of the clan. The fact that many of the new immigrants did not speak English, or spoke it badly, only strengthened the power of the informal community leaders who often determined how the honour of the *biradari* should best be served.

The *biradari* system has become a major source of friction within Muslim communities, creating tensions between the first and second generations. 'At present,' observes Navid Akhtar, 'there is a void between the first generation, who speak for the community, and the second and third generations. This void continues to grow and is a cause of unrest with the young.' Practices such as arranged marriages to other members of the *biradari*, often still living in Pakistan, an honour code that makes the preservation of collective face more important than protecting individual rights, and the frequently contemptuous treatment of women and reluctance to see them grasp opportunities in education, employment or public life – all help deepen that void. 'Forty years after arriving in Britain,' Akhtar concludes, 'we are in danger of going backwards, divided by outdated and divisive practices.' The 'unwritten law of social conduct revolving around ideas of honour' that the *biradari* encapsulates 'necessarily disenfranchises the young', the former Hizb ut-Tahrir member Shiraz Maher points out, especially as the code is 'informally administered by community elders, whose authority cannot be challenged'. The attraction of radical Islamist groups like Hizb ut-Tahrir, Maher writes, is not that they promise a return to the old ways, but that they pledge to rip away the suffocating blanket of *biradari* tradition. Ironically, given popular perceptions of Islamist organizations, women in particular are drawn to radical groups because 'they encourage women to participate in public life, to pursue an education, to oppose arranged marriages and to engage in political activism'.

It would be wrong, however, to overplay the degree to which the new immigrants were cut off from British society or trapped in their traditions. In *Tales from Two Cities*, her celebrated 1987 book about Pakistani and West Indian communities in Bradford and Birmingham, the Irish travel writer Dervla Murphy describes Bradford's Manningham as 'Little Pakistan'. Even 'After decades of living in Britain', Malise Ruthven wrote about the anti-Rushdie demonstrators, 'they still seemed utterly *foreign*' in their 'white hats and long baggy trousers with flapping shirt tails'. But consider a unique collection of photographs of new immigrants taken in a Manningham photographic studio between 1955 and 1960 and reproduced in *Here to Stay*, an oral history of Bradford's south Asian communities collected by the Bradford Heritage Recording Unit. These group photos show the men (and the photos are almost exclusively of men) in smart suits, often with briefcases and rows of pens lining their top pockets. As mill workers or bus drivers few would actually have worn such fancy attire apart from in a photographic studio, but they give an insight into both the aspirations of the migrants and their understanding of British culture – not to mention their desire to show the folks back home how well they were doing.

Sarfraz Manzoor recalls photos of his father taken in the 1960s. By then Mohammed was working at the Vauxhall car plant in Luton, near London. In one of the photographs Mohammed 'is wearing a loose slate grey suit with a black tie and standing next to a vintage automobile'. For Sarfraz, 'what is so extraordinary about the photograph is seeing my father looking so fabulously cool; the image could have been a scene from a thirties gangster flick.' Another photo 'shows my father by a cooker stirring a pot'. The four other men in the shot 'are casually dressed in brown trousers and plain shirts. My father is wearing a tie.'

If photographs such as these show that Pakistani migrants were not as socially isolated or culturally backward as they are often perceived to be, their attitudes to religion were perhaps even more surprising. The first mosque in Bradford was opened in 1959, in the back room of a Victorian semi in Howard Street. It was run by the Pakistani Welfare Association and trustees included both West and East Pakistanis from a variety of sectarian traditions. It was used mainly on Sunday afternoons, not just for religious but also for more practical activities. English speakers among the gathering would translate official documents for their peers and address their letters home.

Over the next half-century, another forty-three mosques were built in Bradford, and the various Muslim communities and traditions all created their own places of worship. The Howard Street mosque was taken over by Pathans and Punjabis from the Chhachh region of the Punjab. In 1968 they installed a Deobandi as their first full-time *alim*. Yet, as one academic study has observed, migrants in the 1950s and 1960s 'suffered an almost total lapse of religious observance'. It was not that they were not pious, more that they did not see Islam as an all-encompassing philosophy.

The writer and director Pervaiz Khan, whose family came to Britain in the 1950s, remembers his father and uncles going to the pub for a pint. 'They did not bring drink home,' he says. 'And they did not make a song and dance about it. But everyone knew they drank. And they were never ostracized for it.' His family belong to the Sufi tradition – as do the majority of subcontinental Muslims in Britain – and were very easy-going. 'They rarely fasted at Ramadan,' Khan says, 'and never went to Friday prayers. They did not boast about it. But they were not pariahs for it. It was very different from today.' His parents had no objection to him attending Christian assemblies at school, joining in the harvest festival concert or taking part in Nativity plays. Again, he says, 'It was so different from what Muslim parents are like today.'

The first mosque for Bradford's Bangladeshi community was not opened until 1970, in two houses in Cornwall Road; it was almost fifteen years before a second one was built. By 1990 the much larger Mirpuri community had built eighteen mosques in the city, but fourteen of them had been constructed in the previous ten years. One reason why so many new mosques began sprouting up in the eighties was the growing self-confidence of Muslim communities. But that is only half the story. For what the pattern of mosque building in Bradford reveals is that it was not the piety of first-generation Muslims that led to the Islamization of the town. It was, rather, the power, influence and money that accrued to religious leaders in the 1980s as a result of Bradford City Council's multicultural policies. Multiculturalism helped paint Bradford Muslim green.

3

On 17 April 1976 the far-right National Front (NF) organized a march through the center of Manningham, the main Asian area in Bradford. It was to end with a rally at a local school. The NF was in the late 1970s a minor force in British politics, but more than a bit unpleasant. In 1974 it took 44 percent of the vote in a parliamentary by-election in Deptford in south London; three years later more than 120,000 voters supported it in London-wide elections. It was on the streets, however, rather than at the ballot box, that the NF preferred to strut its stuff. It had a cadre of thugs often involved in racial assaults and was fond of organizing provocative marches through predominantly black and Asian areas. And it was on the streets that a new generation of blacks and Asians decided to take on the NF. This brought them into conflict not just with the neo-fascists but often with their own community leaders too.

In response to the NF march in Manningham, local politicians and activists organized a counter-rally in the center of Bradford. Frustrated by the fact that while racist brutes were marching past their homes in Manningham, the opposition was rallying several miles away in the safety of the city center, hundreds of young Asians broke away from the main demonstration, fought their way through police lines and attacked the NF marchers. Bricks were hurled, police vans overturned and twenty-four people arrested. It was seen by many as the blooding of a new movement. 'It was there that we really started thinking that we've got to get our own house in order,' remembers the novelist Tariq Mehmood, one of those who took part in the breakaway march that day. 'We can't have this, we can't leave our future in the hands of people we hated like community leaders or the Labour Party types.' That was when, he says, 'the seeds of the Asian Youth Movements began to be formed'.

About a year after the anti-NF riot, a group of young Asians met in a pub to form the Indian Progressive Youth Association. Why did men and women whose origins lay in Pakistan or Bangladesh call themselves Indian? In large part it was an acknowledgement of their debt to the Indian Workers Association (IWA). The IWA had originally been formed in the Midlands town of Coventry in 1938 to agitate for Indian independence. It had been wound down after the demise of the Raj, but in the late 1950s it was re-formed to give a voice to the new wave of immigrants from the subcontinent. The IWA organized both as a trade union, in factories, on the buses and in hospitals, and as an anti-racist campaigning organization within Asian communities. It had close links to the labour movement in Britain and to the Communist Party of India, and its members invariably supported any action that local trade unions were taking, because, as the author and playwright Dilip Hiro put it, 'they believed that the economic lot of Indian workers was intimately intertwined with that of British workers'.

The IWA was, in fact, often forced to organize industrial action itself, usually to the consternation of mainstream trade unions. In May 1965 it led the first significant post-war 'immigrant strike', at Red Scar Mill in Preston, Lancashire, involving Indian, Pakistani and African-Caribbean workers. Over the next decade, the IWA was involved in dozens of industrial disputes, trying to roll back the impact of the first major post-war recession. The economic downturn of the early seventies gutted many of the sectors into which immigrants had been recruited, such as the textile mills. In 1965 there were 50,000 textile workers in Bradford, a third of all those in Britain. Fifteen years later the number had fallen by two thirds. Asians had always got lower wages and worse conditions than whites. Theirs were the first jobs to go when the cutbacks came. Racism shut the door on any other job prospects. The result was a series of stormy strikes in the mills, led by immigrant workers.

For black and Asian workers, taking industrial action often meant facing down not just the employer but the casually bigoted attitudes of union officials too. In one famous and bitter dispute at Imperial Typewriters in Leicester in 1974, the local union organizer refused to back the mainly Asian women strikers on the grounds that 'They have got to learn to fit into our ways, you know. We haven't got to fit into theirs.' But 'fitting in' was exactly what black and Asian workers were doing. Despite the hostility it faced from the local union, the strike committee at Imperial Typewriters insisted that 'black workers must never for a moment entertain the thought of separate black unions. They must join the existing unions and fight through them.'

Such strikes, and such attitudes, give the lie to the myth that Asian workers did not wish to integrate. They also challenge the belief that Britain became a multicultural nation because minorities demanded that their differences be recognized. For much of the 1960s and 1970s, black and Asian immigrants were concerned less about preserving cultural differences than about fighting for decent wages, proper conditions and equal rights. They recognized that at the heart of the fight for political equality was a commonality of values, hopes and aspirations between blacks and whites, not an articulation of unbridgeable differences. Only later were ideas of cultural and religious separateness to take hold within minority communities.

The IWA was important to Asian communities because it gave voice to the notion of the common interests of immigrant and indigenous workers, and acted upon it. It was, in the 1960s and 1970s, the most influential Asian political organization in Britain. In Southall, a west London borough with a large Asian population, the branch had a membership of 12,500 in the late sixties. Little wonder that the IWA provided an inspiration for a new generation of activists like Tariq Mehmood.

The very name of the Indian Progressive Youth Association showed how insignificant in the 1970s were the markers of 'identity' that appear so important today. Young Pakistanis and Bangladeshis were so open-minded about their origins and identity that they were quite willing to call themselves 'Indian', notwithstanding the bloodshed and turmoil of Partition. But while they were happy to be labelled 'Indian', it never entered their heads to call themselves 'Muslim'. As Mehmood puts it, 'In the 1970s, I was called a black bastard and a Paki, but not a coloured bastard and very rarely was I called a Muslim.'

Nevertheless, recalls Mehmood, there were problems in calling themselves the Indian Progressive Youth Association, because 'there was this contradiction that we weren't Indians'. In any case, for all the inspiration that the IWA provided, many young Asians had come to be critical of its activities. Its leaders were seen as part of the old guard of community spokesmen who had lost touch with the needs and problems of the youth. Indeed, the IWA had helped organize the anti-NF rally in Bradford city center, the timidity of which young Asians had so despised. So, the following year the organization was renamed the Asian Youth Movement. Defining itself as Asian was not a way of cutting itself off from African-Caribbeans or whites, but an attempt to create a conscious break with the sectarian forms of subcontinental politics that often still corrupted many first-generation organizations. In its own way, the AYM was to become to a new generation what the IWA had been to the old.

Soon Asian Youth Movements had sprung up all over Britain, in east London, Luton, Nottingham, Leicester, Manchester, Sheffield. Their slogans – 'Come what may, we are here to stay' and 'Here to stay, here to fight' – revealed a generation determined to be both seen and treated as British citizens. The youth movements challenged many traditional values too, particularly within Muslim communities, helping establish an alternative leadership which confronted traditionalists on issues such as the role of women and the dominance of the mosque. 'Asian women are the most oppressed section of our community,' observed *Liberation*, the magazine of the Manchester AYM, perhaps the most progressive of all the AYMs. 'Although we are living in an industrialized society, most of our people retain feudal values and customs. AYM will struggle against these reactionary aspects of our culture. AYM believes that the emancipation of women is a prerequisite for the liberation of society at large.'

AYM activists were not necessarily atheists. But religion never shaped their politics. The AYMs were secular organizations. 'I had grown up in a profoundly secular environment,' recalls Balraj Purewal. 'As a Punjabi I did not think about Muslim or Sikh. At school the person next to me was never a Muslim or Hindu. It never occurred to me to think like that.' Not only did AYM activists not distinguish themselves as Muslim, Hindu or Sikh, many did not even see themselves as specifically Asian, preferring to call themselves 'black'. Indeed, the very first 'Asian' Youth Movement, which Purewal helped found, did not call itself Asian. On 4 June 1976, Gurdip Singh Chaggar was stabbed to death by racists outside the Dominion Theatre in Southall, in west London. In the wake of the murder, local youths formed themselves into the Southall Youth Movement, the aim of which was both to campaign against discrimination and to provide physical defence for the area. What was developing here was a peculiarly British notion of 'blackness' and the fermentation of a very British identity. In America, 'black' meant 'of African origin'. On the Indian subcontinent no one would have defined themselves by their color. In Britain young blacks and Asians were attempting to forge a more inclusive identity rooted in politics rather than ethnicity or skin color, while at the same time trying to highlight the divisive character of racism.

The Asian Youth Movements drew inspiration from two different models of political organization. The first was traditional class-based politics in Britain. Activists did not only draw upon the history of organizations such as the IWA. Many had cut their political teeth in far-left Trotskyist groups. Mehmood himself was a member of the International Socialists, the forerunners of the Socialist Workers Party. The other model on which the AYMs drew was the Black Power movement in America, from which came the notion of 'black self-organization', the idea that blacks should organize independently of white groups. The clenched fist symbol of the AYM came straight from the Black Panthers.

These two guiding spirits were often in tension. 'Most of us were workers and sons of workers,' Mehmood recalls. 'For us race and class were inseparable.' Yet he, like many AYM members, was deeply suspicious of what he called the 'white left' and stressed 'the need for our own organization'. Indeed, the very 'formation of the Asian Youth Movement in Bradford', Anandi Ramamurthy, a historian of the AYM, suggests, 'was also an expression of the failure of "white" left organizations in Britain to effectively address the issues that affected Asian communities'. Despite the racist hostility they had faced from white trade unionists, the strikers at Imperial Typewriters rejected the idea of a separate black union. Their children, who formed the backbone of the Asian Youth Movements, rejected the idea that they should work within organizations that they saw as racist. 'We had to put our own house in order,' Mehmood observes, before it was possible to 'unite as equals' with the 'white left'.

Such attitudes were understandable given the sense of isolation that many blacks and Asians felt. But they could also all too easily lead to what the writer Mala Dhondy has called 'ghetto politics'. Today Dhondy is better known as Mala Sen, biographer of India's 'Bandit Queen',

Phoolan Devi. In the 1960s and 1970s, she was one of the leaders of Britain's Black Panther movement, which modelled itself closely on the American version and provided a political education for a whole generation of black British radicals. The writers Darcus Howe and Farukh Dhondy (then Sen's husband), and the dub poet Linton Kwesi Johnson, were among her contemporaries in the Panthers.

In the late 1970s Mala Dhondy helped organize Bengalis in east London into the Bengali Housing Action Group (BHAG), a militant squatting movement the aim of which was to end discrimination against Asians in housing allocation. Under pressure from the BHAG, the Greater London Council proposed in 1977 that 'we might continue to meet the wishes of the community by earmarking blocks of flats, or indeed whole estates if necessary, for their community'. Jean Tathan, the Conservative chair of the GLC housing committee, told newspapers that 'I am prepared to consider applications from all-white or all-West Indian groups.' The plan for color-coded housing estates caused uproar and was eventually defeated. At the time, Mala Dhondy claimed that 'The GLC has gone beyond what we asked for in a potentially dangerous way.' Later, however, she was to defend the idea of ghetto politics. 'Some people said, "You are creating a ghetto,"' Dhondy argued. 'We said, "Fine, we prefer the ghetto, at least you have each other to defend yourself" ... So that's what it was and we advanced it, and today you walk around Brick Lane [the street that lies at the heart of east London's Asian community] and it's totally Bengali.'

For Asians who often felt under siege from racists, there was indeed safety in numbers. The story of Nasreen Saddique and her family was all too familiar to any Asian who moved into a predominantly white area. And thanks to discriminatory housing policies, most housing estates, especially the good ones, were in those days overwhelmingly white. A 1982 report on housing allocation in east London reported that Bengalis made up just 0.3 percent of tenants on the best estates, and concluded that 'effectively the GLC has picked out certain old estates' in which to house Bengalis, while keeping newer housing stock 'almost exclusively white'. In a follow-up report two years later it found little change and suggested that 'Somewhere, somehow deliberate decisions must have been taken over which estates Bengalis were going to be "allowed" to live on.'

What Mala Dhondy called 'ghetto politics' was, however, more than simply a pragmatic response to such racism, more than simply a question of finding protection in numbers. It was also an attitude that came to celebrate the ghetto as an expression not just of the segregation of immigrants through poverty or racism but also of the cultural distinctiveness of a community. The idea of 'self-organization' originated as a strategy through which to combat racism: 'We have to get our own house in order before uniting as equals.' But over time it mutated into a celebration of cultural separation: 'We are different because we are black and Asian.' The idea of temporary organizational separation for political reasons gave way to the notion of permanent cultural distinctiveness as a fact of life. In the 1980s these ideas moved out of the ghetto of radical anti-racist politics and into mainstream public policy.

4

On 6 April 1981 London's Metropolitan Police launched Operation Swamp in Brixton, south London, the heart of Britain's African-Caribbean communities. The name of the operation had echoes of an infamous interview that Margaret Thatcher had given as leader of the opposition in 1978, in which she had warned about British culture being 'swamped' by foreigners. The operation's aim was to cut down street crime. Hundreds of plain-clothes policemen stopped and searched mainly young black men. The so-called 'sus laws', which allowed the police to stop and search people on 'suspicion', had already exacerbated tension between the police and the African-Caribbean communities because of the way they were used to harass black youths. During Operation Swamp almost a thousand people were stopped in the space of four days and some 118 arrested. The local council leader, Ted Knight, condemned the police action as that of 'an invading army'.

Today, Brixton is the epitome of metropolitan rough chic. Then, it was just rough. Today, terraced houses can fetch close to £1 million. Then, living in Brixton burdened you with unremitting poverty rather than a monstrous mortgage. Today, TV producers lunch on sushi in cool Japanese bars in Brixton market. Then, nearly half the young black men in the area were unemployed and lived on the streets. And on one street in particular. Railton Road, a long terraced street of largely squatted houses, was Brixton's 'front line'. It was there that drugs were sold and politics dispensed. The Black Panthers met there. There was an anarchist bookshop, and an office for the radical black Race Today Collective, above which the great West Indian Marxist, historian and cricket lover C.L.R. James lived. His neighbours included activists, writers and musicians such as Olive Morris, Darcus Howe and Linton Kwesi Johnson.

On the afternoon of Friday, 10 April 1981 the police stopped Michael Bailey, a nineteen-year-old black man bleeding from a knife wound. Witnesses alleged that he was bundled into a police car and no ambulance was called. A crowd gathered, surrounded the car and eventually freed Bailey. Soon there were running battles with the police. The arrest the following day of another black man sparked off a full-scale riot. At 5 p.m. on the Saturday an abandoned police car was set on fire. An hour and a half later, the first petrol bombs were thrown. Shocked viewers watched on the TV news that night scenes they had previously witnessed only on the streets of Belfast or Derry. By the following day thirty buildings had burned down, and another 120 had been damaged. More than a hundred cars and vans, including fifty-six police vehicles, were torched. Three hundred policemen and sixty-five civilians were seriously injured. Up to five thousand people were said to have been involved in the riot.

The Brixton riot was only one in a series of confrontations between black youth and the police. Some, like the Manningham riot in 1976, arose out of attempts to stop far-right marches. The most notorious of these came in Southall in May 1979. An anti-fascist demonstration organized by the Southall Youth Movement degenerated into violent battles with the police, during the course of which the teacher Blair Peach was bludgeoned to death by a member of the infamous Special Patrol Group, a newly created anti-riot squad. Other confrontations, such as the almost annual eruptions at London's Notting Hill Carnival and the riot that shook St Paul's in Bristol a year before Brixton, grew out of a sense of resentment at being treated as second-class citizens, not just through the grinding everyday discrimination in employment, education and housing, but, most explosively, out of the constant, unforgiving harassment that young blacks faced at the hands of the police.

It was, however, the Brixton riot of April 1981 that came to symbolize the breakdown of race relations in Britain. It was the first in a series of violent eruptions that rippled out from Railton Road through the rest of London and well beyond. From Brixton the violence touched Peckham, Southall, Wood Green, Finsbury Park, Woolwich, Forest Gate and Notting Hill in London. It reached into Liverpool, Birkenhead, Sheffield, Manchester, Hull, Newcastle and Preston in the north of England. It sparked off riots in the Midlands towns of Coventry, Birmingham, Leicester, Derby and Nottingham. Towns in the south of England rarely thought of as racial tinderboxes caught alight too: Southampton, Cirencester, High Wycombe, Gloucester, Luton, Reading and Aldershot. In Wales rioting broke out in Cardiff. Finally the violence returned to Brixton, in July 1981. 'Measured by any standards,' Darcus Howe has written, 'this revolt assumed serious insurrectionary proportions . . . Not since the insurrection of the 1830s – the Chartist movement – has English society experienced such extensive revolt.'

The summer of riots became the first major political challenge for Margaret Thatcher's Conservatives, who had swept into power in May 1979. The Iron Lady had a well-earned reputation for being tough on the issues of race and immigration. She was eager to bring National Front supporters 'back behind the Tory party', she claimed in her infamous 1978 'swamping' interview. To do so, the Conservative party had to 'talk about this problem [of immigration] and we must show that we are prepared to deal with it'.

Thatcher also had a reputation for being inflexibly ideological ('The lady's not for turning,' as she put it in her party conference speech in

1980, helping to write her own myth). Yet she could pirouette on the proverbial sixpence when necessity willed. Faced with major urban unrest, the Thatcher government responded in a typically pragmatic fashion, throwing resources not at more riot police but at inner-city communities. The effect of the riots, wrote the criminologist Marian Fitzgerald, then a Home Office researcher, was to 'transform pleas for more political opportunities for black people into the received wisdom that the black electorate *should* be more involved in politics'. There was a widespread recognition that unless black activists were given a political stake in the system, their frustration could threaten the stability of Britain's inner cities. But not all activists, nor all black people. The aim, as Sir George Young, who had been made Britain's first minister for race relations in the wake of the Brixton riot, put it the following year, was to 'back the good guys, the sensible, moderate, responsible leaders of ethnic groups. If they are seen to deliver, to get financial support from central government for urban projects, then that reinforces their standing and credibility in the community. If they don't deliver, people will turn to the militants.' The government's aim, in the words of a *Sunday Times* profile of Young, was 'the creation in Britain of a small but prosperous black middle class'.

The day after the Brixton riot, the home secretary, William Whitelaw, established a public inquiry into the disturbances under the chairmanship of former top judge Lord Scarman. When Scarman delivered his report in November, he dismissed the suggestion that the riots had been the product of 'institutional racism', blaming instead 'complex political, social and economic factors' for creating a 'disposition towards violent protest'. Without 'urgent action', Scarman concluded, racial disadvantage could become an 'endemic, ineradicable disease threatening the very survival of our society'.

It was difficult for the Conservative government to take such action because even those whom George Young called the 'good guys' did not trust what they regarded as the party of racism. Unlike the Tory central government, Labour-controlled local authorities possessed not just the hard cash but also the moral currency to help rebuild the inner cities.

In the late 1970s many radicals had left their tiny Trotskyist organizations to join the Labour Party. By the early eighties the Conservatives seemed dominant nationally and the Labour Party a broken institution, so many of those radicals looked to local councils as the path to political power. As a result such councils began to acquire a radical reputation. In South Yorkshire the local authority revelled in the nickname 'the Socialist Republic of South Yorkshire'. (Its leader, David Blunkett, was later to become, in Tony Blair's Cabinet, one of Britain's most illiberal home secretaries.) In 1981 a palace coup made the radical Ken Livingstone (who, like Blunkett, was to gain national prominence two decades later, in his case as the first Mayor of London) the leader of the Labour group on the Greater London Council (GLC), and eventually leader of the council too. The GLC, with its radical postures, was a constant thorn in the side of the Thatcher government, so much so that it was abolished in 1986. But the GLC was also an invaluable bridge between the political elite and the black and Asian communities. In 1981 the House of Commons home affairs committee encouraged local authorities to 'make as much direct contact as possible with ethnic minorities'. No institution did this more assiduously than the GLC. Many of its policies were derided as 'loony left' by the Conservative press in the 1980s. Within a decade they had been rebranded as 'multiculturalism', and had become as unexceptional as curry and chips on a Friday night.

Between 1981, when Labour regained control of the council, and 1986, when it was abolished, the GLC pioneered a new strategy of making minority communities feel part of British society. It arranged consultations with them, drew up equal opportunities policies, established race relations units, and dispensed millions of pounds in grants to minority groups. On average, fewer than forty people attended each consultation meeting organized by the GLC's newly established Ethnic Minorities Unit. Yet these came to be seen as representing the authentic voice of each community, and the means by which to identify both the needs of the community and the leaders best placed to represent it.

Once the GLC had established a political structure with which to engage minority communities, cash tumbled out of its myriad institutions. In 1980/81 the GLC dispensed some £5 million to voluntary organizations. Five years later, in its final year before abolition, the figure had climbed to £77 million. In 1983/84, its first full year of operation, the Ethnic Minority Unit dispensed more than £2.3 million to 247 groups. In its final year more than £6.2 million was allocated to some three hundred groups. Other council institutions joined in, too. The industry and employment committee, the arts and recreation committee, the police committee and the enterprise board – all these and many others provided finance for minority groups.

At the heart of the GLC's anti-racist strategy was not simply the reallocation of resources but also a redefinition of racism. Racism now meant not the denial of equal rights but the denial of the right to be different. Black people, so the argument went, should not be forced to accept British values or to adopt a British identity. Rather, different peoples should have the right to express their own identities, explore their own histories, formulate their own values, pursue their own lifestyles. In this process, the very meaning of equality was transformed: from possessing the same rights as everyone else, to possessing different rights appropriate to different communities.

Scepticism about the idea of a common national identity arose in part from cynicism about the idea of 'Britishness'. There was widespread recognition among blacks and Asians that talk about Britishness was a means not of extending citizenship to all Britons, whatever their color or creed, but of denying equal rights to certain groups. When Margaret Thatcher suggested, in her infamous 'swamping' interview, that 'The British character has done so much for democracy, for law, and done so much throughout the world, that if there is any fear that it might be swamped, people are going to react and be rather hostile to those coming in', she seemed to be equating Britishness with whiteness. In Conservative eyes, as Rushdie put it in his essay 'The New Empire within Britain', 'a black man could only become integrated when he started behaving like a white one'.

The GLC's anti-racist strategy did not, however, simply question the idea of Britishness. It challenged the very notion of common values, drawing on the ideas of the 'New Left' that had emerged in the 1960s. The New Left was a loose association of groups and individuals that was self-consciously opposed to the 'old left' of the communist parties and trade unions. Where the old left looked to the working class as the agency of change, the New Left found new, surrogate proletariats in the so-called New Social Movements – Third World liberation struggles, civil rights organizations, feminist groups, campaigns for gay rights, and the peace movement. Where the old left talked of class and sought to raise class-consciousness, the New Left talked of culture and sought to strengthen cultural identity.

The New Left was shaped by cultural success and political failure. The sixties heralded a cultural sea change. The rise of youth culture and of mass culture, the transformation of the role of women, more liberal attitudes to sex and sexuality, the creation of more diverse societies through immigration, the ease of mass travel – all helped transform Western culture.

Conservatives railed against the breakdown of traditional moral codes and the rise of the 'permissive society'. Politically, however, they were in the ascendant. By the end of the seventies, both the social democratic and the communist left were in crisis. The election triumphs of Margaret Thatcher in Britain in 1979 and of Ronald Reagan in America the following year signalled a new era in politics, characterized by aggressive free-market economic policies, harsh Cold War rhetoric and a full-frontal assault on trade unions. By the end of the 1980s working-class organizations were in decline, Third World liberation movements had largely disintegrated and even the new social movements of the 1960s were in disarray. The fall of the Berlin Wall in 1989 confirmed the seismic shift in politics.

The cultural critic Todd Gitlin remembers how this combination of cultural success and political failure shaped left-wing attitudes. Since 'society as a whole seemed unbudgeable', so the demand grew for 'separate organizations [acting] on behalf of distinct interests'. The idea of self-organization emerged initially from the struggle for black rights in the US. Accusing the left of indifference to their cause, many black activists ceded from integrated civil rights organizations and set up separate movements. Black self-organization soon gave way to the idea of black identity, a 'recognition of those things uniquely ours which separate ourselves from the white man', as the Black Power activist Julius Lester put it. Soon, Native Americans, Puerto Ricans, Chicanos, Chinese Americans, not to mention a myriad white ethnics, all set up their separate cultural organizations, using the template established by Black Power activists. Women and gays became surrogate ethnics, each with their own particular cultures, identities and ways of thinking. 'The demand is not for inclusion within the fold of "universal humankind" on the basis of shared human attributes; nor is it for respect "in spite of one's differences",' wrote feminist and sociologist Sonia Kruks. 'Rather, what is demanded is respect for oneself as different.'

By the 1970s, Gitlin observes, the old left-wing dream of collective action in pursuit of universal values was already passé. 'One belonged to a caucus, cultivated a separate culture, and dismissed the idea of the human condition, or the republic or the common good, or citizenship as hopelessly pre-postmodernist.' Separatism had become 'more than an idea'; it had become 'a structure of feeling, a whole way of experiencing the world. Difference was now felt . . . more acutely than commonality. Initiative, energy, intellectual ingenuity went into the elevation of differences.' Social solidarity became increasingly defined not in political terms – as collective action in pursuit of certain political ideals – but in terms of ethnicity or culture. 'The very language of commonality', Gitlin writes, 'came to be perceived by the new movements as a colonialist smothering – an ideology to rationalize white male dominance.'

It was through municipal anti-racism that such ideas became entrenched in Britain. The black and Asian population was smaller in Britain than in the US, and its political and economic clout less significant. The attempts at self-organization were weaker, while the authority of both the moderate and the radical left was greater. As a result, until the 1980s, the influence of identity politics remained weak. The Asian Youth Movement had been built on the model of self-organization drawn from America, but it was nevertheless more outward-looking, working closely with other anti-racist and radical organizations.

GLC policy changed both the character of anti-racism and the meaning of self-organization. For AYM activists, self-organization had been a political strategy: they wanted to separate themselves from other political movements not because they saw themselves as permanently different, but as a practical means of organizing collective action at a particular time. Self-organization was part of a wider political programme.

GLC strategists, however, talked not so much of self-organization as of cultural self-development. They viewed separation not as a political matter but as a cultural necessity, not as a means to an end but as an end in itself. As Gita Sahgal and Nira Yuval-Davis of the Asian women activists' group Southall Black Sisters have observed, the GLC reduced the fight against racism 'to preserving the "traditions and cultures" of the different ethnic minorities'. 'Rather than tackling the central problem of racism itself', municipal anti-racists insisted that 'cultural differences between various groups in society [were] of paramount importance'.

The GLC activists did not call themselves 'multiculturalists'. But the policies they fashioned became central to multicultural thinking. In 2000, more than a decade after the GLC had been abolished, the Commission on the Future of Multi-Ethnic Britain published its report. The commission had been set up by the Runnymede Trust, an independent think tank devoted to the cause of promoting racial justice in Britain, and was chaired by the political philosopher Bhikhu Parekh. The commission's remit was to 'analyse the current state of multi-ethnic Britain and propose ways of countering racial discrimination and disadvantage and making Britain a confident and vibrant multicultural society at ease with its rich diversity'. The Parekh report concluded that Britain was 'both a community of citizens and a community of communities, both a liberal and a multicultural society'. Since citizens had 'differing needs', equal treatment required 'full account to be taken of their differences'. Equality, the report insisted, 'must be defined in a culturally sensitive way and applied in a discriminating but not discriminatory manner'.

The Parekh report has come to be seen as defining the essence of multiculturalism. But the two arguments at its heart – that Britain is a 'community of communities', and that equality must be defined 'in a culturally sensitive way' – emerged out of the policies of municipal anti-racism.

The GLC strategy of the 1980s combined the distribution of council largesse with the celebration of cultural distinctiveness. 'Here's the cash, now go off and do your own cultural thing. Just don't cause a commotion on the streets.' That was the essence of municipal anti-racism. It proved a winning formula in getting militants off the streets, and often into the town halls. Between the Broadwater Farm riot of 1985 and the violence that ripped through the northern mill towns of Bradford, Burnley and Oldham in 2001, Britain's inner cities were free from large-scale violence. As a means of bridging racial divisions and differences, however, it was far less successful. Multiculturalism helped create new divisions and more intractable conflicts which made for a less openly racist but a more insidiously tribal Britain.

5

On 9 September 1985 police arrested a young black man near the Acapulco Café in the Handsworth area of Birmingham. A few hours later they launched a drugs raid on the nearby Villa Cross pub. Hundreds of people – blacks, whites and Asians – took to the streets in protest, attacked police and property, looting, smashing and setting off fire-bombs. Two people were killed and dozens injured. It was almost the last flicker of the eighties inner-city conflagrations.

Almost exactly twenty years later, on 22 October 2005, another riot erupted in Lozells, next door to Handsworth. This time the fighting was not between youths and police but between blacks and Asians. It began with a rumour that an African-Caribbean girl had been gang-raped by a group of Asian men in Beauty Queen, an Asian-owned shop selling African-Caribbean hair products. Kirk Dawes is a black former drug squad officer in Birmingham who now runs a mediation service that negotiates between rival street gangs. He was approached by the police to try to defuse the tension in Lozells. When the rumour began, he says, 'it was about a woman of thirty-two being raped by two Asian men. It was only barber-shop talk. But over time the age of the woman came down and the number of rapists went up.' Soon the African-Caribbean community was buzzing with stories about a fourteen-year-old girl, a Jamaican illegal immigrant, having been assaulted by twenty-five Asian men. 'We asked people how they knew about the rape,' he said. 'It was always, "I heard it from a woman who heard it from a woman at One-Stop."'

Soon the rumour was being broadcast on local black pirate radio stations. Warren G, a DJ on Sting FM, gave a graphic account of the supposed rape and called for a demonstration outside the shop. It was then picked up by two websites, Blacknet and Supertrax, which reported that Lozells was swarming with 'Paki gangs'. 'I hope Asian women are getting their throats cut as we speak' was a typical comment in the chat room. According to Mohammed Saleem of the Birchfield Traders' Association, the discussion on the airwaves was no less incendiary. One caller rang Sting FM to say, 'There are not enough of you pussies out there in the street! This is between blacks and Pakis.'

The following week there were pickets outside the shop and activists distributed leaflets within the African-Caribbean community urging blacks to boycott all Asian shops. The police took the owner of Beauty Queen and four other men into custody for questioning. An extensive investigation could not unearth any evidence of a rape nor, indeed, discover the girl who was supposed to have been raped. The men were released without charge. Meanwhile, according to Kirk Dawes, black gangs were flooding into Lozells from across the country, thinking that 'black people couldn't walk the streets of Birmingham'. It had already turned 'from being about the so-called rape into something about the exploitation of the black community by the Asian community'.

On Saturday, 22 October there was a demonstration outside Beauty Queen. Around five hundred people turned up. Warren G spoke first, urging a boycott of the shop. Bini Brown, a local community leader, told the crowd that 'there was a systematic programme to drive the black people out of certain areas of Birmingham'. Itabarica Naphthali, a Rastafarian who runs the Haile Selassie Peace Centre, called it 'ethnic cleansing'. Another demonstration took place that evening outside the New Testament Church on Lozells Road. It degenerated into a riot. According to the African-Caribbeans, a group of Asian men attacked the demonstration, shouting 'Kill the niggers'. Asians claim that black demonstrators armed with baseball bats and bricks rampaged through the area attacking Asian shops. What is beyond dispute is that for two days blacks and Asians fought each other on the streets, with guns and petrol bombs, smashing cars and burning shops. A young black man, Isiah Young-Sam, who happened to be walking home through Lozells on Saturday evening, was set upon by a gang of Asian men and murdered.

On the Monday after the riot, Britain's main black newspaper, the *Voice*, published a front-page story with the headline 'Gang of 19 Rape Teen', claiming that Birmingham had 'erupted after sex attack on black girl, 14'. An editorial urged a boycott of Asian-run shops. The following week the *Voice* published a retraction and an apology.

Why did two communities that had fought side by side in 1985 fight against each other twenty years later? Why did an area that had twice the national average of 'mixed-race' children splinter so suddenly? Why did virtually every African-Caribbean take as true a malicious rumour – and continue to do so even after an intensive police investigation had turned up no evidence? Why did so many African-Caribbean community leaders call for a boycott of *all* Asian shops in retaliation for the alleged rape?

The answer lies largely in the policies introduced by Birmingham City Council after the original riots of 1985. The council borrowed the

GLC blueprint to create a new political framework through which to reach out to minority communities. It created nine so-called 'Umbrella Groups', organizations based on ethnicity and faith, which were supposed to represent the needs of their particular communities and help the council develop policy and allocate resources. They included the African and Caribbean People's Movement, the Bangladeshi Islamic Projects Consultative Committee, the Birmingham Chinese Society, the Council of Black-led Churches, the Hindu Council, the Irish Forum, the Vietnamese Association, the Pakistani Forum and the Sikh Council of Gurdwaras.

The council hoped that by setting up these groups it could draw minority communities into the democratic process and so keep anger off the streets. The trouble was, there was precious little democracy in the process. The groups themselves had no democratic mandate – indeed, no mandate at all. After all, why should the Council of Black-led Churches presume to speak for the needs and aspirations of African-Caribbeans in Birmingham? Why should all Bangladeshis be represented by an Islamic organization, or all Sikhs by the gurdwaras? Indeed, what is *the* Bangladeshi community, or *the* Sikh community, and what are their needs and aspirations?

Imagine if the council had set up a 'White Forum' to represent the needs of the white community in Birmingham. Could such a group have represented the interests of all white people in Birmingham? Clearly not. Some whites vote Conservative, some Liberal, some for the Labour Party, and a few for the communists or the neo-fascists. And some don't vote at all. Some whites are religious, others militantly secular. And most whites would not see their interests as specifically 'white'. A white Christian probably has more in common with a black Christian than with a white atheist. A white communist would think more like a Bangladeshi communist than like a white Conservative. And so on. Why should we imagine that Bangladeshis or Sikhs or African-Caribbeans are any different? They are not. It is simply that the council's policies, like all multicultural policies, seemed to assume that minority communities had somehow arrived in Birmingham from a different social universe. Cosmologists believe that the physical universe in its infancy was homogeneous and uniform. Multiculturalists seem to think the same about the social universe of minority groups. All are viewed as uniform, single-minded, conflict-free and defined by ethnicity, faith and culture. As the council's own report put it, 'The perceived notion of homogeneity of minority ethnic communities has informed a great deal of race equality work to date. The effect of this, amongst others, has been to place an over-reliance on individuals who are seen to represent the needs or views of the whole community and resulted in simplistic approaches toward tackling community needs.'

Birmingham's policies, in other words, did not respond to the needs of communities, but to a large degree *created* those communities by imposing identities on people and by ignoring internal conflicts which arose out of class, gender and intra-religious differences. They empowered not individuals within minority communities, but so-called 'community leaders', who owed their position and influence largely to the relationship they possessed with the state. The 'new class of "ethnic representatives" [that] entered the town halls from the mid-1980s onwards', observes Arun Kundnani of the Institute of Race Relations, became 'the surrogate voice for their own ethnically defined fiefdoms'. This new black elite 'entered into a pact with the authorities': in return for 'managing and containing anger from within the ranks of black communities', the authorities gave them 'free rein in preserving their own patriarchy'.

Such ethnic fiefdoms were at the heart of local politics in Birmingham. In the 1960s and 1970s, says Pervaiz Khan, who grew up in the Sparkbrook area, not far from Handsworth, the first generation of immigrants were involved largely in Pakistani politics. Most were supporters of the Pakistan People's Party, presided over by the Bhuttos – first Zulfikar, and subsequently his daughter Benazir. Political support was organized largely on *biradari* lines, and PPP meetings in Birmingham often degenerated into physical fights between different clans. By the 1980s interest in Pakistani politics had waned. In 1977 General Muhammad Zia-ul-Haq overthrew the then prime minister Zulfikar Ali Bhutto in an army coup and later executed him. By the 1980s Zia had fully consolidated his power in Pakistan. PPP supporters in Birmingham turned their attention from Pakistani to local politics.

The Labour Party took advantage of this shift in focus by recruiting from the Asian communities. It did so, however, largely on clan lines. 'What the Labour Party was really interested in', says Khan, 'was recruiting clan elders who could deliver votes en masse. At election time, the elders would simply tell everyone in the clan to vote for their candidate.' He tells the story of his uncle, who came to Britain in the 1950s and who became, a decade later, the first non-white shop steward in the Transport and General Workers' Union in Birmingham. He developed strong relationships with the local Labour Party hierarchy and had, by the 1980s, become an essential cog in the Labour Party machine. 'He was never an elected councillor,' says Khan, 'but he was treated as if he was. He had his own office in the council building, a pass and a parking space. He effectively acted as a "whip", making sure that other Asian councillors voted the "right way". In return, he got council grants for the Asian community, for community centers and other projects.' Second-generation Asians, who had little interest in Pakistani politics and despised the *biradari* system, also accommodated themselves to what Khan calls 'machine politics', recognizing it as a useful way of gaining resources for their communities.

Such machine politics inevitably created conflicts between minority communities. The 'ethnically defined fiefdoms' were constantly skirmishing with one another. As one academic study of Birmingham observes, the 'model of engagement through Umbrella Groups tended to result in competition between BME [black and ethnic minority] communities for resources. Rather than prioritizing needs and cross-community working, the different Umbrella Groups generally attempted to maximize their own interests.'

Once political power and financial resources became allocated by ethnicity, then people began to identify themselves in terms of their ethnicity, and *only* their ethnicity. 'People are forced into a very one-dimensional view of themselves by the way that equality policies work,' says Joy Warmington of the Birmingham Race Action Partnership, a council-funded but independent equalities organization. 'People mobilize on the basis of how they feel they will get the resources to tackle the issues important to them. And in Birmingham it helps to say you're campaigning for the needs of your ethnic or faith community, because policies have tended to emphasize ethnicity as a key to entitlement. It's become accepted as good practice to allocate resources on ethnic or faith lines. So rather than thinking of meeting people's needs or about distributing resources more equitably, organizations are forced to think about the distribution of ethnicity. And people begin to think in those terms too. If somebody in Handsworth or Lozells wants a community center or a health center it is often easier to get funding if they say "We want an Asian community center" or "We want an African-Caribbean health center." They are forced to see themselves in terms of their ethnicity, their race, their culture and so on rather than in broader terms that might bring people together.'

Imagine that you are a secular Bangladeshi living in a run-down area of Birmingham. You don't think of yourself as a Muslim, you may not even think of yourself as Bangladeshi. But you want a new community center in your area. It is difficult to get the council's attention by insisting that your area is poor or disadvantaged. But if you were to say that the Muslim community is deprived or lacking, then council coffers suddenly open up – not because the council is particularly inclined to help Muslims, but because being 'Muslim', unlike being 'poor' or 'disadvantaged', registers in the bureaucratic mind as an authentic identity. Over time, you come to see yourself as a Muslim and a Bangladeshi, not just because those identities provide you with access to power, influence and resources, but also because those identities have come to possess a social reality through receiving constant confirmation and affirmation. It is how you are seen, so it is how you come to see yourself. You come to fear and resent African-Caribbeans and Sikhs and the Irish, partly because they are competitors for that pot of council largesse and power, and partly because the rules of the game are that your identity has to be affirmed as distinctive and different from the identities of other groups. Being Muslim also means being not Irish, not Sikh and not African-Caribbean.

'Plural monoculturalism'. That is Nobel Prize-winning economist Amartya Sen's apt suggestion for the proper name for multiculturalism. What we call multiculturalism, he observes, is really policy driven by the myth that society is made up of a series of distinct, uniform cultures which dance around one another. He might have been describing the assumptions underlying policy in Birmingham. What Birmingham reveals is the way that policy can make the myth a reality. Multicultural policy creates the segmented society and fixed identities to which it is supposedly a response. The term 'multicultural' has come to define both a society that is particularly diverse, usually as a result of immigration, and the policies necessary to manage such a society. It has come to embody, in other words, both a *description* of a society and a *prescription* for managing it. Multiculturalism is both the problem and the solution – and when the problem and the solution are one and the same we can only be dealing with political snake oil.

In applying multicultural snake oil to the problems of Birmingham, the council created rifts between communities where none had previously existed and exacerbated divisions that had previously been managed. The greatest estrangement was between the Asian and African-Caribbean communities. African-Caribbeans resented the economic success of many Asians and, in particular, felt aggrieved that many shops selling what were regarded as 'black' goods, such as African-Caribbean beauty products or West Indian food, were Asian-owned. Asians had achieved their success, many believed, by manipulating the council funding process and by strangling African-Caribbean political influence.

To a degree they were right. The *biradari* system had allowed Asians to influence the political machine far more successfully than the more individuated African-Caribbean communities. 'We have a South African situation here,' claimed Maxi Hayles, chair since 1989 of the council-funded Birmingham Racial Attack Monitoring Unit and one of the city's most respected African-Caribbean leaders. 'White on top, coloured Asian in the middle and African at the bottom. If you want a taxi – Asian. If you want petrol – Asian. Off-licence – Asian. Access to banks – Asian. Even Afro-Caribbean food – Asian. Our community feels trapped.' The Asians, Hayles claimed, 'have an unfair advantage: they came from Uganda and Kenya with money. I cannot condone what Idi Amin is supposed to have done – I stress supposed to have done – but the fact is that the Afro-Caribbeans were here first, then the Asians came and built an economy based on the millions they had made in Africa.' Another black community leader, Bini Brown, chair of the African-Caribbean Self-Help Centre, which describes itself as the 'most powerful Pan-African Organization in Birmingham that inspires African people to take their rightful place on earth', talks of the 'deep racism' in the Asian community, 'which is sometimes hidden . . . and sometimes out there, throwing change on the counter, and disrespect for our women'. On the streets black teenagers talk of 'Paki rapists', while Asians contemptuously dismiss blacks as 'kalas', blaming African-Caribbeans for their own misfortunes and suggesting that they are too lazy and feckless to be successful.

A few months after the riots I went to Birmingham to make a TV documentary about community tensions. Most African-Caribbean leaders, including Maxie Hayles and Bini Brown, refused to talk to me, not because they found the cameras too intrusive but because I was Asian and therefore 'on the other side'. One of the few who was willing to talk was Anthony Gordon, chair of the Partnership Against Crime. Before I could interview him, however, he wanted me to account for what he saw as the crimes of the Asian community. I can only speak for myself, I told him, I cannot speak for all Asians. He snorted. 'But Asians have always had it in for the black man. It was like that in South Africa. It was like that in Kenya and Uganda. And it's like that here. It's in your blood.'

Birmingham City Council began with the intention of bringing minority communities into the democratic process. It ended up with communal politics so deeply entrenched that it eventually led to communal rioting. Hostility is not in the blood of Asians or African-Caribbeans. It is in the DNA of multicultural policies.

6

In Bradford, it was not a riot but a trial that shook the town. In the summer of 1981 Bradford's Asian communities were flush with rumours of an impending attack by neo-fascists. A group of young Asians, including Tariq Mehmood, made and stashed away petrol bombs to be used in the event of any such attack. They were all members of the United Black Youth League, a group that had broken away from the Asian Youth Movement, which they felt was not sufficiently radical. Police discovered the petrol bombs on some waste ground and twelve members of the UBYL were arrested and charged with conspiracy to cause an explosion and endanger lives. The trial of the 'Bradford 12' the following year created a national sensation. The defendants put up an audacious defence. They openly admitted making the petrol bombs – but argued that they were acting legitimately to protect their communities. Astonishingly, the jury agreed and acquitted all twelve.

The sheer bravado of the Bradford 12 and their bold, confident self-assertion won them respect and support from communities across the country that similarly felt under siege from racists. It also unnerved both local politicians and Muslim religious leaders. 'Our children were growing up hating our culture', observed Sher Azam of the Bradford Council of Mosques. 'They were being drawn to Western values and Western lifestyles. We knew such values and ways of doing things could only harm them. Without Islam they had no foundations, no home. They were angry, withdrawn, we could not reach them.'

The reverberations of the Bradford 12 case were also felt within the town's political elite. The trial had revealed not just an unprecedented degree of self-assertiveness among young Asians but also a yawning gap between Asian communities and mainstream political structures. A few months after the arrest of the Bradford 12, a council report observed that 'we have no direct knowledge of Asian needs and requirements, and we have no automatic way of knowing the issues they feel important'. They needed 'some new channel of communication between the council and the communities – something to compensate for the lack of political representation'.

Today, Ali Hussein is a casually dressed graphic designer living in a newly built loft apartment in Leeds. In the eighties he lived in Manningham in Bradford and was deeply immersed in the political battles of the time. The atmosphere in the town hall was, he says, like something from the popular British TV sitcom *Dad's Army*. The series told the story of a platoon of the Home Guard in the Second World War, local volunteers ineligible for military service, usually because they were too old, whose job it was to protect the British mainland from invasion. The humour came from the pompousness of their leader, Captain Mainwaring, and the incompetence of the volunteers. 'Don't panic!' the elderly corporal Jones would shout, flapping as the platoon blundered into yet another mishap. In 1981 the spirit of Corporal Jones stalked the committee rooms of Bradford town hall. 'They were shit-scared,' remembers Hussein. 'They were staring at the possibilities of widescale riots and they were looking for people to talk to. Anyone, anywhere. They pulled people off the streets and said, "Come and talk to us."'

The council reached for the GLC template. It drew up equal opportunities statements, established race relations units and threw money at minority organizations. A twelve-point race relations plan declared that every section of the 'multiracial, multicultural city' had 'an equal right to maintain its own identity, culture, language, religion and customs'. The first aim of its 'race relations initiative' was to 'bring about social justice' by ensuring 'Equality of esteem between different cultures'.

To create its 'new channel of communication', in 1981 the local authority helped set up and fund the Bradford Council of Mosques. The six founding members of the Council represented various Islamic traditions and sects, such as the Deobandis, the Barelwis and Jamaat-e-Islami. But the Council of Mosques was not primarily a religious organization. It was designed, rather, to present itself as the true voice of the 'Muslim community', and to be the conduit between that community and public bodies in the city. With the singular exception of Pir Maroof, the Sufi mystic, none of the prime movers behind the Council were *ulema*, or religious scholars, nor has one ever become its president. It was not imams but businessmen who pulled the strings. The most prominent of these was Sher Azam. He had been chairman of the Howard Street mosque, the first in Bradford, was one of the founders of the Council of Mosques and served as its chairman for more than half its first decade, and was the man who helped torch *The Satanic Verses*. He was also one of Bradford's leading businessmen, running the Al Halal Supermarket and Cash & Carry, an Islamic cooperative with a turnover, in the 1980s, of more than £2 million.

One of the myths around which much policy has revolved (and not just in Britain) is that of the all-powerful imam. The 'preacher of hate' has become a potent image in both the media's and policy-makers' discussions of how Islamic terrorists get 'brainwashed'. An important strand of British policy has been about 'taming' the imam, ensuring that he speaks good English and has been trained in the virtues of liberal democracy. There are certainly firebrand preachers, such as Abu Hamza, who is said to have converted the 7/7 bombers to terrorism through his incendiary sermons at the Finsbury Park mosque in north London. But these are the exceptions rather than the rule. Most imams in most British mosques are timid creatures, badly paid, treated not particularly reverently, and whose lack of English is likely to make them not more fiery but less assertive.

In *The Islamist*, Ed Hussain's account of his descent into radical Islam, he tells of how he and his fellow radicals in the Young Muslim Organization took over Stepney mosque in east London. Hussain was at that time estranged from his father, who was hostile to radical Islam. The imam at Stepney was a friend of Hussain's father and was equally opposed to radicalism. Yet he felt unable to challenge even sixteen-year-old Hussain. Imams, Hussain observes, 'tend to be meek' and 'very rarely rock the boat. The YMO was perceived in Stepney as a well-connected, educated group of young men, outside the domain of a mosque imam. He humbly led the prayers, then left us to listen to the lectures of Sami [a university graduate and supporter of Jamaat-e-Islami who was training the YMO radicals].' The real power in a mosque rests with the mosque committee, and the real power in the mosque committee rests with the businessmen who hold the purse strings, both in the mosque and in the community.

In Bradford, the local authority backed the Council of Mosques with an initial grant to help it buy the semi-detached Victorian house that was to serve as its headquarters. But its real gift was the funding it provided for mosque-based social projects, including two centers for the elderly, a variety of advice workers, and a service for women in hospitals and clinics. It also funded a series of Muslim youth and community centers.

Such funding provided mutual benefits. Bradford City Council was able to define the needs of the Asian community without having to think about the political changes necessary to ensure real equality. What the community needed was a bit more of its own culture, a lot more of its faith and a good ladle of welfare. And it was not council leaders who said so, but Muslim men of faith. 'What we wanted from the council', Sher Azam told me, 'was their support for our efforts to make sure that our children were not lost to our culture or Islam. We were worried that they had become so Westernized that they no longer saw themselves as Muslims or wanted to practise their faith. We had lots of problems with no jobs, lots of drugs, even fighting. We told the council that the best way to help us was to restore pride in our culture and our religion.'

Because such arguments came from Muslim leaders, Bradford City Council did not even have to accept responsibility for the new strategy. This was not the only responsibility of which the local authority washed its hands. By subcontracting its mandate for providing welfare services, the local authority expected the Council of Mosques not just to attend to the well-being of Muslims in the town but also to maintain peace and decorum within its community. Council officials saw Islam, rather than any secular ideology or political policy, as the best way of keeping angry young men in check. As Dervla Murphy put it her account of 1980s Bradford:

> The prospect of thousands of jobless young Muslims, untamed by Islam, adrift in the inner-cities alarms me much more than that other problem – at present attracting so much attention – of thousands of jobless young Blacks on the loose. The virtues of the Muslim community – industry, forward-planning, group-loyalty, agile thinking, efficient teamwork, purposefulness – could, if deprived of a legitimate arena, produce a law and order problem that would make the Blacks' sporadic outbursts of despairing violence seem trivial.

Mohammed Ajeeb, then a Labour councillor, who was later to become Bradford's first Asian lord mayor, had noted in a radio interview that 'our children are bound to be influenced by the values of their British counterparts', and may not be able to 'withstand . . . Western values and culture'. Murphy was appalled. 'If Mohammed Ajeeb's forecast is proved correct,' she warned, 'then my forecast is Big Trouble Ahead.'

Why should Islam be a panacea for the social ills of young men of Pakistani and Bangladeshi origin, but irrelevant to everyone else? What is it about Western values that would poison the souls of young Muslims, and seemingly only of young Muslims? Why would it not have been more rational to provide jobs and equal opportunities for the alienated youths and to treat them as one would treat everyone else? Murphy does not say. Nor did the myriad policy-makers whose views she echoed. They simply accepted that 'Western values' were a form of virus within Asian communities and that the best inoculation was a good dose of Islam. Over time, what became subcontracted out, as we shall see in Chapter 4, was not simply the provision of welfare but political authority too. Rather than appeal to Muslims as British citizens, and attempt to draw them into the mainstream political process, politicians and policy-makers came to see them as people whose primary loyalty was to their faith and who could be politically engaged only by Muslim 'community leaders'. It was a policy that encouraged Muslims to view themselves as semi-detached Britons – and that inevitably played into the hands of radical Islamists.

The Bradford Council of Mosques, of course, seized its opportunity with great zeal. The local authority had effectively installed it as the custodian of the Muslim community, a community that did not exist in this form until council policy had parcelled it up and given it as a gift to the Council of Mosques. Few, apart from a handful of religious leaders and mosque officials, had thought of themselves as 'Muslim'. They might have seen themselves as Pakistani, or Bengali, or Kashmiri, or Sylheti, or Asian – or, perhaps, British – but very rarely Muslim. But once the mosques became the voice of the community, then Muslim became the identity stamped upon every individual within that community. And, as in Birmingham, people began to accept that identity as their own, because it was the way to relate to the outside world. Just as the Council of Mosques became the channel of communication between the Muslim community and local organizations, so Muslim identity became the interface between individuals within that community and the outside world.

At the same time as the Council of Mosques was installed as the voice of the Muslim community, a new generation of secular politicians was being groomed too. The local Community Relations Council, observed Philip Lewis, lecturer in peace studies and former advisor to the bishop of Bradford, 'functioned as a nursery for Muslim politicians, where the necessary skills, confidence and contacts were developed'. The new breed of politicians did not provide an alternative leadership to the mosques, as, say, the Asian Youth Movement had done. Rather, they turned into the secular wing of the Bradford Council of Mosques. Take Mohammed Ajeeb. He became the first south Asian chairman of the CRC, from 1976 to 1983. He was elected a councillor in 1979. In 1983 he became senior supervisor of a local authority-funded Council of Mosques project. In 1985 he was installed as Bradford's first Asian lord mayor. The CRC, Lewis writes, 'was the main forum where officers of the Council of Mosques and Muslim councillors met and where support for Muslim concerns in the wider community could be tested'. Ali Hussein takes a more cynical view. 'There developed a mutual relationship between the religious leaders, the secular leaders and the council,' he says. 'The religious leaders delivered the votes. The secular leaders delivered the money. And for the council it has meant a few years of relative peace on the streets.'

As part of its brief to allow different communities to express their distinct identities, Bradford City Council helped set up not just the Council of Mosques but also two other religious umbrella groups: the Federation for Sikh Organizations and the Vishwa Hindu Parishad, both created in 1984. What happened in Birmingham found its echo in Bradford. As each community fought for a greater allocation of council funding, so new divisions and tensions were created within and between different communities. There had always been residential segregation between the black and white communities in Bradford, thanks to a combination of racism, especially in council house allocation, and a desire among Asians to find safety in numbers. But within Asian areas Muslims, Sikhs and Hindus lived cheek by jowl for much of the post-war period. In the 1980s, however, the three communities started dividing. They began increasingly to live in different areas, attend different schools and organize through different institutions. New council-funded community organizations and youth centers were set up according to religious and ethnic affiliations. By the early 1990s even the Asian business community was institutionally divided along community lines, with the creation of the largely Hindu and Sikh Institute of Asian Businesses in 1987, the Hindu Economic Development Forum in 1989 and the Muslim-dominated Asian Business and Professional Club in 1991.

The real segregation, however, was not physical or organizational but in the mind. Multiculturalism transformed the character of anti-racism in Bradford. At the end of the 1970s the main issues that concerned black and Asian communities were largely political: opposing discrimination

in the workplace, organizing against racist attacks, preventing deportations and ending police brutality. By the mid-1980s, however, the focus
had shifted to religious and cultural issues. What convulsed Bradford
now were demands for separate Muslim schools and for separate education for girls, a campaign for halal meat to be served at school, and, most
explosively, the confrontation over *The Satanic Verses*.

Political struggles unite across ethnic and cultural divisions; cultural
struggles inevitably fragment. As different groups began asserting their
particular identities ever more fiercely, so the shift from the political
to the cultural arena helped to create a more tribal city. The Asian
Youth Movement, a beacon in the 1970s of a united struggle against
racism, split up, torn apart by such multicultural tensions. Mukhtar
Dar was a founder of the AYM in Sheffield and was deeply involved in
the Bradford 12 campaign. In the late 1980s, he says, 'The AYM's symbolic
black secular clenched fist split open into a submissive ethnic hand
with its divided religious fingers holding up the begging bowl for the
race relations crumbs.'

CHAPTER THREE

The rage of Islam

That night I lay awake, holding his fate in my hands as well as my own. If I allowed myself to be destroyed I could destroy him, too. I had to choose, on that awful night, whether I preferred death with revenge to life without anything.

Salman Rushdie, *The Satanic Verses*, p.368.

1

The number 30 bus from Hackney Wick to Marble Arch had been diverted from its normal route because of a logjam of traffic near King's Cross station. The driver was unsure where he was. He stopped and called to a parking attendant walking along the side of the road. 'The bus stopped and the driver asked me the name of the street,' said Ade Soji. 'I told him Tavistock Square.' It was 7 July 2005. The time was 9.47 a.m. The day before, London had been awarded the right to host the 2012 Olympics, to great joy in the city. Five days earlier the Live 8 concert had taken place at Wembley. That morning prime minister Tony Blair was about to address the G8 summit of world leaders at Gleneagles. 'Just as I was about to go,' remembers Soji, 'I heard the bus explode. I ran for my life. I looked back and saw the roof flying over.'

The explosion on the number 30 bus was one of four almost simultaneous suicide attacks on London's transport system. At 8.50 three bombs had exploded on Underground trains within fifty seconds of each other: one between Liverpool Street and Aldgate stations, a second near Edgware Road station and a third between King's Cross and Russell Square stations. The bomb on the bus was also meant for the Tube, but the bomber was late and could not enter King's Cross station because of the mayhem caused by the three explosions. He caught a bus instead. And so it was that the smouldering, red, twisted metal of the number 30 bus, blown up in a square famous for its statue of that apostle of non-violence Mahatma Gandhi, came to symbolize the carnage of 7/7.

Fifty-six people, including the four bombers, were killed in the attacks and seven hundred injured. It was the deadliest single act of terrorism in Britain since the bombing of Pan Am flight 103 over Lockerbie in 1988, in which 270 people had perished. More people died on 7/7 than in any single IRA attack in Britain or Ireland.

But it was not the death toll that made 7/7 so chilling. Nor even the fact that these were the first-ever suicide-bomb attacks in Europe. It was the recognition that the bombers were not foreigners but British citizens, steeped in this country's life and culture. Three of the four men involved, Mohammad Sidique Khan, Shehzad Tanweer and the bus bomber Hasib Hussain, had been born and bred in the Yorkshire town of Leeds. The fourth, Jamaican-born Germaine Lindsay, had lived in Britain since the age of five.

In the days following 7/7, thousands of journalists decamped to Beeston, the suburb of Leeds where the three Yorkshire bombers had spent much of their lives, most apparently believing that they were about to walk into a kind of ersatz Kabul. 'I came here expecting lots of angry young men,' wrote Urmee Khan in a major spread for the *Observer*. 'But there was not one Free Palestine flag in sight.' Khan was a Muslim but, in her own words, came from the sheltered leafy lanes of Surrey in southern England. Beeston was as alien territory to her as it would have been to most people in Britain. Her 'first impressions of Beeston' were a 'surprise': 'The housing was looking grim but far more normal than the menacing streets I expected. Maybe I had envisaged eerie gothic pathways with shuffling clerics spreading words of hate. No, it was all drab but very normal.' Later, Khan went to the town center, 'expecting it to be run-down and shabby. Instead I found a vibrant and colorful building in what used to be a church. Notice boards advertise Pilates classes, Muslim women-only gym work-outs, police drop-in sessions and a sign advertising cut-price car-window tinting. It was slightly surreal – this could have been any community center in Britain, yet this was Beeston.'

Not just the town but the people, too, seemed normal. The 'young men are no more religiously observant than an equivalent group of white men'. Teenage boys 'often get drunk on vodka in the park. But their talk tends to be about girls and football, not international jihad.' At a sewing class at the local community center, women chat about *Big Brother* and read *Heat* magazine. 'All the women,' Khan writes, 'including those wearing headscarves and saris, are reading celebrity gossip enthusiastically.' Khan concludes the essay by observing that she came to Beeston, 'looking for mullahs bent on destruction'. Instead, she 'found kind, decent people: young mums, bored kids, community cohesion'.

Far from being a 'little Lahore', Beeston is very British. It is a working-class area, slightly rough at the edges, whose inhabitants have the same dreams, hopes, aspirations, problems and confusions as those of any similar part of the country. And if Beeston was normal, so, it seemed, were the bombers. The leader of the group, Mohammad Sidique Khan, was born a few miles away, in St James's University Hospital, Leeds. He was popular at school, and nicknamed 'Sid'. 'He was friends with the in-crowd,' remembers one of his fellow pupils, Robert Cardiss. 'He had white mates as well as Asian and he would quite often be round the back of the gym at breaktime smoking a fag with the rest of us. He didn't have any girlfriends that I know of, but he'd talk to girls. He was friendly.' Cardiss added that 'Some of the other Pakistani guys used to talk about Muslim suffering around the world but with Sidique you'd never really know what religion he was.'

Until a few months before the bombings, Khan had worked at Hillside primary school in Leeds as a 'learning mentor' with the children of immigrant families who had just arrived in Britain. His colleagues commented that he had been a quiet individual who rarely talked about his religious or political beliefs. 'He seemed a really kind man,' remembered one child, 'he taught the really bad kids and everyone seemed to like him.'

Khan's wife Hasina Patel came from a family with a strong tradition of community involvement, charity work and activism. She herself was a so-called 'community enrichment officer' who worked in schools with special needs pupils. The two had met at Leeds Metropolitan University, where Khan had taken a business degree and Patel studied sociology. They married in 2001 and their daughter, Maryam, was born three years later. It was a love-match, not an arranged marriage, which led to friction with Khan's family, not just because he had refused to marry his cousin, as his parents had desired, but also because Patel was an Indian Deobandi whereas the Khan *biradari* were Pakistani Barelwis.

Khan's mother-in-law, Farida Patel, worked as a council liaison officer at a school in Dewsbury. In 1998 she had become the first Asian woman to be invited to a Buckingham Palace garden party, meeting the Queen and other members of the royal family, in recognition of her work within the Muslim community in Dewsbury. She was invited to another royal garden party in July 2004. While Farida Patel was sipping tea and eating cucumber sandwiches in the grounds of Buckingham Palace, her son-in-law was being shown round the Houses of Parliament by Jon Trickett, MP for the Yorkshire constituency of Hemsworth, whose wife Sarah was headmistress of Hillside school.

2

There was nothing unusual about Beeston. Nor about Mohammad Sidique Khan. So how did a man with such a background turn into a killer seemingly without pity or conscience? By what strange path did radical Islamists travel to go from burning books in Bradford to committing mass murder in London?

There have in recent years developed two kinds of explanation for the rage of Islam. The first is that there is something about Islam that makes it irredeemably violent, even evil. 'Islam is not just a religion,' the journalist Mark Steyn tells us. 'There's a global jihad lurking within this religion', which is 'a bloodthirsty faith in which whatever's your bag violence-wise can almost certainly be justified'. In Islam, Martin Amis has suggested, 'the West confronts an irrationalist, agonistic, theocratic/ideocratic system which is essentially and unappeasably opposed to its existence'.

The second explanation takes the opposite view: the problem is not Islam but the treatment of Muslims. The Western hatred of Islam makes for Islamic hatred of the West. In his 'martyrdom video', released by al-Qaeda a year after 7/7, Shehzad Tanweer, who blew himself up near Aldgate Tube station, put the blame four-square on Western imperialism. 'To the non-Muslims of Britain,' he proclaimed, 'you may wonder what you have done to deserve this. You are those who have voted in your government, who in turn have, and still continue to this day, to oppress our mothers, children, brothers and sisters, from the east to the west, in Palestine, Afghanistan, Iraq and Chechnya.' Many journalists and anti-war activists agreed. 'The principal cause of this violence', the radical writer and film-maker Tariq Ali wrote, 'is the violence being inflicted on the people of the Muslim world.' 'What we are confronting here', the distinguished foreign correspondent Robert Fisk similarly suggested, 'is a specific, direct, centralized attack on London as a result of a "war on terror".'

Neither explanation holds up. Muslims have been in Britain in large numbers for more than half a century. It is only in the past twenty years that radical Islam has gained a foothold. Blaming it all on Islam or on the Qur'an does nothing to explain the changing character of Muslim communities and their evolving beliefs. Islam, like every religion, comprises not just a holy text but also a history, a culture and a set of institutions, not to mention a clergy and a body of believers. All these and more help define how the holy text is interpreted. 'The key question', Olivier Roy points out, 'is not what the Koran actually says, but what Muslims say the Koran says.' Muslims continually disagree on what the Qur'an says, he adds dryly, 'while all stressing that the Koran is unambiguous and clear-cut'.

Equally unconvincing is the idea that terrorist rage has been driven by Western foreign policy. Just as Muslims were in Britain long before they turned to radical Islam, so Western governments were attacking Muslim lands long before Osama bin Laden took to a cave in Afghanistan. From

Winston Churchill ordering the use of mustard gas against Iraqi rebels in the 1920s, through the CIA-engineered coup against the democratically elected government of Mohammed Mosaddeq in Iran in 1953, the brutal attempt by the French to suppress the Algerian independence movement in the late 1950s, and the West's backing for Saddam Hussein in his war against Iran in the 1980s, to America's continuing economic and military support for Israel, there is a long history of Western intervention. There has always been resistance to such intervention, and often violent resistance, but Islamic opposition is relatively new, and nihilistic terrorism newer still. In any case, the actions of the terrorists belie their supposed political beliefs. In July 2007 Islamic terrorists parked two car bombs outside Tiger Tiger, a central London nightclub. The bombs failed to detonate. Had they done so, they could have created far greater devastation than the 7/7 attacks. Just two minutes' drive from Tiger Tiger are the Houses of Parliament and the Foreign Office. Yet the bombers chose to park their deadly load outside a building full of partygoers – hardly the actions of political soldiers driven to fury by Britain's foreign policy.

There is something else that fits oddly with the attempt to pin all the blame on Western foreign policy. No Western nation draws more Islamist ire than America. Yet, since 9/11, the Great Satan has not had a hair singed. There have been devastating attacks in London, Madrid, Bali, Casablanca and elsewhere. But not in the USA. More than that: American Muslims seem far less interested in Islamism than do their European counterparts. In the five years following 9/11, 2300 Muslims were arrested in Europe on suspicion of terrorist activity; there were just sixty such arrests in the USA. Even taking into account the much larger proportion of Muslims in European societies, European Muslims are six times as likely to take part in suspicious activities as their transatlantic brethren. American Muslims are certainly more middle-class than those in Europe. Yet so are the terrorists: Islamic terror, as we have seen, is the work not of the dispossessed of the earth but more of the well-educated, middle-class professional.

Europe is not a single entity, and there are major differences between the ways in which, say, British Pakistanis and French *beurs* relate to their respective societies. Yet to cross the Atlantic is to move between two distinct social philosophies about the nature of immigration. American Muslims, like many immigrant groups before them, have largely bought into the promise of the American Dream. Seventy-one percent think that people who want to make it in America can do so with hard work – a higher figure than for the US population as a whole. They tend to see themselves as assimilated Americans, not as disgruntled Muslims. Fewer than half think of themselves as Muslims first and Americans second. In Britain the corresponding figure is 81 percent, in Spain 69 percent and in Germany 66 percent. Only in France – the one European country that has as strict a separation of faith and state as America – do a comparable number see themselves as citizens first, Muslims second. Unlike in Europe, most American Muslims are happy to view Islam as a private faith, rather than as an all-encompassing social ideology.

We should not exaggerate the social width of the Atlantic; nevertheless, in America the myths and perceptions of immigration help to inoculate against Islamism to a degree, whereas in Europe they help to raise the fever. The difference shows how the rage of Islam is a political, not a religious, phenomenon, and one shaped less by Western foreign policy, however misguided such policy may be, than by domestic political attitudes and social experiences.

The two main explanations for Islamic rage – 'blame it on Islam' and 'blame it on the West' – are both variants of the 'clash of civilizations' argument: the belief that the world is caught in a mortal struggle between Islam and the West. The trouble is that not only is there no such as thing as 'Islam' and 'the West' as singular, uniform entities, but contemporary Islam, especially in its more radical forms, is as much the product of Western societies as it is their supposed nemesis. 'Fundamentalism and radical violence', Olivier Roy observes, 'are more linked with Westernization than a return to the Koran.' Roy, together with his fellow professor at the Centre national de la recherche scientifique (CNRS) in Paris, Gilles Kepel, have been among the most astute observers of the Muslim world and their work has done much to challenge many of the myths about Islamic militancy. At the heart of the work of both Roy and Kepel is an insistence that radical Islam is a modern philosophy, not a throwback to an ancient past, and one whose very attempt to cleanse itself of corrupting Western ideas and attitudes is given shape by those same ideas and attitudes.

It is often said that there are four broad 'schools' of Islam today: the traditionalists, the fundamentalists, the Islamists and the modernists. This kind of taxonomy does capture something of the character of contemporary Islam. Yet it also obscures many of the changes taking place. The relationships between these schools are anything but straight-forward, and their affiliations to Western values and to ideas of modernity can be surprisingly unsettling.

Islamic traditionalists have a deep attachment both to the literal word of the Qur'an and to the cultures and institutions of Islam. Over the centuries, however, those cultures and institutions have transformed the reading of the Qur'an and the practice of Islam. Religions, like all social forms, cannot stand still. Islam today can no more be like the Islam of the seventh century than Mecca today can look like the city of Muhammad's time.

Islam has been transformed not just through time but across space too. The spread of the faith from the Atlantic coast to the Indonesian archipelago and beyond incorporated peoples who fitted into Qur'anic scripture many of their old religious and social practices. What Pakistani Mirpuris see as traditional Islam is very different from that of North African Bedouins. And what British Mirpuris see as traditional is different from the traditions of Mirpuris still in Mirpur.

It is this transformation of Islam over time and space to which fundamentalists object. 'True Islam', Ayotallah Khomeini argued, 'lasted only for a brief period after its inception. First the Umayyids [the first Arab dynasty, who ruled the caliphate for a hundred years from shortly after Muhammad's death in 632] and then the Abbasids [who overthrew the Umayyids in 750] inflicted all kinds of damage on Islam. Later the monarchs ruling Iran continued in the same path; they completely distorted Islam and established something quite different in its place.'

'True Islam', however, has proved difficult to define, especially as both Sunnis and Shiites see themselves as true believers. The division between Shia and Sunni dates back to the struggle to take over the leadership of the Muslim nation after the death of Muhammad. Shias believe that the only true caliphs are Muhammad's descendants, beginning with his cousin Ali. Shia means 'party' and is a shortened form of 'Shia't Ali', or 'party of Ali'. Throughout history, Shias have refused to recognize the authority of elected Muslim leaders, choosing instead to follow a line of imams whom they believe to have been appointed by Muhammad or by God Himself.

Sunnis, on the other hand, take a more pragmatic view, arguing that leadership should rest with whoever is most capable. Unlike Shias, they accepted Muhammad's close friend and advisor, Abu Bakr, as the first caliph. When Ali, who had eventually become the fourth caliph, was defeated in battle by Mu'awiya Ummayad, the governor of Damascus, Sunnis accepted the Ummayad dynasty, and subsequently the Abbasids, who defeated the Ummayads at the battle of Zab in Egypt in 750.

Sunnis do not have a formal clergy, just scholars and jurists, who may offer non-binding opinions. Shias, on the other hand, believe that the supreme imam, such as Ayatollah Khomeini, is imbued with pope-like infallibility and is an inerrant interpreter of law and tradition. The Shia religious hierarchy is not dissimilar in structure and religious power to that of the Catholic Church. Sunni Islam, in contrast, more closely resembles the myriad independent churches of American Protestantism. Today about 85 percent of the world's 1.4 billion Muslims are Sunni. There are some 150 million Shiites, concentrated mainly in Iran, Iraq, Bahrain, Azerbaijan and the Lebanon.

Like the majority of Muslims, the majority of fundamentalist groups are Sunni. One study found that of 175 Islamic groups identified as fundamentalist between 1970 and 1995, only thirty-two were Shiite. As in the squabble over Muhammad's succession, so today's conflict between Sunnis and Shias, and between Sunni and Shia strands of fundamentalism, is political as much as theological, shaped by the struggle between Saudi Arabia and Iran for leadership of the Muslim world.

The religious philosophy of the House of Saud is drawn from the ideas of the eighteenth-century Arab writer Muhammad ibn Abd-al-Wahhab, a 'Salafi'. Salafis, whose name comes from an Arabic word meaning 'predecessor' or 'first generations', believe, like Khomeini, that Islam was perfect and complete during the time of Muhammad, but has been corrupted and needs reviving by restoring the true Prophetic tradition. In the 1970s, buoyed by money from the oil boom, the Saudi government started funding Salafi organizations worldwide. The Iranian revolution of 1979, when the Shiite Khomeini toppled the Shah and claimed political power, challenged the political supremacy of the Saudis within the Muslim world. The meaning of 'fundamentalism' became part of that political struggle. Both may be 'fundamentalists', both may yearn for a return to the purity of the original faith, but Iran and Saudi Arabia, the Khomeinists and the Salafis, are as two dogs fighting over a single bone. Even fundamentalists cannot agree on what is fundamental.

Fundamentalists are often seen as 'traditionalists' and as hostile to modernism because of their obsession with the purity of faith and the literal word of the Qur'an. But, as Olivier Roy points out, to a fundamentalist 'the enemy is not modernity but tradition, or rather, in the context of Islam, everything which is not the Tradition of the Prophet'. The celebration of the authentic Prophetic tradition expresses not a desire literally to return to the past but an attempt to use the past to reshape the present. For all the yearning for an authentic Islam, fundamentalists are quite at home in the modern world. They have embraced not just new technology, such as the Internet, but also contemporary political ideas. Muslim activists, particularly in Europe, call upon modern Western legal concepts, such as group rights, to demand official recognition for their identity and state support for their communities. When Muslim organizations make a case for the introduction of sharia law into Western jurisprudence, they talk of pluralism and minority rights, notions that would have been meaningless to Muhammad. The very name of the London-based Islamic Human Rights Commission is absurd in traditional Islamic terms – human rights are an invention of the past century – but significant in the contemporary debate about the place of Islam in modern Western society.

Even more than the fundamentalists, radical Islamists speak the political language of Western modernity. Radical Islam is an offshoot of fundamentalism which emerged in response to the collapse of the Ottoman empire and the break-up of the caliphate in the wake of the First World War. Because Sunni Muslims were most attached to the caliphatic tradition, they felt its collapse most strongly, and radical Islam emerged from the Sunni tradition. Its ideas were shaped by the writings of Sayyid Abul A'la Maududi, the Pakistani founder of the Jamaat-e-Islami party, the Egyptian Sayyid Qutb, a leading member of the Muslim Brotherhood, and the Palestinian Taqiuddin al-Nabhani, who set up Hizb ut-Tahrir in 1953. Such radicals viewed Islam less as a religion and more as a complete socioeconomic system, and were driven as much by political sentiments as theological arguments.

Political Islamists reject liberal democratic values. But they are equally hostile to traditional religious cultures. It is just this detachment from traditional religious institutions and cultures that forces them into a literal reading of the Holy Book and to a strict observance of supposedly authentic religious norms. Disconnected from traditional cultures and institutions, they look to the very word of the revealed text for anchorage and to rigid cultural forms – such as, for instance, the veil – to mark themselves out as distinct and to provide a collective identity.

The fourth school of Islam, the modernists, openly espouses liberal democratic ideas and has, for obvious reasons, won the greatest sympathy from Western liberals. But the modernizers often have more in common with radical Islamists than they have with traditionalists. Indeed, in promoting the idea of the *khalifa* and of Islam as a global religion, radicals pose a challenge to the parochial, clan-based politics of the traditionalists, and so help open the way towards a more liberal democratic politics. Some modernizers promote secularism and the idea of Islam as a private faith. Others, such as Ziauddin Sardar, are deeply sceptical about the virtues of secularism. Yet others, such as the Iranian Abdul

Karim Saruch, call for the separation of faith and state but want civil society to remain religious. And some modernizers, such as Tariq Ramadan, have close links with Islamist groups – in Ramadan's case, with the Muslim Brotherhood.

The back story of the London bombings – and of the Beeston bombers – cannot be confined within the conventional boundaries often used to understand radical Islam. There were many roads that led to Tavistock Square on that morning of 7 July. One of them ran through Tehran in February 1979.

3

A frail old man, wearing a black turban and ankle-length robes, stepped out of an Air France 747 into a chill February morning. His back hunched, he clutched the arm of a purser as he took faltering steps down a portable ramp to touch Iranian soil. After fifteen years in exile, the seventy-eight-year-old Ayatollah Ruhollah Khomeini had come home, the spiritual leader of a popular revolution that had toppled the Shah of Iran and humbled SAVAK, his American-backed secret police force. Several million people from all across the country thronged into the capital to welcome him, lining the twenty-mile route out to Behesht-Zahra cemetery, where many of the martyrs of the revolution were buried. 'The holy one has come!' they shouted triumphantly. 'He is the light of our lives!' At the cemetery Khomeini prayed and delivered a thirty-minute funeral oration for the dead. Then a boys' chorus sang, 'May every drop of their blood turn to tulips and grow forever. Arise! Arise! Arise!'

It is difficult today to give a sense of the hope and expectation created by the overthrow of the Shah. 'It made dreamers of us all,' recalls Ziauddin Sardar. 'It seemed natural for me and my friends to support the revolution. I understood the deep emotional roots from which it sprang, and the aspirations it aimed to fulfil.' Even I felt elated. I was no dreamer of Islamic dreams. But even to a militant non-believer like me, the overthrow of the brutal, undemocratic Shah seemed a good thing, especially as radical secularist groups were at the heart of the opposition – until they were crushed by Khomeini.

The Iranian revolution of 1979 was to radical Islam as the Russian revolution of 1917 had been to revolutionary communism. Each gave life to a political philosophy that until then few had believed capable of flesh-and-blood expression. Just as with the Russian revolution, the shock of the Iranian revolution was that it was so unexpected. Marxists had never dreamt that the world's first communist revolution would happen in an industrially backward, peasant-based society, rather than in one of the advanced nations of western Europe with their well-organized proletariats and strong revolutionary traditions. Similarly, the last place that Muslims had imagined a radical Islamic revolution was in Iran, a largely Shiite nation, a tradition famous for its religious piety and political quiescence. Just as revolutionaries flocked to Moscow after the October revolution, Tehran now became a magnet for frustrated Islamists.

In the decade between Khomeini's return to Tehran and the imposition of his fatwa on Salman Rushdie – and it was almost ten years to the day that the one followed the other – Islamism mutated from being a minor irritant to nationalist regimes in Muslim countries into a major threat to the West. The Rushdie affair – and the fatwa in particular – seemed like a warning that the seeds of the Iranian revolution were being successfully scattered across the globe, not least into the heart of the secular West. Through the nineties, Islamist parties grew in influence in Turkey, Palestine and elsewhere, shaking the very foundations of secular government. In Algeria a vicious and bloody civil war broke out in 1991 between the Groupe Islamique Armé (GIA) and the secular military government, a war that spilled over into acts of terror in France. The Taliban imposed its medieval rule on Afghanistan. The creation of Hamas in Palestine and Hezbollah in Lebanon posed a mortal threat not just to Israel but also to secular organizations such as the PLO. Radical groups like Hizb ut-Tahrir gained a foothold within Muslim communities in western Europe. And terror worked itself into the political landscape, from suicide bombings in Palestine and Lebanon, to bombings on the Paris Métro, the attack on American embassies in Kenya and Tanzania, and eventually the horror of 9/11.

While all this was happening the Berlin Wall collapsed, and with it the vision of global socialism. Many young Muslims who had previously been attached to left-wing radical movements were now left politically homeless and searching for new ideological shelter. The collapse of the Soviet Union had also opened the way for the *umma* physically to extend its reach beyond the old Iron Curtain to embrace the new Muslim states of Central Asia, the Caucasus and the Balkans.

Most analysts expected Islamists to sweep to power across the world. The former US ambassador to Algeria, Christopher Ross, who in the wake of 9/11 would become a 'special coordinator for public diplomacy and public affairs', declared in 1993 that the Middle and Near East were 'fated to witness a wave of Islamist revolutions, successful or failed, over the next decade'. A decade later, a CIA report predicted that Islamists would 'come to power in states that are beginning to become pluralist and in which entrenched secular elites have lost their appeal'.

It never happened. There was no second Iranian revolution. In places like Egypt, Jordan and Malaysia, where the Islamists once held high hopes of repeating Khomeini's success, their influence has been curtailed, admittedly often through brutal repression. Outside of the rare cases where social convulsions shaped the political landscape for a short period, such as in Algeria in 1991, when elections took place on the eve of civil war, and with the single exception of Hamas in Gaza in 2006, no Islamist party has ever won more than 20 percent of the popular vote. Twenty percent was what Iran's Mahmoud Ahmadinejad won in the first round of the presidential elections in 1995. Parties that have broken through the 20 percent barrier – like Turkey's AK, Algeria's FIS and Tunisia's Nahda – have done so largely by shedding their Islamist trappings, renouncing their dreams of a caliphate, and becoming ordinary political parties with Muslim leanings – and in the process often becoming better democrats than the secularists they toppled.

We are left, then, with a paradox. On the one hand, Western societies have become increasingly fearful of Islamic terror, and politicians and commentators often talk as if the West is under siege from radical Islam. From the Rushdie affair to the electoral success of Hamas in Gaza, from the worldwide protests over the Danish cartoons to the increasing calls for the introduction of sharia law not just in Muslim countries but in secular Western nations too, Muslims seem increasingly drawn to radical arguments. On the other hand, not only has Tehran failed to export its revolution, but Islamist parties have failed to win mass support. 'For all its political successes in the 1970s and 1980s,' Gilles Kepel observes, 'by the end of the twentieth century the Islamist movement had signally failed to retain political power in the Muslim world, in spite of the hopes of supporters and the forebodings of enemies.'

How can we explain this paradox? Terror is an expression of the impotence of Islamism; unable to win for themselves a mass following, jihadists have become impresarios of death, forced into spectacular displays of violence to gain the attention they cannot win through political means. Nothing reveals the moral squalor of radical Islam better than its celebration of the suicide bomber. Traditional political and military movements nurtured as their greatest asset the people who supported them. For jihadists people are like firecrackers to be lit and tossed away.

And yet this weakness has been transformed into a strength by the political uncertainty and self-doubt that has seeped into Western societies. The key question, as Bill Durodie, a lecturer in risk and security at Cranfield University, puts it, is not 'what it is that attracts a minority from a variety of backgrounds, including some who are relatively privileged, to fringe Islamist organizations, but what it is about our own societies and culture that fails to provide aspirational, educated and energetic young individuals with a clear sense of purpose and collective direction through which to lead their lives and realize their ambitions, so that they are left looking for this elsewhere – including, for some, among various arcane and distorted belief systems'.

Consider the Rushdie affair. The initial campaign against *The Satanic*

Verses had minimal impact and drew little support from Muslim communities beyond Britain and the Indian subcontinent. It was Ayatollah Khomeini's fatwa that drew global headlines. But the fatwa itself was a sign of weakness rather than of strength, an attempt by Khomeini to distract attention from defeat in the war with Iraq and the erosion of political support at home. In the West, it was not theological distress about blasphemy but political despair about belongingness and identity that stoked up anti-Rushdie sentiment. Someone like my old comrade Hassan was not moved to campaign against *The Satanic Verses* because the Qur'an insisted that 'those that deny Our revelations shall be punished for their misdeeds'. I doubt if he even knew of Allah's promise to 'cast terror into the hearts of those who disbelieve', to 'Smite them above their necks, and smite off all their fingertips'. What he did know was racism; and anger about racism created in him resentments towards British society out of which radical arguments about the Muslim community could breed. Disenchantment with the left eroded his ideas about universal values and beliefs in struggles across communities, not least because the left itself was abandoning those ideas and beliefs. Multicultural policies suggested the inability, even unwillingness, of British politicians and institutions to reach out to him as a citizen rather than as a member of a 'community of communities'. The reluctance of politicians to speak to his resentments, and their aversion to talking in a language of common citizenship, inevitably pushed Hassan towards an Islamist identity, even if there was little within that identity to pull him in.

4

It is not simply the uncertainties of secular politicians that Islamists have been able to exploit. It is also their cynicism. Time and again over the past four decades politicians in both Muslim countries and Western nations have encouraged the growth of Islamist groups, because they have regarded radical Islam as less threatening than secular radicalism.

In June 1967 Arab armies from Egypt, Jordan and Syria were routed by Israel in the Six Day War. The greatest humiliation was heaped upon Egypt's President Nasser, the figure most identified with the assault on Israel. The main beneficiary of Nasser's fall was the left. In February 1968 – three months before the famed *événements* in Paris – students and workers took to the streets of Cairo, and other Egyptian cities, in violent protest against what they regarded as the generals' treachery. These protests grew in scope and ferocity over the next few years.

Fearing the radicals more than the Islamists, Anwar Sadat, who became president after Nasser's death in 1970, came to a rapprochement with the Muslim Brotherhood, an organisation that Nasser had savagely repressed and whose leader, Sayyid Qutb, he had executed in August 1966. Sadat released the Brothers and their associates from prison and encouraged them to organize against the left in the universities. 'Sadat's gamble', Gilles Kepel observes, 'was to encourage the emergence of an Islamist movement which he perceived as socially conservative.' In exchange for allowing the 'Islamist intelligentsia considerable cultural and ideological autonomy', Sadat expected them 'to hold the line against more radical groups whose goal was to subvert society.' The Islamists certainly held secular militants in check. But Sadat was unable to do the same with radical Islamists who now flourished in the spaces from which nationalists and radicals had been forced out. In the end Sadat paid the ultimate price. In October 1981 he was assassinated by members of Islamic Jihad – a group that he himself had encouraged – during a military parade in Cairo.

This has been a common story over the past thirty years. Secular governments unleash the dogs of militant religion to keep in check left-wing radicals, believing that the dogs can be tethered again after they have done their job – only to be savaged themselves by the beasts they have let loose. 'By making concession after concession in the moral and cultural domains', Kepel writes, governments in Muslim countries 'gradually created a reactionary climate of "re-Islamization". They sacrificed lay intellectuals, writers, and other "Westernized elites" to the tender mercies of bigoted clerics, in the hope that the latter, in return, would endorse their own stranglehold on the organs of state.'

It was not just regimes in Muslim countries that went down this path. In the 1970s the Israelis encouraged the growth of the Muslim Brotherhood in Gaza to counter the influence of the secular Palestine Liberation Organization. A decade later the Brotherhood created Hamas. Not only did the Islamists visit terror upon Israel far bloodier than that ever envisaged by the PLO, but their success also encouraged the PLO itself to loosen its secular moorings and instead increasingly to look to Islam to guide the destiny of Palestinians.

After the Soviet invasion of Afghanistan in 1979 America helped fund international jihadists to drive out the Red Army – including Osama bin Laden and the groups that eventually became the Taliban. 'Moslem countries will be concerned,' the US National Security Advisor Zbigniew Brzezinski wrote in a memo to President Jimmy Carter the day after the invasion, 'and we might be in a position to exploit this.' Carter himself went on television to denounce the Soviet action as 'a deliberate effort by a powerful atheistic government to subjugate an independent Islamic people'. America's hope was to use the battle against the Red Army not simply to humiliate Moscow but also to stem Iranian influence on the Muslim world by reasserting the power and prestige of Saudi Arabia, with whose conservative, Wahhabist regime Washington was now closely allied. Arab states, still divided by the Cold War, were unable to take a united stand against the Soviet invasion. Washington and Riyadh took advantage by jointly funding transnational organizations to fight the Afghan jihad.

The war in Afghanistan helped create not just a physical network of jihadists but also a symbol of Muslim struggle. In the 1990s, Western powers tacitly allowed Afghani jihadists to come to Bosnia to fight against the Serbs and establish a new focus for Muslim radicalism. 'Some of the most important factors behind the contemporary radicalization of European Muslim youth can be found in Bosnia-Herzegovina,' the terrorism expert Evan Kohlman has written, 'where the cream of the Arab mujahideen from Afghanistan tested their battle skills in the post-Soviet era and mobilized a new generation of pan-Islamic revolutionaries.'

Domestic policy has mirrored international policy. Britain, as we have seen, turned to Muslim groups to stifle militancy on the streets – only to help create the Rushdie affair and worse. And despite its professed secularist tradition and distaste for 'Anglo-Saxon communalism', France, too, has not been averse to using Islamists to undermine militant secularists. When France was rocked by a series of major strikes in the late seventies, largely involving immigrant workers, the French government encouraged the building of prayer rooms in factories, because they saw Islam as a useful way to quieten rebellious workers.

Flirting with Islamism has proved costly. Fundamentalism, terrorism and jihad – the rage of Islam has all too often been stoked by Western cynicism, not to mention Western funding.

5

It was not the Qur'an but crack cocaine that first led Mohammad Sidique Khan down the path to jihad. Not crack cocaine that he injected into his own veins, but crack cocaine that he tried to stop others from injecting. In the late 1980s drug-dealers moved into Beeston. The dealers were mainly young Asian men with flash cars, loud hip hop and even louder bling, who set up shop in crack houses and in the local park. The long-time residents of the area had no idea how to deal with them. Then the Mullah Crew showed up. The Crew, or the Mullah Boys as they sometimes called themselves, were a group of second-generation young men, British-born but of Pakistani origin, who decided to clean up the neighbourhood. One of their tactics was to kidnap young drug addicts and, with the consent of their families, give them cold-turkey treatment in a flat near the Wahhabi-inclined mosque on Stratford Street. Mohammad Sidique Khan was a Mullah Boy.

The Mullah Crew did not simply sweep the dealers off their turf. They were also contemptuous about the ways of the older generation. They saw themselves as Muslim, but rejected most of the traditions of Islam. Despite their campaign against the dealers, the Boys were happy to smoke dope and drink vodka, and often used the local massage parlour cum brothel. But the tradition that most grated with the youths was that of arranged marriages. The Mullah Crew encouraged love-matches (though only between Muslims), and even started conducting marriages from the premises of Iqra, a local Islamic bookshop, which soon became a kind of drop-in center for the Boys.

On the face of it, the activities of the Mullah Crew might seem to be a way that second-generation Asians, fully integrated into British society and no longer accepting the restrictions of first-generation Pakistani-based traditions, had forged to take control of their lives and their community. In that sense the Crew might appear to be like a local version of the Asian Youth Movements of a decade earlier – except that the AYM was a political movement, and the Mullah Crew was little more than a street gang with pretensions.

One of the Mullah Boys' victims was Tyrone Clarke, a sixteen-year-old black teenager from Beeston. In April 2004 he happened to be walking with his friend Rafael Lovick through Brett Gardens, a local park that the Boys had decided was Asian territory. A pack of about twenty Asians, many of them wearing balaclavas, chased them. The two friends got separated, and the mob set upon Clarke with cricket bats, scaffolding poles and planks of wood. He was then stabbed three times. By the time the mob had finished, his mother told reporters, all that was left was 'a bloody pulp'.

A year later four men – Islamur Rahman, Anjum Amin, Kamer Akram and Liaquat Ali – received sentences of between nine and twelve years' imprisonment for the murder. All were said to be Mullah Crew members. Shehzad Tanweer, one of the 7/7 bombers, was reported to have been questioned about Clarke's murder, though Tanweer's father has denied the story. Tanweer did, however, receive a caution for a public order offence arising out of the gang battles.

Both the police and the trial judge denied that Clarke's murder was racially motivated, insisting that it was gang-related violence. But Britain's new tribalism has cleaved gangs along racial lines. Shortly after 7/7, an American journalist visited Brett Gardens and talked to five white teenagers. They were hovering at the edge of the park, smoking joints, and fearful of stepping inside. The park 'used to be ours', said one, 'but now the Pakis won't let us cross'. 'They start fights with us because we're white,' said another. 'They're fucking racist.' 'The Asian kids here are very well community-minded,' said a local community worker. 'They get together, back each other up. It makes them powerful. They can control something: the streets.'

Being 'community-minded' clearly meant something very different to the Mullah Boys from what it had meant to the Asian Youth Movement. The identity of the AYM, and of its members, came from its political vision and from its relationship to broader political movements, working-class organizations at home and national liberation struggles abroad. 'The only real movement capable of fighting the growth of organized racism and fascism', the Bradford AYM declared in its magazine *Kala Tara*, 'is the unity of the workers' movement, black and white.' The AYM also saw the fight against racism as part of a wider set of struggles such as those 'in Ireland, South Africa, Zimbabwe and Palestine'. Those struggles (like the AYM itself) had all but disappeared by the 1990s – not just physically in the sense of the decline of the organizations, but intellectually, too, as the ideas that had fired them burned out.

A decade earlier, Sidique Khan or Shehzad Tanweer might well have joined the AYM, or even the Socialist Workers Party. But these were now lost causes. Far from being plugged into a wider political network, as the AYM had been, the Mullah Crew existed primarily because its members were cut off from wider society. Their aim was not to change the world but to protect their turf on the streets of Beeston. In that difference – in the degeneration of political campaigning into gang ritual – lies much of the change that has taken place within Muslim communities in Britain over the past twenty years. And out of that difference have come the reasons that a number of Muslims have turned jihadist.

The Mullah Crew was different not just from an earlier generation of secular activists but from an earlier generation of Islamists too. In his teenage years, Pervaiz Khan had been an Islamist, an activist for the

Jamaat-e-Islami. Between 1974 and 1977, he was secretary of the Birmingham branch of the Islamic Youth Movement (IYM) and on the national organising committee. It was through the IYM that the UK Islamic Mission (UKIM), the prinicipal Jamaati organization in Britain, organized its youth work. As a child he had read the whole of the Qur'an, but had not been particularly religious. He was drawn to the mosque as a teenager not by the sermons but by the youth club, run by Jamaati activists. 'They introduced me to a much wider world,' he says. 'They also introduced me to politics. It was through them that I learnt about colonialism and imperialism. It was also through them that I learnt about universal values and the possibilities of social change.'

Like many first-generation immigrants, his parents were 'quite inward-looking. They wrapped themselves up in the culture that they had left. They weren't anti-white, but they did not think much of them. Or of blacks. Whereas the Islamists said, "There is nothing wrong with white people, or black people. It's not skin color that matters but what they believe." It was liberating to hear that.' Khan's parents were horrified by his involvement with the Islamic Youth Movement. 'They called them Wahhabis, which was meant as an insult. But as a working-class Pakistani kid I was excited because what the Islamists taught me about the world and how to change it was much more inspirational than what I was learning at school or at home.'

By the end of the seventies Khan had left the Jamaatis. 'They trained me to think about the world. And when I did I found that I no longer believed in God.' But while he lost his faith in God, he retained his belief in the importance of social change and in the idea of a common humanity, becoming active in left-wing organizations. 'Islamists in the seventies were outward-looking, political, and had a desire to change the world. Today, Islamic radicals have much narrower minds. Even when I was with the Islamic Youth Movement, my best friends were Hindus, Sikhs and Afro-Caribbeans. We used to go round to each other's houses. It doesn't happen any more. Today Pakistani Muslims only know other Pakistani Muslims. Islamists today are obsessed by things like beards and the niqab but have little knowledge about the world and little desire for political struggle. They don't even have much knowledge about Islamic traditions.'

Multicultural policies in the 1980s had helped create a more tribal Britain by encouraging people to see themselves in narrower ethnic or cultural terms. Muslim inhabitants of towns such as Beeston adopted a more rigid Islamic identity, becoming more isolated from other communities. Second-generation Muslims like the Mullah Boys would, just a decade earlier, have probably been far more secular in their outlook, and more willing to forge friendships with people of different faiths and cultures. Now they saw themselves as tribal Muslims, and most of the people they knew, liked and trusted came from within the tribe. But not only were they segregated from the wider social world, they were also cut off from the traditional institutions and structures of Islam. Even though the Boys saw themselves as Muslim, they wanted nothing to do with the subcontinental Islam of their parents. In challenging the old ways, they isolated themselves from their families and often became pariahs in the community. So disgusted were Sidique Khan's family about his relationship with Hasina Patel that they moved from Beeston to Nottingham, in the hope that their errant son would follow them. He didn't.

It is a common story. In *The Islamist*, Ed Hussain tells of how his attraction to radical Islam led to a battle with his pious but traditional father. Eventually his father gave him an ultimatum: leave Islamism or leave my house. Hussain decided to leave his house. He stole out in the middle of the night and crept down to the East London mosque, which was controlled by the Jamaat-influenced Islamic Forum. He was taken in by 'the brothers' and treated like a 'family member'. For people like him, Hussain observes, 'cut off from Britain, isolated from the Eastern culture of our parents, Islamism provided us with a purpose and place in life'.

'My generation of young British Muslims', Hussain writes, 'was torn between two cultures.' This has become an all-too-common explanation for the alienation of British Muslims, repeated by everyone from Islamists to intelligence experts, to explain everything from the rise of drug-taking to the popularity of jihadism. But people like Hussain and Sidique Khan were not caught between two cultures. They were caught between no cultures. Rejecting traditions from back home is a common feature of second-generation immigrant life. I did it, and so did most of the people with whom I grew up. For us, though, it was not such a big deal. We were defined less by our culture than by our politics; our sense of belongingness and identity emerged out of the collective struggle for our political ideals.

Multiculturalists assumed that minority groups would want not to jettison the past but to embrace it, that those born here would want to define themselves through their parents' cultures and traditions. They imagined Britain as a 'community of communities', and pushed second-generation Britons of migrant stock back into the traditional cultures that they had rejected. And so those second-generation migrants found themselves adrift, without any cultural ballast.

The most degraded form of tribal life is the gang. It is not surprising that, as Britain has become more tribal, so gang culture has taken over much of inner-city life. In the space between no cultures, a gang such as the Mullah Crew provided something to which to belong. Such tribalism is not confined to working-class areas like Beeston. Mohamed Atta's Hamburg cell, the group of educated, Westernized professionals who went on to form the core of the 9/11 bombers, was as much a gang as Mohammad Sidique Khan's Mullah Crew. Each was a self-selecting group, cut off from broader social networks, with a single figure of authority, brought together by ties of personal friendship, common activity and routine tasks, and bonded through danger and adventure.

For the Mullah Crew, as for the Hamburg cell, Islam provided the ideas and rituals that bound its members together. What the Boys found in Islam was less a theology of faith than the sacraments of street life. Friday prayers and halal meat were to the Mullah Crew what blue bandanas and British Knights trainers are to the LA Crips. But having rejected the traditions of their parents' Islam, the Mullah Crew had to find a new kind of Islam to which to relate. Islamism filled the gap. Hassan Butt was a former spokesman for the radical Islamic group al-

Muhajiroun, who claimed to have organized training for two hundred British Muslims to join the jihad, though he later also claimed to have exaggerated his role for the sake of publicity. Like Sidique Khan, Butt was a youth worker. Unlike Sidique Khan, he recanted his former views and now calls on Muslims to 'renounce terrorism'. Islamism, he says, filled the gap for those caught with no culture. 'When I went to Pakistan,' he says, 'I was rejected. And when I came back to Britain, I never felt like I fitted into the wider white community.' He was a stranger in Pakistan because he had rejected traditional Islam. He was a stranger in Britain because he saw himself as a Muslim, not a British citizen, and others saw him that way too. Islamism gave him an identity. 'You don't need Pakistan or Britain. You can be anywhere in the world and this identity will stick with you and give you a sense of belonging . . . When you're cut off from your family, the jihadi network then becomes your family. It becomes your backbone and support.'

6

Until the Iranian revolution, radical Islam had been viewed by most Muslims as the property of Sunnis. Unlike Shiites, Sunnis had a deep attachment to the caliphate as the living expression of the Muslim nation. The destruction of the Ottoman caliphate after the First World War, and its replacement in 1924 by the secular republic of Turkey under Kemal Atatürk, created great turmoil among Sunnis. Out of this emerged radical Islam. It is an ideology with twin roots in the soils of Egypt and the Indian subcontinent, and in the works of Sayyid Abul A'la Maududi and Sayyid Qutb.

Maududi was born in 1903 in what was then British India. The founder of the Jamaat-e-Islami party in 1941, he is often regarded as the man who began the task of Islamic renaissance in the twentieth century. Much of his work was in opposition to Muslim nationalists and their project for a separate Muslim state, Pakistan. The nationalists wanted to unite all the Muslims of the subcontinent into a single nation; but they envisioned Pakistan as a 'Muslim state', rather than as an 'Islamic' one, in much the same way as secular Zionists wanted Israel, which came into being the year after Pakistan was born in 1947, to be a 'state of the Jews' but not a 'Jewish state'. The nationalist project was to create a modern democracy whose institutions would be modelled on those of the old colonial power, Britain.

For Maududi, nationalism implied impiety. The Holy Prophet, Maududi wrote, 'has positively and forcefully forbidden the Muslims to assume the culture and mode of life of the non-Muslims' because such cultural miscegenation rots the essence of Islam, 'destroys its inner vitality, blurs its vision, befogs its critical faculties, breeds inferiority complexes, and gradually but assuredly saps all the springs of culture and sounds its death-knell'. Politics, for Maududi, was 'an integral, inseparable part of the Islamic faith'. The five pillars of Islam (shahada or profession of the faith, prayer five times a day, the fast at Ramadan, the Haj or pilgrimage to Mecca, and almsgiving) were merely preparation for jihad, the struggle against those who had usurped Allah's sovereignty. Despite his distaste for 'European' ideas, Maududi was deeply influenced by the organization of European communist parties, and Jamaat-e-Islami, founded to carry out jihad, was modelled on the Leninist party as the vanguard of the Islamic revolution.

Jamaat-e-Islami never achieved popular support, even in Pakistan. But in the 1950s Maududi's ideas were picked up by Sayyid Qutb, the leading intellectual of the Egyptian Muslim Brotherhood. The Brotherhood had been founded in 1928 by Hassan al-Banna to reclaim Islam's political dimension which had been lost with the abolition four years earlier of the Ottoman caliphate. It developed over the years to be the largest and most influential political Islamist organization and a model for twentieth-century Islamist thought. Islam, for the Brotherhood, was a total system and Muslims should not look to Europe for political ideas. 'Allah is our objective,' it declared. 'The Prophet is our leader. Qur'an is our law. Jihad is our way. Dying in the way of Allah is our highest hope.' This remains the slogan of the Muslim Brotherhood.

The problem for the Brotherhood was not just the abolition of the caliphate but also the erosion of the *umma*. Nationalism was now the driving force throughout the Third World, including those lands in which Muslims lived. And nationalism was like political acid to the Muslim *umma*, dissolving the historic land of Islam (*dar al-Islam*) into distinct communities. Egypt and Syria, Turkey and Iran, Pakistan and Indonesia – every nation now had its own specific priorities and pursued its own goals. And where they were bound together in a common project, that project embodied secular, not religious, values. Liberation meant not submission to Allah but emancipation from injustice and the pursuit of political ideals, such as freedom and equality, which had their roots in the secular European Enlightenment.

The triumph of the nationalist politician over the religious scholar was felt particularly acutely in Egypt, the home of the Brotherhood. In 1952 Gamal Abdel Nasser led an army coup which overthrew the Western-backed King Farouk and established a secular republic. Nasser became the symbol of the godless modernism that was sweeping through Muslim lands. Nationalists and Islamists were soon in bloody conflict, and Nasser savagely repressed the Brotherhood, imprisoning and executing many of its leaders. Qutb himself was eventually hanged in 1966.

In response to the repression, Qutb declared that the Muslim world had reverted to an age of *jahiliyyah*, or ignorance. This was the term that Muhammad had used to describe the state in which Arabs lived before the revelation of Islam. It was also the name that Salman Rushdie gave to the holy city of Mecca in *The Satanic Verses* (in Rushdie's hands it is rendered as Jahilia). The modern *jahiliyyah* must be struck down, Qutb wrote, just as the Prophet had struck down the original state of ignorance and built his Islamic state on its ruins. Traditionally Muslims had divided the world between believers and unbelievers, Muslims and *kuffar*. But for Qutb, most Muslims themselves were corrupt and igno-rant and therefore subject to *takfir*, or excommunication, a highly charged act in Islamic terms and consequently one that traditionally had been used very sparingly. Following Qutb, however, *takfir* became the weapon of choice for Islamists. A new generation of Islamists also became enraptured by the idea of jihad, which Qutb, like Maududi, believed to be the only way of overcoming modern-day barbarism. Qutb's brother Muhammad moved to Saudi Arabia after being released from prison by Nasser and became a professor of Islamic studies. He was a mentor to al-Ayman Zawahiri, founder of the Egyptian Islamic Jihad group, and Zawahiri in turn was a mentor to Osama bin Laden.

7

The British government's official account of the 7/7 bombings, published in May 2006, suggests that 'after an incident in a nightclub, [Sidique Khan] said he turned to religion and it changed his life'. This is almost certainly, in the words of Sidique Khan's brother Gultasab, 'bullshit'. Sidique Khan's conversion was more gradual and had little to do with nightclubs. In the traditional, community-run mosque on Beeston's Hardy Street, which Sidique Khan's family attended, the imams spoke and wrote in Urdu, a language most second-generation Muslims understand only poorly, and thought the way to attract young believers was to get them to recite the Qur'an by rote in Arabic. Disenchanted with this old-fashioned Barelwi faith and indifferent to its theological message, Sidique Khan drifted away from religion. Afzal Choudhury, a community worker who in 1997 helped Khan organize summer workshops for young people, remembers that he sometimes got 'what we call the Friday feeling' and would go to mosque for Friday prayers, but otherwise he didn't pray much. Gradually, though, he was drawn back to faith, not to the traditional faith of his family, but to an intoxicating mixture of Wahhabism and Islamism. Theologically the two groups frequently despise one another with a sect-like intensity. Conservative Wahhabis, often funded by the Saudis, fear the social radicalism of the Islamists. On the other side, Farid Kassim, one of the leaders of Hizb ut-Tahrir, once told me with contempt that he saw little difference between Wahhabis and Hindus, which for an Islamist is about as great an insult as he could throw. But to the teenagers on the streets of

Beeston such theological niceties were meaningless. What mattered was how faith felt, and this home-brewed Islam induced an intoxicating sense of belonging.

This was not Islamism as Maududi or Qutb would have understood it. The Islamism of the founding fathers drew upon recognizable traditions and appealed to distinct social groups. It was not even a kind of Islamism that the creators of Hamas or Hezbollah would recognize. Terrorist organizations they may be, but they are also mass movements with deep roots in their communities, whose social and welfare needs they often meet. This was a form of Islamism that had grown up in the space between no cultures, fertilized neither by politics nor by theology but by a yearning for identity in a society that could not inspire loyalty.

For Sidique Khan the pull of fundamentalism came from several directions. His sweetheart Hasina Patel's family belonged to the Indian Deobandi tradition, which has links to Wahhabism. Radical Islamist groups, such as Hizb ut-Tahrir, organized at Leeds Metropolitan University where both he and Patel were students. Many members of the Mullah Crew were also looking for a new kind of faith. And the Wahhabists and Islamists seemed to know what made young Muslims tick. They delivered sermons in English, took their recruitment drives out of the mosques and on to the streets, and into the gyms, cafés and parks, and, despite their 'fundamentalism', were flexible enough to indulge second-generation concerns. They insisted, for instance, that arranged marriages were un-Islamic and a cultural import from Hindu India. It was not just love-matches that Islamists were happy to accept. 'When I said I've been clubbing, I've smoked some weed, he was cool,' former Hizb ut-Tahrir member Shiraz Maher recalls of his mentor in the organization. 'At a traditional mosque in the Pakistani community they would have told me I was going to hell, but he just said, "If it wasn't fun people wouldn't do it."' Hizb ut-Tahrir was also happy to accommodate members with a penchant for pornography, fast cars, forged documents; even prayer was seen as a distraction to be 'dropped' rather than a crucial act of piety.

The Mullah Crew did not receive its Islamist ideas by attending sermons given by preachers of hate, a favourite media explanation for the 'brainwashing' of the London bombers. Rather, such ideas perco-lated through a small group of friends as they talked in gyms and youth clubs. Khan used his position as a youth worker to win public money to build facilities for Asian youth. In 2000, for instance, he received a £4000 EU grant through Leeds City Council to set up a gym under the Jamia mosque on Hardy Street. Another gym was set up in Lodge Lane in the name of the youth programme of the nearby Hamara Centre. It was here that Sidique Khan would meet with Shehzad Tanweer and Hasib Hussain and sketch out the plans for the 7/7 bombings.

What the Mullah Boys yearned for was not God but, like members of any gang, respect and recognition. Martin Gilbertson was an IT tech-nician who did a lot of work for the Iqra bookshop and got to know the three Beeston-based bombers quite well. Sidique Khan, he says, 'wasn't the ranting type; what he seemed to want was kudos within the group, and among people on the street outside. Khan's way was to be a "cool dude"; it was all about kudos in the Muslim community.'[33] The same words crop up in Ed Hussain's account of the Islamist groups to which he belonged in east London. He began his radical journey with the Jamaat-influenced Young Muslim Organization based at the East London mosque. The YMO, he writes, 'had gained in Tower Hamlets and beyond a reputation as being tougher than the toughest gangsters. The Brick Lane Mafia, Cannon Street Posse and Bethnal Green Massive shrank to the stature of playground bullies when compared with the rising star of the YMO. YMO had several members in prison. They won fights, deployed kung-fu experts in the mosque hall, defied the police, and were "bad boys" too . . . They were as bad and cool as the other street gangs, just without the drugs, drinking and womanizing.'

Hussain later gave up on the YMO for the more radical Hizb ut-Tahrir. Again, he seemed drawn by the scent of macho glamour and kudos. The YMO 'seemed little more than an insignificant local group of unsophisti-cated young Bangladeshi men' compared to the 'young, articulate, self-assured' members of Hizb ut-Tahrir. One such was Maajid Nawaz, who would later become a leader of the movement in Britain and subse-quently spend four years in Cairo's notorious jails, having injudiciously gone to study, and proselytize, in Egypt, where Hizb ut-Tahrir is a proscribed organization. Nawaz, Hussain writes in awed tones, 'oozed street cred. He wore the latest baggy jeans, expensive trainers, and had good hair. He had once worn an earring and the empty piercing spoke volumes to east London rude boys. Maajid was equally at home among aspiring black rappers and budding Asian bhangra singers. His clothes, attitudes, and street speak made him very popular, very quickly.'

Hussain and Nawaz have both now left Hizb ut-Tahrir to found the Quilliam Foundation, a Muslim think tank that aims to wean people away from Islamism. But one can still hear in Hussain's autobiography the voice of the star-struck teenager for whom the radical chic of Islamism was the path to street cool.

8

On 19 November 2004, Mohammad Sidique Khan and Shehzad Tanweer boarded Turkish Airlines flight TK1056 from Heathrow, bound for Karachi. They stayed at a hotel in Karachi's central Saddar area for a week before leaving for Lahore by train and apparently splitting up. Tanweer visited a number of madrasas, in Karachi and Lahore, trying to make contact with militants. He is thought to have stayed at one run by Lashkar-e-Taiba, a banned Sunni group, in Mudrike, twenty miles outside Lahore, before visiting a training camp in Mansehra, a remote area near the Kashmir border, organized by Harkat-ul-Mujahideen (the Movement for Holy Warriors), the group that had been involved in the kidnapping and beheading of *Wall Street Journal* reporter Daniel Pearl in 2002. Khan's trail goes cold after Karachi. However, it was not the first time he had gone to Pakistan on jihadist activity. The previous year he had spent two weeks at a training camp in the Swat valley, a beautiful jumble of mountains, forests and villages in the Malakand area of Pakistan's North-West Frontier province, not far from the badlands of the Afghan border where Osama bin Laden is believed to be hiding out, and where al-Qaeda and the Taliban have established their camps.

A trip to a Pakistani training camp has become a staple in the making of a jihadist. The spectre of dozens, perhaps hundreds, of Western jihadists jetting off for terror training has given rise to much speculation about a sophisticated, international jihadist conspiracy, financed by al-Qaeda. 'Up to sixteen thousand British Muslims either are actively engaged in or support terrorist activity,' the British commentator Melanie Phillips wrote in her book *Londonistan*, citing a government paper on *Young Muslims and Extremism*, 'while up to three thousand are estimated to have passed through al-Qaeda training camps, with several hundred thought to be primed to attack the United Kingdom.'

The same year as Sidique Khan went to Malakand, Omar Khyam held a barbecue in north London to raise funds to take another group of jihadists to the same camp. Khyam, a college dropout from Crawley, Sussex, was the leader of the Operation Crevice plot. Named after the operation that foiled their plans, Crevice was one of the biggest terrorist conspiracies of recent years, involving a complex network of dozens of individuals, five of whom, including Khyam himself, were found guilty in April 2007 of conspiracy to cause explosions and to endanger life.

The barbecue raised £3500, sufficient for Khyam to take a small group to Pakistan later that year. After flying to Lahore, they stayed at the Avari Hotel. A seventeen-hour drive in a hired minivan took them to Kalam, a trekking resort at the northern end of the Swat valley. Another two days of hiking – during which one of the group collapsed from the heat and altitude – and they finally reached their camp. It was not quite what they had expected. 'I was thinking about something with ranges and assault courses, like I'd seen on TV,' one of group said later. 'But it wasn't like that at all.' The training camp comprised a field and two tents, one for the local organizers and one for the British trainees. The would-be jihadists had to dig their own latrine. The first day was spent doing physical exercises. Then, on day two, the local men brought out some AK47s, a light machine gun and a rocket launcher. 'It was wicked,' one of the plotters said later.

Operation Crevice was one of the biggest police surveillance operations against jihadists, involving hundreds of officers and hours of tape.

The picture that emerges is not one of a sophisticated jihadist conspiracy. Omar Khyam's plot was a DIY exercise, and a highly amateurish one. He and his fellow would-be warriors raised their own funds, took themselves to Pakistan, found suitable terrorist trainers and set up their own training camp. In Pakistan, the Crevice plotters fired off machine guns under the gaze of total strangers, exploded home-made bombs in the back garden of their suburban safe house, refused to move to another house until the carpets were cleaned, and tried to smuggle vital bomb-making ingredients through airport customs while carrying a collection of knives. Their Pakistani landlord spotted that they were terrorists. In Britain, they talked openly in their homes and cars about targets for bombing. Sophisticated it was not.

None of this should surprise us. Jihadists who have been fighting for years in Afghanistan or Bosnia are often tough, experienced soldiers. But wannabe terrorists like Omar Khyam and Sidique Khan are naive, disaffected young men (and the occasional woman), who are defined not by their engagement with broader social currents but by the very opposite: their sense of isolation from the rest of the world. Islamism punched a hole through that isolation. Not only did it afford a set of ideas and rituals to bind together the local gang, it also provided entry into a worldwide gang of jihadists. But, as the American historian Faisal Devji points out, this sense of being part of a global movement is a cruel illusion. The jihadist network has moved away from 'a politics of intentionality and control that is organized around some common history of needs, interests or ideas, to create a landscape of relations in which very little, if anything, is shared'. The global jihad 'brings together allies and enemies of the most heterogeneous character, who neither know nor communicate with each other, and who in addition share almost nothing by way of prior history'.

In the past, an organization such as the IRA was defined by its political aims (in its case the creation of a united Ireland). It had an exclusive membership. Not just anyone could become an IRA volunteer: you had to be chosen for your skills, beliefs and attitudes. The activities of the members were tightly controlled by the leadership. The IRA saw itself as part of both a historical tradition of struggles for a united Ireland and a political tradition of national liberation movements. And however misguided we might think its actions, there was a close relationship between cause – in the sense both of the IRA's political cause and of the Army Council as the cause of its volunteers' actions – and effect – in the sense of its military and terrorist activities.

The jihadi network possesses none of these attributes. There is no such thing as al-Qaeda as an organization. Originally it referred to the handful of jihadists who swore personal loyalty to Osama bin Laden. Today there is little more than what Marc Sageman calls al-Qaeda Central – men such as bin Laden himself and his deputy Ayman al-Zawahiri – and even their importance has greatly receded. The jihadis have no explicit political aim, no defined membership, and no leadership exercising control. Instead, al-Qaeda operates as a kind of brand. There is no link between cause and effect. An act of terror is not related to a political demand, nor is it controlled by any organization. There is no common political history or relationships between different jihadists. The Hamburg cell, the Beeston bombers, and the Salafia Jihadia terrorists, who brought carnage to Casablanca in May 2003, are all seen as Islamic terrorists, often even described as al-Qaeda operatives, but there is little tangible that links them. They are not united even by ideology, for it is impossible to know what their ideology is. All that connects them is their desire to sow terror.

Of course, jihadists do not see themselves in this fashion. The story that they tell themselves, and the outside world, is of Islamist terror as a reaction to unconscionable Western policy, a response in kind to the West's murderous hatred of the Muslim world. Yet through all Islamist writing runs a chasm between the grand claims for their actions and a lack of intellectual curiosity about the world upon which they act. When the Islamic Youth Movement trained Pervaiz Khan in the 1970s, it broadened his mind, he says, and gave him a deeper understanding of the world. There is little sign of that today. When contemporary Islamists talk about the West, they rarely move beyond overworked clichés about decadence or Islamophobia. They seem to lack curiosity even about the Islamic world. The horrors of Bosnia, Chechnya and Palestine have become standard explanations for radicalism and terror. 'The Balkan crisis truly radicalized many Muslims in Britain,' writes Ed Hussain. 'I desperately wanted to help, to do something to stop the killing.' Yet for most Islamists their understanding of these conflicts rarely goes beyond TV footage or video clips. This is true even of the Palestinian conflict, the issue that Muslims usually cite, together with Iraq, as the one than most inflames their hatred of the West. One study found that fewer than one in five Muslims could name the president of the Palestinian Authority and that barely one in seven knew who was the prime minister of Israel. Younger Muslims, who were more upset about Palestine, were least knowledgeable about it. Nearly a third of over-fifty-five-year-olds knew that Mahmoud Abbas was the Palestinian president; just 9 percent of sixteen- to twenty-four-year-olds did. In fact non-Muslims were as knowledgeable about these issues as young Muslims.

In 2002 London-born Ahmed Omar Saeed Sheikh was convicted in Pakistan of beheading the *Wall Street Journal* reporter Daniel Pearl. His road to terror began with Bosnia Week at the London School of Economics, where he was a student. It was November 1992 and according to Sheikh, 'various documentaries on Bosnia were shown. One such film, *The Destruction of a Nation*, shook my heart. The reason being that Bosnian Muslims were being shown being butchered by the Serbs.' The forty-five-minute film depicting the castration of Muslim prisoners in Serb detention camps moved Sheikh so much that the following March he joined the Convoy of Mercy, a relief operation for Bosnia. There he met jihadists from Afghanistan and decided that it was better being a warrior than a relief worker. Sheikh flew to Pakistan with, in his own words, 'zeal and intention to undergo arms training and join the mujahideen'. He went to Afghanistan to join the terror group Harkat-ul-Mujahideen. The following year, he kidnapped four Westerners in India as a bargaining tool with which to free Harkat leaders imprisoned in India. It was a laughably amateurish operation. Sheikh brought the demands in person to an Indian newspaper and had to run away when the recipient started opening the envelope. Indian police freed the prisoners and captured Sheikh, who spent five years behind bars. After his release he maintained his contacts with Harkat-ul-Mujahideen. In 2002 he took part in another operation, the kidnapping and brutal murder of Daniel Pearl.

What is striking about Sheikh's journey to jihad is how it was fuelled not by political anger but by emotional anguish. He seems to have had little understanding of, or curiosity about, the history of the Balkans or the roots of the civil war, just a gut revulsion at the treatment of Muslims and a sense that what pains one Muslim must pain all Muslims, so that the atrocities done to Bosnian Muslims were felt viscerally by Sheikh himself. In Sheikh's writing one almost gets a sense of jihad as therapy, as a way of cutting out the emotional distress created by the worldwide treatment of Muslims.

Perhaps it is no coincidence that virtually every Islamist documentary on Bosnia includes a section on the Serbs' supposed penchant for castrating Muslim men. Such documentaries have the same smell to them as anti-abortion films that depict in graphic detail the destruction of an embryo, or the infamous ad about Willie Horton, a black felon who committed rape while on weekend furlough from a Massachusetts prison, which the Republicans used to attack the Democratic candidate Michael Dukakis in the 1988 US presidential election. Each is designed to lodge in some dark recess of the mind and to conjure those terrifying ghosts that all too often distort thought and unbend reason. Anti-abortionists know that once anyone sees pictures of an embryo being broken up, there is little room for reasoned debate about rights. The Republicans were happy to play on old fears about black men and rape. 'With Rushdie, all those sleeping demons about Muslims have come awake,' Sher Azam of the Bradford Council of Mosques had told me in 1989. With Bosnia, Islamists brought to life all those slumbering ghosts about Christians and crusades.

The intensely personal, deeply emotional response to the Bosnian conflict was not new. Ziauddin Sardar read a copy of *The Satanic Verses* on a plane from Kuala Lumpur to London. By the time he landed at

Heathrow, 'It felt as though Rushdie had plundered everything I hold dear and despoiled the inner sanctum of my identity. Every word was directed at me and I took everything personally. This is how, I remember thinking, it must feel to be raped.' Sardar's friend Gulzar Haider, professor of architecture at Carleton University in Ottawa, and a fellow editor of the Islamic magazine *Inquiry*, was 'lying on a sofa' when he heard the news of Ayatollah Khomeini's fatwa. 'So catastrophic was the effect,' Sardar reports, 'he couldn't move, it was as though his body had been struck down by a disease. He was sofa-bound for almost a year.' Sardar's friend and colleague Merryl Davies 'bellowed like a fiery dragon goaded by a million arrows, writhing by turns with sorrow and rage'. It is almost as if Sardar and his friends were driving themselves into a kind of self-induced hysteria, as if they felt that they had to suffer personally for their faith to be meaningful.

The British sociologist Frank Furedi coined the term 'therapy culture' to describe the growing emotionalism of our age and its tendency to 'cultivate vulnerability'. Other scholars, such as the philosopher Charles Taylor and the sociologist Olivier Roy, have described how such emotionalism has become central to new forms of 'expressive' faith. 'All religious revival movements of the late twentieth century', Olivier Roy writes, are marked by an 'anti-intellectualism that favours a more emotional religiosity', so that 'feelings are more important than knowledge'. This is true not just of radical Islam but also of other 'born again' religions, such as charismatic Christianity, the Lubavitch, one of the largest Jewish Hasidic communities and the Hindutva, a Hindu revivalist movement. Such faiths 'play on emotion through ritual and collective expressions of faith, using symbolic and ostensible markers of belonging'. This is one reason for the importance of the veil to radical Islamists. Islamists like flaunting a piece of clothing that traditionally was of little concern to Islamic scholars, because it is such a visible 'marker of belonging' and of difference.

Revivalist religions place a stress not only on emotion but also on the individual who is enraptured by that emotion. The new forms of religion appeal less to the collective than to the individual self.

Blasphemy used to be regarded as a sin against God. Now it is felt as an assault on the individual believer – which is why Sardar was cut by the barbs of *The Satanic Verses* so personally and so painfully.

9

The young man is dressed in an olive-green jacket with a red-and-white *keffiyeh*, the Arabic scarf, wrapped around his forehead, clutching a pen and glancing at his notes. He looks at the camera and reads in a monotonous tone, leavened by a Yorkshire accent. 'I'm going to keep this short and to the point,' he begins, 'because it's all been said before by far more eloquent people than me. And our words have no impact upon you, therefore I'm going to talk to you in a language that you understand. Our words are dead until we give them life with our blood.'

It is Mohammad Sidique Khan speaking on his so-called 'martyrdom video'. It is not clear when or where the video was made. It came to light two months after the 7/7 bombing, when it was broadcast on the Al Jazeera channel. Khan's statement, which was apparently filmed in Britain, was spliced together with a video of Ayman al-Zawahiri, al-Qaeda's second-in-command, who calls the 'blessed London battle' a 'sip from the glass that the Muslims have been drinking from'. Zawahiri does not refer directly to Khan, and there is no evidence that Khan was working under al-Qaeda orders. It is likely that Khan's martyrdom tape would have been passed from hand to hand after the London bombings until it reached al-Qaeda, which then added Zawahiri's retrospective blessing.

I'm sure by now the media's painted a suitable picture of me. This predictable propaganda machine will naturally try to put a spin on things to suit the government and to scare the masses into conforming to their power and wealth-obsessed agendas. I and thousands like me are forsaking everything for what we believe. Our driving motivation doesn't come from tangible commodities that this world has to offer.

Our religion is Islam – obedience to the one true God, Allah, and following the footsteps of the final Prophet and messenger Muhammad. This is how our ethical stances are dictated.

By now Khan is wagging his finger quite ferociously.

Your democratically elected governments continuously perpetuate atrocities against my people all over the world. And your support of them makes you directly responsible, just as I am directly responsible for protecting and avenging my Muslim brothers and sisters. Until we feel security, you will be our targets. And until you stop the bombing, gassing, imprisonment and torture of my people we will not stop this fight. We are at war and I am a soldier. Now you too will taste the reality of this situation.

Khan concludes with a paean to his heroes.

I myself, I myself, I make *dua* [pray] to Allah to raise me amongst those whom I love like the prophets, the messengers, the martyrs and today's heroes like our beloved Sheikh Osama bin Laden, Dr Ayman al-Zawahiri and Abu Musab al-Zarqawi and all the other brothers and sisters that are fighting in the name of this cause. With this I leave you to make up your own minds and I ask you to make *dua* to Allah almighty to accept the work from me and my brothers and enter us into gardens of paradise.

What jumps out of the video is not Khan's righteous anger, still less any sense of religious piety. Rather it is the narcissism that oozes out of every line. 'I'm going to keep this short and to the point . . . I'm going to talk to you in a language that you understand . . . I and thousands like me are forsaking everything for what we believe.' And so on. In a two-minute rant, Khan says 'I' nine times – about once every fifteen seconds.

Terrorists have always sought publicity for their causes and have never been shy of issuing public justifications of their actions. After virtually every bombing or shooting the Provisional IRA would put out a statement claiming responsibility and demanding political change – the withdrawal of British troops from Northern Ireland. Occasionally the Provos taunted their victims. 'You were lucky today,' the IRA told Margaret Thatcher after the Brighton bomb in 1984, when it attacked the hotel in which Conservative leaders were staying during a party conference, killing five people, but leaving the prime minister herself unharmed. 'We only have to be lucky once.' Yet even when terror was recast as a personal grudge, there was little doubting the concrete political cause that was held to justify the bombing. The contrast with the Islamic terrorists is striking. For Mohammad Sidique Khan, the actor is clearly more important than the action. His farewell video is a justification not so much of his bombing as of himself. It craves publicity not for the deed but for the man.

'I'm sure by now the media's painted a suitable picture of me,' Khan moans. The IRA often accused the media of bias, but it was angered less by the demonization of individual volunteers than by the portrayal of its collective struggle. For Khan there is no collective struggle, just individual gestures. What seems to dismay him is the thought that journalists might impugn his personal integrity.

'I and thousands like me are forsaking everything for what we believe,' Khan tells us. For IRA members, any personal sacrifice they might have had to make was something to be accepted, not boasted about. For Khan, the sacrifice appears to *be* the struggle. The jihad has, for him, become an individual journey rather than something that is part of a collective movement. Unlike political activists of the past, today's jihadist does not submit himself to the will of the collective; each decides for himself what that will is. Common among radical militants who claim to fight for the *umma*, Olivier Roy observes, 'is the belief that jihad is a compulsory individual duty (*fard al-ayn*) while traditionally it has always been considered a collective duty (*fard al-kifaya*)'. Only through death do jihadists join their imagined community.

CHAPTER FOUR

Bargains, resentments and hatreds

> But to be raised in the house of power is to learn its ways, to soak them up, through that very skin that is the cause of your oppression. The habit of power, its timbre, its posture, its way of being with others. It is a disease, Bilal, infecting all those who come too near it.
>
> Salman Rushdie, *The Satanic Verses*, p.211.

1

In the run-up to the first anniversary of the 7/7 bombings, in July 2006, a row broke out between the prime minister Tony Blair and Muslim leaders. Sadiq Khan, Labour MP for the south London constituency of Tooting, was one of a number of prominent Muslims who lambasted the government for ignoring their advice on how to deal with extremists. Few of the proposals put forward by an Extremism Task Force set up after the bombings had been acted upon, Khan complained. 'What has happened to all the good ideas?' he asked. 'Why hasn't an action plan been drawn up with timelines? There has been limited progress but there is an air of despondency. Only three recommendations have been implemented, and group members feel let down.'

The prime minister responded to the criticisms by insisting that the real problem lay with Muslims themselves. Moderate Muslims had taken insufficient responsibility for unmasking extremists. 'Government itself cannot go and root out the extremism in these communities,'

Blair told a parliamentary liaison committee of senior MPs. 'I am not the person to go into the Muslim community and explain to them that this extreme view is not the true face of Islam.'

The debate carried on for a week or two before petering out. But while much of what Blair suggested was challenged by his Muslim critics, no one dissented from his central point that he was not the person to venture into the Muslim community to challenge extremism.

The starting point for both sides – as it seems to be in any discussion today about extremism – was the belief that Muslims constitute a distinct community with its own views and beliefs, and that real political authority for British Muslims must come from within the Muslim community. Mainstream politicians, so the argument goes, are incapable of reaching out to Muslims. Only authentic Muslim leaders can engage with them. So there has to be a bargain between the government and the Muslim community. The government acknowledges Muslim leaders as crucial partners in the task of confronting extremism and building a fairer society. In return Muslim leaders agree to keep their own house in order. The argument between Tony Blair and his critics was really about who was, or was not, keeping their side of the bargain.

In the same week as the row, two polls on Muslim attitudes were published, one for *The Times* newspaper conducted by Populus, the other an NOP survey for Channel 4's *Dispatches* programme. The polls showed why such multicultural bargains are a bad idea. There is no such thing as a Muslim community to be bargained over, no token of which all Muslims would say, 'That's mine.' Should Muslim women wear the hijab? Is it better to live under sharia law or British law? Should people be free to say what they want, even if it offends religious groups? Is polygamy acceptable? Must wives always obey their husbands? Is it preferable to have Muslim neighbours? Should Muslim children go to state schools or faith schools? Should they attend single-sex schools? Are public displays of affection offensive? Do the police disproportionately stop and search Muslims? Should police be allowed to monitor mosques?

Are the 7/7 bombers martyrs? Will there be another 7/7? Does Tony Blair deserve respect? On all these and many other questions Muslims are deeply divided.

For instance, half of those polled thought that the invasion of Iraq was the principal reason for the London bombings; more than one in four disagreed. Almost exactly the same numbers believed it right for the security services to infiltrate Muslim groups (48 percent) as thought it unacceptable (47 percent). Fifty-six percent thought the war on terror was a war against Muslims; a third dismissed that as nonsense. Thirty-six percent wanted Muslim neighbours; 40 percent did not mind who lived next door. More than half (56 percent) were happy with Islamic ideas about women, but one in four thought that Islam treated women as 'second-class citizens'. Not surprisingly, more women than men were critical of Islam. Around half of those polled thought that wives must always obey their husbands; a third disagreed. Forty-three percent wanted to send their children to Muslim schools, while 44 percent preferred state schools.

The only issue on which virtually all Muslims seemed to agree was the importance of Islam. Yet even here, the response was not as straightforward as it may seem. Nine out of ten respondents in the Channel 4 poll felt strongly attached to Islam. Yet half never attended mosque; fewer than one in ten attended every day. More than 50 percent did not want Britain to be an Islamic state; around 17 percent were 'strongly' attracted to the idea. Thirty percent wanted the introduction of sharia law; 54 percent did not. One in five would move to a country governed by sharia; 70 percent preferred to stay in Britain. Whatever their attachment to Islam, it was not for straightforwardly religious reasons.

Tony Blair seemed to be suggesting that the aims and aspirations of Muslims were so different from those of non-Muslims that he could not connect with them. The polls painted a different picture. Three quarters of non-Muslims thought Muslims should do more to integrate. So did two thirds of Muslims. One in four Muslims thought that hostility towards them had increased since 7/7; more than 60 percent of non-Muslims agreed. Just over half of both Muslims and non-Muslims were offended by public drunkenness; the proportion of Muslims offended by same-sex couples kissing in public was not much greater than for non-Muslims (36 percent as against 27 percent). A third of the general population had close friends who were Muslims – a high figure given that Muslims make up less than 4 percent of the population. Nearly nine out of ten Muslims had close non-Muslim personal friends.

Tony Blair's insistence that he was 'not the person to go into the Muslim community' was based less on the reality of Muslim attitudes than on a political reality. It was an acknowledgement that the government had abandoned its responsibility for engaging directly with Muslim communities and instead had subcontracted those responsibilities to so-called community leaders. The organization that for more than a decade has 'represented' the Muslim community is the Muslim Council of Britain. It was founded in 1997, with considerable support from the newly elected Labour government of Tony Blair. Its roots, however, go back to the Rushdie affair.

2

Inayat Bunglawala, one of the leaders of the Muslim Council of Britain, suggests that the campaign against *The Satanic Verses* was 'the catalyst for the forging of a more confident Islamic identity among many British Muslims'. What it really catalysed was a transformation of Islamism in Britain. The Rushdie affair provided an opportunity to bring order to the chaos of the fissiparous Islamist landscape – and for Islamists to stake a claim for the leadership of British Muslims and to present themselves as their true representatives.

In October 1988 the Saudi government helped set up the United Kingdom Action Committee on Islamic Affairs to promote its campaign against *The Satanic Verses*. Based at the Saudi-run Islamic Cultural Centre in London, it brought together many Islamist groups, such as the UK Islamic Mission, founded in 1962 as the British arm of Jamaat-e-Islami, the Maududist Islamic Foundation, and the Union of Muslim

Organizations, which was funded by the World Muslim League, a body set up by Saudi Arabia in 1962 to promote Wahhabism and often seen as a wing of the Saudi foreign ministry. The UKACIA's two convenors were the Saudi diplomat Mughram al-Ghamdi, director general of the Islamic Cultural Centre, and Iqbal Sacranie from the Balham mosque in London, the man who said of Rushdie, a few days after the fatwa, that 'death, perhaps, is a bit too easy for him'. Sacranie would later become the first secretary general of the Muslim Council of Britain and eventually Sir Iqbal, in 2005.

No sooner had the Saudis constructed their Islamist edifice than the Iranians rolled a grenade under the door. The fatwa undid the Saudis' carefully mapped-out strategy, not only transforming at a stroke the whole debate about Rushdie, but giving voice to a more assertive, more radical form of Islamism. 'I was truly elated,' Bunglawala recalls about the day that Khomeini delivered his death edict. 'It was a very welcome reminder that British Muslims did not have to regard themselves just as a small, vulnerable minority; they were part of a truly global and powerful movement. If we were not treated with respect then we were capable of forcing others to respect us.'

Pro-Iranian Islamists now set up the Muslim Parliament to challenge what they saw as the caution of the UKACIA. The Parliament was the brainchild of one man – Marxist-turned-Muslim, and one-time *Guardian* journalist, Kalim Siddiqui. Like many British Muslims, Siddiqui had been enraptured by the Iranian revolution. In 1973 he had set up the Muslim Institute, a foundation for research into Islamic affairs. Originally funded by the Saudis, it became after 1979 a mouthpiece for Tehran.

Until the fatwa, the Muslim Institute, like most Muslims even in Britain, had paid little attention to the furor over Rushdie, dismissing it as a 'non-event'. According to the Institute of Contemporary Islamic Thought's hagiography of Siddiqui, 'Dr Kalim took the view that campaigning for a ban on *The Satanic Verses* would be a major and pointless distraction from the main work of the Muslim Institute, and would serve only to give the book more status and publicity than it deserved.' Once the ayatollah had delivered his death sentence, however, the

Institute discovered the Rushdie affair to be the most important issue facing Muslims. 'The imam's intervention on February 14', Siddiqui wrote in *Crescent International*, the magazine of the Muslim Institute, 'will go down in history as one of the greatest acts of leadership of the *umma* by any political or religious leader in the history of Islam. The imam spoke on behalf of the one thousand million Muslims of the world, and the world's Muslim community did not disappoint him. Virtually every Muslim man, woman and child agreed Rushdie should die.'

'The conflict over Rushdie was never about religion,' says Ghayasuddin Siddiqui, one of the Institute's founders. 'It was about politics. It was not a battle about blasphemy but a battle between Saudi Arabia and Iran about winning the hearts and minds of Muslims.' The aim of the Muslim Institute 'was to stop the Action Committee'. As a student in Pakistan, Siddiqui had been a member of the youth wing of Jamaat-e-Islami, an organization deeply embedded within the UKACIA. 'I knew how they thought and how to stop them. We let them organize demonstrations, so we didn't have the burden of doing so, and then we took it over and made it into our protest.' Kalim Siddiqui, wrote another of the Institute's founders, Ziauddin Sardar, who by now was a bitter opponent, 'could not believe his luck: he was handed a conflict on a platter . . . He took over the Muslim leadership – not a difficult task since most Muslims are inarticulate and terrified of the media – and projected himself as *the* Muslim leader ("I have been advising the Muslim community . . ." is his favourite opening line).'

In 1990 the Institute issued the Muslim Manifesto, which 'laid out both the problems facing Muslims here and the duties and responsibilities the Muslim community had living in a non-Muslim country'. And in 1992 it set up the Council for British Muslims, an organization that would 'act as a "Muslim parliament" in Britain'. That phrase captured the media's imagination and the organization came to be known simply as the Muslim Parliament. 'It was an unfortunate name because it frightened people,' said Ghayasuddin Siddiqui. 'It was not meant to be a democratically elected parliament, just a council of appointed members to help work out Muslim demands and put pressure on the government.' It nevertheless had grandiose aims. The Parliament set out 'to empower Muslims with their separate and distinctly Islamic institutions to meet their needs independently of the British government and local authorities'. It 'sought to discourage Muslims from entering mainstream politics or even from voting in elections'. Instead, it wanted 'to create a "non-territorial Islamic state" in Britain'.

The fatwa fired the imagination of British Muslims, especially those who had been born and brought up here; but despite this, few were drawn towards the Muslim Parliament. This has been a recurring theme of the past twenty years. Disaffection among large swathes of the Muslim population has often led them to applaud big, anti-Western gestures, such as the fatwa, that have made Muslims appear capable of giving their opponents a bloody nose. But political organizations that have sought to exploit such disaffection have rarely succeeded in winning a mass base.

In one sense it mattered little that neither the UKACIA nor the Muslim Parliament had popular support. The desire of both groups was not to act as democratic representatives of Britain's Muslims, but to influence government policy. Their model was the Board of Deputies of British Jews, the umbrella organization that seeks 'to protect, to promote and to represent UK Jewry' through a close relationship with the government, including 'the privilege of personal approach to the Sovereign on state occasions'. The Muslim community, the Islamic scholar Mohammad Raza wrote in 1991, 'has not yet learnt how to approach the British political system. It lacks the political experience which is practised by other communities like the Jews.' Or, as the British Muslim philosopher Shabbir Akhtar put it, had Muslims 'been a powerful, well-organized lobby like the Jews, Rushdie's outrages would never have got into print'.

Mainstream politicians were, in turn, keen to find credible Muslim leaders to whom they could talk. They wanted to replicate at national level the success of a local organization such as the Bradford Council of Mosques. In March 1994 the Conservative home secretary Michael Howard appealed to Muslims to form a 'representative body' that he could 'support and recognize'. The UKACIA was too closely associated with the Rushdie affair and with the Saudi government. No one took the Muslim Parliament seriously; it was, in any case, seen as too confrontational, and as Tehran's creature. In 1994 a conference of Muslim organizations at the Golden Hillock mosque and community center in Birmingham set up a National Interim Committee on Muslim Affairs to sketch a blueprint for an organization that Whitehall might find appealing. In November 1997 the Muslim Council of Britain was born. Iqbal Sacranie, one of the joint convenors of the UKACIA, became its first general secretary.

The MCB was soon accepted by both central government and the national media as the authentic voice of the Muslim community. It would become particularly useful to the New Labour government which had swept to power in May 1997, just a few months before the founding of the MCB. Martin Bright, former political editor of the left-leaning *New Statesman*, describes the Labour government and the MCB as 'joined at the hip'. According to Bright, when foreign secretary Jack Straw and MCB leader Iqbal Sacranie shared an international platform shortly after the 7/7 bombings, 'both men's speeches were written by the same man: Mockbul Ali'. Ali is the government's senior Islamic advisor. A former student at London University's School of Oriental and African Studies (SOAS), and one-time political editor of the Muslim magazine *Student Re-Present*, he is now a civil servant who runs the Engaging with the Islamic World Group (EIWG) within the Foreign Office and is largely responsible for shaping government attitudes to Muslim organizations and communities. *Student Re-Present* was seen as a hard-line magazine, once praising a Palestinian suicide bomber as 'a bride in the dress of martyrdom' and promoting the work of clerics such as the Egyptian Yusuf al-Qaradawi, the spiritual leader of the Muslim Brotherhood. A contemporary at SOAS is reported as saying that 'Mockbul was a straightforward Islamist, loyal to something like the Brotherhood tradition'.

Much of Bright's information came from documents sent anonymously in brown envelopes by Derek Pasquill, a Foreign Office civil servant, who had become 'increasingly unhappy about the activities of Mockbul Ali' and his insistence 'that Islamist organizations such as the Muslim Brotherhood and its south Asian offshoot Jamaat-e-Islami [were] mainstream'. Pasquill was arrested in January 2006 and eventually charged under the Official Secrets Act for leaking the documents. Two years later, in January 2008, the prosecution dropped the case after it was revealed that the Foreign Office had failed to disclose emails that showed that many of its civil servants sympathized with Pasqualli and opposed his prosecution.

One of Pasquill's jobs within the EIWG was to help organize the Festival of Muslim Cultures, a celebration in Britain of Muslim arts from around the world, which ran from January 2006 to the summer of 2007. Its trustees included a number of prominent Muslims, such as the lawyer, writer and broadcaster Raficq Abdulla, Mahmood Ahmed of the Ismaili Council of the UK, and the BBC governor and former commissioner of the Commission for Racial Equality, Shahwar Sadeque. The organizing committee applied for government funding. Money would only be available, they were told by Mockbul Ali, if they did business with Whitehall-approved organizations. 'Within the FCO [the Foreign Office]', Pasquill remembers, 'certain individuals were sceptical about the festival's value and worried that it was not "Islamic" enough. It was felt that certain key organizations, such as the Muslim Council of Britain, would have to be squared off before we gave the go-ahead.' Not only did the festival have to accept an MCB representative on its board of trustees, it also had to forge links with many Jamaat-influenced MCB affiliates such as Young Muslims UK, the Islamic Society of Britain, the Islamic Foundation and the Muslim Welfare House. 'If any activities are seen to contradict the teachings of Islam then we will oppose them,' insisted MCB general secretary Iqbal Sacranie. Hardliners objected to the festival inviting Sevara Nezarkhan, an Uzbek singer who does not wear a headscarf and has worked with Jewish klezmer musicians. Gay Muslims were refused permission to stage an event after Sacranie described homosexuality as 'harmful' and 'not acceptable'.

There is nothing wrong, or unusual, in government ministers talking to Islamist, or even jihadist, groups. But the British government went further: it presented such organizations as authentic representatives of British Muslims and used its financial muscle to force independent Muslim bodies to deal with its pet projects. The MCB is no more representative of British Muslims than the UKACIA or the Muslim Parliament were. It boasted, at its founding, 250 affiliated organizations (today there are 350). But, as with the UKACIA, the core of the MCB remains Islamist. The independent Muslim magazine *Q-News*, the first Muslim publication in Britain not linked to any denomination or funded by any state, observed in 1998 that the majority of the MCB's central working committee 'belong to or have sympathies with a UK organization which is a sidekick of the Jamaat-e-Islami in Pakistan'. The sociologist Chetan Bhatt of Goldsmiths College, University of London, an expert on religious extremism, points out that 'the overwhelming number of organizations that the government talks to are influenced by, dominated by or front organizations of the Jamaat-e-Islami and the Muslim Brotherhood. Their agenda is strictly based on the politics of the Islamic radical right, it doesn't represent the politics or aspirations of the majority of Muslims in this country.'

Indeed it doesn't. An NOP/Channel 4 poll of Muslims in 2006 found that less than 4 percent thought that the MCB represented British Muslims, and just 12 percent felt it represented their political views. This is in line with many other surveys. An NOP poll for the Conservative think tank Policy Exchange found only 6 percent of Muslims thought the MCB represented their views. 'Who elected them?' asked one respondent. 'Who put them there? I don't know. I don't even know who they are.' Less than half the sample in the Channel 4 survey 'respected' Iqbal Sacranie – barely more than the number who respected Tony Blair and considerably less than the 69 percent who respected the Queen. Astonishingly, a quarter of Muslims had never heard of the recently knighted Sacranie, probably the most prominent mainstream Muslim leader in the country. Little wonder that *Q-News* acidly described the MCB as 'Dad's Muslim Army'.

The 'joined at the hip' relationship between the MCB and the government helped reproduce at national level all the problems already seen through the implementation of multicultural policies at local level. 'Why should a British citizen who happens to be Muslim have to rely on clerics and other leaders of the religious community to communicate with the prime minister of the country?' asks the Nobel Prize-winning economist Amartya Sen, whose 2006 book *Identity and Violence* provided a penetrating critique of multiculturalism and the politics of identity. It is a policy that encourages Muslims to see themselves as semi-detached Britons. After all, if the prime minister believes that he can only engage with them by appealing to their faith, rather than through their wider political or national affiliations, who are Muslims to disagree? Is it surprising that, if mainstream politicians abdicate their responsibility for engaging with ordinary Muslims, those Muslims should feel disenchanted with the mainstream political process? Or that such disenchantment should take a radical religious form?

The multicultural bargain designed to keep the Muslim house in order helped open the door to a new generation of Islamic radicals. Worse, the so-called community leaders were as clueless as national politicians about how to deal with such radicalism. Tony Blair believed that he was not equipped to talk to Muslims about extremism. Unfortunately, neither was Iqbal Sacranie. The MCB may be deeply influenced by the Jamaat-e-Islami and other Islamist groups. But 'Dad's Muslim Army' is as oblivious to the rumblings on Radical Street as are the politicians in Westminster or the policy-makers at the Home Office. Britain's multicultural bargain created the space for radical Islamism, but not the means to reach it.

3

In 1996 the famous Stone of Scone was removed from Westminster Abbey in London and returned to Edinburgh. The Stone is an oblong block of red sandstone which was originally kept at the now-ruined abbey of Scone, near Perth in Scotland, and used for the coronation of Scottish monarchs. In 1296 it was captured by the English king Edward I, the 'Hammer of the Scots', and taken to Westminster Abbey, where it was fitted to a wooden chair, known as St Edward's Chair, on which all subsequent English monarchs (with the exception of Mary II) have been crowned.

The return of the Stone to Scotland brought no joyous celebrations north of the border. Few attended the ceremony when the Stone was reinstalled in Edinburgh Castle, and no one applauded. Why such coolness towards a relic for the return of which Scots have yearned for centuries? Because, suggests the Scottish writer Andrew O'Hagan, 'Over time the Stone's importance had become essentially that of the grievance it evoked. What mattered about the Stone was precisely its absence: the fact that it had been carted off by an English king in an act of plunder which was also intended to be a symbolic act of conquest.' O'Hagan adds that 'A half-hearted nation will want to hold fast to its grievances and in that sense Scotland has done well.'

Grievance is not a Scottish speciality. It hangs in the air of political debate and gives grit to the soil in which identity is rooted. And few grievances weigh more heavily than Muslim grievances. From the offence caused by Salman Rushdie to the injustice of Western foreign policy, resentment is the rendering in which Muslim identity is clad. It even has a special name: Islamophobia, the stuff in which all that grievance and resentment and bitterness and blame has become wrapped. Ten years ago no one had heard of it. Now everyone from Muslim leaders to anti-racist activists to government ministers wants to convince us that Britain – and, indeed, every Western society – is in the grip of an irrational hatred of Islam, a hatred that leads to institutionalized harassment, physical attacks, social discrimination and political alienation. More than that – it is leading to a Holocaust.

'The next time there are gas chambers in Europe,' the philosopher Shabbir Akhtar wrote during the Rushdie affair, 'there is no doubt concerning who'll be inside them.' 'Unless something is done urgently at governmental level,' Massoud Shadjareh, chair of the Islamic Human

Rights Commission, said at the launch of the IHRC's report on *Anti-Muslim Discrimination and Hostility in the United Kingdom* in 2000, 'Muslims in Britain face the same fate this century as Jews in Europe in the last.' According to Salma Yaqoob, a Respect party councillor in Birmingham, Muslims in Britain 'are subject to attacks reminiscent of the gathering storm of anti-Semitism in the first decades of the last century'.

There is clearly ignorance and fear of Islam in most Western countries. Muslims do get harassed and attacked because of their faith. But the idea that a storm is brewing in Europe that is about to sweep Muslims into gas chambers is – and there is no other way of putting this – hysterical to the point of delusion. Akhtar, Shadjareh and Yaqoob are not marginal figures. Akhtar is a well-respected Muslim intellectual. Shadjareh's IHRC has the support of the Equality and Human Rights Commission as well as various United Nations bodies. Yaqoob has a national reputation, particularly for her campaigning work against the Iraq war. That such figures need a history lesson about the real Holocaust reveals how warped the Muslim grievance culture has become.

Jews were, in Hitler's Germany, *Untermenschen* – sub-humans. Jewish shops were marked with a yellow star or had 'Juden' written on the window. SA men often stood outside to dissuade people from entering. Buses, trains and even park benches were marked with separate seating for Jews. In 1935, under the Nuremberg Laws, Jews lost the right to German citizenship, and marriage between Jews and non-Jews was forbidden. Jews were driven out of their jobs and their homes. On 10 November 1938 – Kristallnacht – ten thousand Jewish shops were raided, along with homes and synagogues. The violence was endemic and was orchestrated by the authorities.

If Muslims are singled out in Britain, it is often for privileged treatment. In 2005 the British government passed controversial legislation banning 'incitement to religious hatred', largely to appease Muslim leaders. The BBC stopped referring to 'Islamic terrorists' after protests from the MCB. The Archbishop of Canterbury has suggested that sharia law should be introduced into Britain, as has the former Lord Chief Justice, Lord Phillips. Muslim organizations get special funding from local and national government. Workplaces, schools and leisure centers make special provision for Muslims. Many provide prayer rooms, offer the choice of halal meat and make special dispensation for Muslim women and girls to dress more modestly. Some swimming pools have gender-segregated sessions, and even 'Muslim men only' periods during which non-Muslims and women are excluded.

The 'war on terror' has certainly exacerbated tensions between Muslims and non-Muslims. It has led to a huge erosion of rights and liberties, from domestic British anti-terror laws to the international affront that is Guantanamo Bay. There have been vicious physical attacks on Muslims and on mosques, and verbal onslaughts in the media.

Yet, once again, we need to maintain a sense of proportion. In the summer of 2004 a major political controversy erupted in Britain over government figures about stop and search operations by the police. These revealed a 300 percent increase in the number of Asians being stopped and searched under Britain's anti-terror laws. Journalists, Muslim leaders and even government ministers pinned the blame on Islamophobia. The IHRC described Britain as a 'brutal police state'. When I interviewed Iqbal Sacranie for a TV documentary, he insisted that '95–98 percent of those stopped and searched under the anti-terror laws are Muslim'. The real figure was 14 percent. Of the 21,577 people who had been stopped and searched in the previous year, most – 14,429 – were white. Just 2989 were Asian. Britain classifies by ethnicity but not by religion, so it is impossible to know for certain how many of those were Muslim. We can, however, make an intelligent guess. Muslims constitute about half of Britain's Asians, so it is reasonable to suppose that around half of those stopped and searched were Muslim. In other words, out of a population of around 2 million, some 1500 Muslims were stopped and searched – hardly an example of remorseless Islamophobia.

Asians make up about 6 percent of Britain's population, but 14 percent of those stopped under the Terrorism Act. In part, this disparity is explained by the fact that almost two thirds of terrorism stop and search operations take place in London, where Asians form 12 percent of the population. Stop and search operations also tend to focus on young people, and the Asian population is disproportionately young. Taking all this into account makes the argument about anti-Muslim bias far less plausible.

The treatment of Muslims bears no comparison with the harassment of African-Caribbeans under the 'sus laws' in the 1970s or even the treatment of Irish people under the old Prevention of Terrorism Act. A 2005 parliamentary report on *Terrorism and Community Relations* concluded that 'We do not believe that the Asian community is being unreasonably targeted by stops and searches, but accept that Muslims perceive that they are being stigmatized by the legislation.' The IHRC dismissed the conclusion as serving to 'condone and endorse such targeting of a specific community'. In the looking-glass world of grievance culture the lack of evidence of Islamophobia is itself evidence of Islamophobia.

As it happens, there *was* evidence that stop and search had been used in a racist fashion. But the victims were not Asian. They were black. British police can stop and search people under a number of different laws. Stops and searches under the Terrorism Act formed only a tiny proportion of the total 869,164 stops and searches that took place in the year 2002/03. Of that number 58,832, or just under 7 percent, were of Asians – roughly proportional to the Asian population. Blacks, on the other hand, formed just 3 percent of the population but 14 percent of those stopped and searched. An African-Caribbean was five times more likely to be stopped and searched than an Asian. One of the consequences of the exaggeration of anti-Muslim prejudice was to hide the real discrimination.

What about racist violence? In December 2007, Asad Mahmood Ahmed was beaten to death by a gang of white youths as he walked to the shops near his home in Bolton. The only reason seemed to be that he was a Muslim. Such attacks are, thankfully, rare. Chris Allen is director of research and policy at the Birmingham Race Action Partnership and a lecturer at the University of Wolverhampton. He was co-author of an EU report on racist violence after 9/11, published in May 2002. What evidence, I asked him, was there of a general climate of virulent and systematic attacks on Muslims? 'When you're looking at evidence, hard evidence, it's very difficult to find the data and statistics to actually prove this,' he said. 'It's not to say that it's not happening, but actually regarding the monitoring of these types of attacks it is very difficult to find.' In his research into racist attacks after 9/11, he found, 'There were very few serious attacks.' Rather, hostility towards Muslims 'manifested itself in quite basic and low-level ways'.

After the bombings on the London Underground in July 2005 there were fears that Muslim communities might come under siege. The European Monitoring Centre for Racism and Xenophobia (EUMC) reported an increase in 'faith hate' attacks on Muslims immediately after the bombings, but observed that 'the strong stand taken by political and community leaders both in condemning the attacks and defending the legitimate rights of Muslims saw a swift reduction in such incidents'. The EUMC's annual report added that 'Community and political leaders were quick to distance the actions of a few British-Muslim bombers from the Muslim community in general. This message was picked up and repeated by the British and foreign media and served not to "demonize" the Muslim community in Britain.'

Britain's director of public prosecutions came to similar conclusions in his annual report published in December 2006. Fears 'of a significant backlash against the Muslim community' after the 7/7 bombings, he observed, 'appear to be unfounded'. He noted that 'although there were more cases [of religiously aggravated offences] in July 2005 than for any other month, the rise did not continue into August and overall in 2005–2006 there was an increase of nine cases compared to the previous year'. There were in fact just eighteen cases in which the victim was identified as Muslim, six of which happened in the month following the bombings.

The actual figures for such attacks are undoubtedly significantly higher than those officially recorded. Nevertheless, there is no evidence of any kind of systematic targeting of minorities of the kind that was common in Britain just twenty years ago. Britain has changed hugely in that time. It has become more tribal. But it has also become less racist. Hatred and hostility have not been scrubbed away, but the weekly litany of stabbings, firebombings and murders that defined minority life in the 1970s and 1980s is thankfully no more; no one has to organize the kind of street patrols that were so vital thirty years ago. In 1982, so commonplace was the sort of siege that Nasreen Saddique's family endured that even journalists on the local paper barely bothered reporting it. Today such incidents are so rare that every one makes a national headline.

Britain is emphatically not like Germany in the 1930s. It is not even like Britain in the 1970s. My old comrade Hassan might have been driven into the arms of the mullahs at least partly by righteous anger over racism. Whatever fuelled Mohammad Sidique Khan's anger, it was not the lash of racism that Hassan once felt.

4

Europe, 2020. A dark veil is being drawn across a continent that has been 'remorselessly evolving month by month into Greater Bosnia'. Britain, France, Holland and Denmark have all fallen to the Islamists. It is only time before the rest of western Europe also opens its democratic legs to the mad mullahs. English pubs have stopped selling alcohol. Islamic rather than fashion police ensure that French women are veiled from head to toe. And Holland's gay clubs have been relocated to San Francisco, though where the gays themselves have been relocated, we do not know. What we do know is that Madrid and 7/7 were just the 'opening shots of a European civil war' that eventually led to 'societal collapse', 'fascist revivalism' and a never-to-return journey into 'the long Eurabian night'. As Europe's white population flees, the continent becomes 'reprimitivized'. America alone is left to defend the values of Christian civilization.

This is not a fantasy from some white supremacist website, but a prophecy from the pen of Mark Steyn, a Canadian-born American shock-jock-turned-shock-journalist whose work appears everywhere from the *Washington Post* to the *Daily Telegraph*, from the *Jerusalem Post* to the

Australian. Steyn's delight at baiting Muslims is matched only by his fear of what Muslims might do to Western civilization. The problem with Muslims is that their numbers are 'expanding like mosquitoes'. The 'European races', on the other hand, are 'too self-absorbed to breed'. Their failures in the bedroom are allowing the 'recolonization of Europe by Islam.'

Steyn's demographic arguments are as outlandish as they are crude. There are currently 13 million Muslims in Europe – out of a population of some 491 million. To become the majority population by 2020 they would have to increase their numbers twenty-fold in little over a decade. Even if Muslims continued to breed like mosquitoes, it is unlikely that Steyn's demographic prophecy would come to pass.

According to Steyn, the welfare state is responsible for the poor performance of the 'European races' in the bedroom. State intrusion into 'healthcare, childcare, care for the elderly' has 'effectively severed its citizens from humanity's primal instincts, not least the survival instinct'. Yet the highest fertility rates in Europe are in those nations with the best state childcare provisions – Iceland, Sweden, Norway and Denmark. Countries with poor childcare facilities – such as Poland or Romania – have much lower rates. Steyn makes much of Muslim states such as Niger, with an exceptional fertility rate of six. But he ignores the fact that of the five most populous Muslim countries (Indonesia, Malaysia, Pakistan, Bangladesh and Iran) the figure for all but one stands at three or less, and the figures for all are plummeting. In 1979, before the revolution, the fertility rate in Iran was 6.5. Today it is 1.7, lower than for most Scandinavian countries and below the rate needed to stop the population from falling. Using Steyn's demographic logic, one could argue that the best way of reducing Muslim fertility rates to those of Europeans is by having an Islamic revolution and imposing sharia law.

Convinced that Europe is about to be transformed into Eurabia, Steyn believes that violence is both the inevitable outcome and the only realistic response to the Muslims' looming demographic victory. 'Why did Bosnia collapse into the worst slaughter in Europe since World War Two?' Steyn asks. Because, 'In the thirty years before the meltdown,

Bosnian Serbs had declined from 43 percent to 31 percent of the population, while Bosnian Muslims had increased from 26 percent to 44 percent.' Faced with such figures, the Serbs came to the conclusion that 'if you can't outbreed the enemy, [you have to] cull 'em'. And what the 'Serbs figured . . . out', Steyn warns, 'other Continentals will in the years ahead.'

Steyn has gained a hearing not just among right-wing anti-Islamic activists, but among liberals too. 'Mark Steyn believes that demography is destiny,' Christopher Hitchens wrote in a review of *America Alone*, 'and he makes an immensely convincing case.' Hitchens would not 'concede that Serbo-fascist ethnic cleansing can appear more rational in retrospect than it did at the time'. Nevertheless he could not 'deny Steyn's salient point that demography and cultural masochism, especially in combination, are handing a bloodless victory to the forces of Islamization.'

Martin Amis is another liberal admirer of Steyn's demographic arguments. And while he, like Hitchens, would not sympathize with the Serbs' solution to the 'Muslim problem', he nevertheless has felt 'a definite urge', as he told Ginny Dougary of *The Times* in September 2006, 'to say, "The Muslim community will have to suffer until it gets its house in order." What sort of suffering? Not letting them travel. Deportation – further down the road. Curtailing of freedoms. Strip-searching people who look like they're from the Middle East or from Pakistan . . . Discriminatory stuff, until it hurts the whole community and they start getting tough with their children.'

Dougary described Amis's call for collective punishment as 'hardline, inflamingly so'. He is not alone, however, in expressing such views. The philosopher and neurobiologist Sam Harris is one of the so-called New Atheists – the wave of militantly anti-religious thinkers such as Richard Dawkins, Daniel Dennett and Hitchens himself that has swept into public consciousness in recent years. In a column for the *Los Angeles Times*, Harris flayed fellow liberals for appeasing Islamism, concluding that 'The people who speak most sensibly about the threat that Islam poses to Europe are actually fascists.' Christopher Hitchens (who had previously defended Amis on the grounds that 'the harshness Amis was canvassing was not in the least a recommendation, but rather an experiment in the limits of permissible thought') found Harris's comment 'alarming' and 'irresponsible'.

A best-selling author who seems ambivalent about the use of violence against Muslims; Britain's leading novelist imagining collective punishments against the Muslim community; one of America's most prominent intellectuals praising fascists for their sensible discussion of Islam: the arguments of Steyn, Amis and Harris seem to add credibility to the belief that hatred and revulsion for Muslims are deep-rooted in Western societies. Yet, as in the discussions about police harassment and racist attacks, we need to maintain a sense of proportion. However unpleasant the claims of Steyn, Amis and Harris may be, we should not exaggerate their impact. Their arguments no more make Western societies institutionally Islamophobic than the actions of Mohamed Atta (who piloted the first plane into the Twin Towers) or Mohammad Sidique Khan make Islam an institutionally violent religion.

The attempt to demonize Muslims is matched by the attempt to institutionalize respect for Islam. It has become a mantra from virtually every Western leader that Islam is really a religion of peace and that jihadists distort the message of the Qur'an. 'The most remarkable thing about the Qur'an', Tony Blair has written, 'is how progressive it is. I write with great humility as a member of another faith. As an outsider, the Qur'an strikes me as a reforming book, trying to return Judaism and Christianity to their origins, much as reformers attempted to do with the Christian church centuries later. The Qu'ran is inclusive. It extols science and knowledge and abhors superstition. It is practical and far ahead of its time in attitudes toward marriage, women, and governance.'

Blair is not alone in his enthusiasm for Islam. 'There is much we can learn from Islam,' Prince Charles told a conference organized by the Foreign Office in 1996. 'Everywhere in the world people want to learn English. But in the West, in turn, we need to be taught by Islamic teachers now how to learn with our hearts, as well as our heads.'

While the former prime minister and the monarch-in-waiting enthuse about Islam as a faith, the head of the nation's judiciary and the leader of its established Church are both sympathetic to the introduction of sharia law into Britain. In July 2008, Lord Phillips, Britain's most senior judge, told the London Muslim Council that he was willing to see sharia law operate in the country, so long as it did not conflict with the laws of England and Wales, or lead to the imposition of severe physical punishments. He was echoing comments made five months earlier by Rowan Williams, the Archbishop of Canterbury. In a speech on 'Civil and Religious Law in England', the archbishop argued that in a plural world of divided cultural, religious and ethnic loyalties, it is 'very unsatisfactory' for a citizen 'simply to be under the rule of the uniform law of a sovereign state'. Secular law must be modified to accommodate religious sensibilities. Muslims should not have to choose between the 'stark alternatives of cultural loyalty or state loyalty'. What is needed is a system of 'plural jurisdictions' under which individuals possess 'the liberty to choose the jurisdiction under which they will seek to resolve certain carefully specified matters'. There is a 'danger', the archbishop told the BBC, in saying that 'there's one law for everybody and that's all there is to be said'.

What all this suggests is that the relationship between Western societies and Muslim communities is a highly complex one and not easily reduced to simple formulas such as 'the West is Islamophobic' or 'blame it all on Islam'. There is certainly fear and hatred of Islam. But this is only one of many strands of opinion. Islamophobia is matched by Islamophilia.

What is most troubling is the common desire to play the victim. On the one side, many Muslim leaders view Western societies as institutionally Islamophobic and all Muslims as living under a state of siege. On the other, the likes of Mark Steyn view the West as living under the lash of Islam and seek some form of collective revenge. Neither claim matches reality. But the two sides feed off each other, creating ever more exaggerated fears. Such exaggeration is the life-blood of grievance culture. It helps create a siege mentality, stoking up anger and resentment, and making communities, both Muslim and non-Muslim, more inwardlooking and more open to extremism.

In 1993 Ed Hussain, then the organizer of the Islamic Society at Tower Hamlets College in east London, put on a thirty minute documentary on Bosnia. 'In the dark lecture theatre,' he remembers, 'there were sobs at what people were seeing; gasps of shock at what was going on two hours away from Heathrow airport; the serving of Muslim men's testicles on trays, Serbs slaughtering pregnant Muslim women, reports of group rape within the borders of Europe.' The students reacted as Ahmed Omar Saeed Sheikh had done the previous year when he had watched a similar documentary at the freshers' fair at the LSE, an experience that put him on the road to jihad and eventually led him to murder the American journalist Daniel Pearl in Pakistan. In east London, Hizb ut-Tahrir followed up the film by organising a rally entitled 'Bosnia Today – Brick Lane tomorrow'. The idea that the massacre of Srebrenica could be replicated in Whitechapel might seem a bit far-fetched – except, perhaps, to a community whose leaders constantly claim, seemingly in all seriousness, not only that Britain is a brutal police state but that Muslims are a whisker away from being swept into the gas chambers. Once you begin to hear the echo of jackboots in the high street, once you start believing that your neighbours are really SS guards in waiting, then it is but a small step to imagine that blowing them up on a bus might be a virtuous act.

CHAPTER FIVE

God's word and
human freedom

So he was sentenced to be beheaded, within the hour, and as soldiers manhandled him out of the tent towards the killing ground, he shouted over his shoulder: 'Whores and writers, Mahound. We are the people you can't forgive.'

Mahound replied, 'Writers and whores. I see no differences here.'

Salman Rushdie, *The Satanic Verses*, p.392.

1

Kåre Bluitgen is a soft-spoken but jovial man. A self-proclaimed socialist (and a former member of the far-left Venstresocialisterne or Left Socialists), he lives in Nørrebro, famed as Copenhagen's most ethnically diverse area. He has long been a campaigner on Third World issues and for immigrant rights. His teenage children attend the local state school, 90 percent of whose pupils come from migrant families. Integration, he insists, requires an understanding of different cultures from an early age.

Bluitgen is a successful writer of children's books, with a distinctive, offbeat style. In his most popular work, *A Boot Fell from Heaven*, God, sitting on a cloud and admiring a rainbow, drops one of his boots. Descending to Earth to retrieve it, He is met with uncomprehending hostility. Two policemen, thinking Him crazy, throw him in jail. God escapes and meets the boy who has found his boot, the only human being willing to listen to Him.

Bluitgen is likely to be remembered, however, less as a writer of quirky children's stories than as the man whose fruitless search for illustrations for one of his books led eventually to riots, death threats and a worldwide diplomatic storm. In 2005 Bluitgen was writing a children's book on Islam, *The Qur'an and the Life of the Prophet Muhammad*, which he hoped would bring greater understanding of the religion to a new generation of Danes. He looked for an illustrator. The first three he approached refused to take on the job, the fourth would do so only on condition of anonymity. All were worried that they would end up like Theo van Gogh, the Dutch film-maker ritually murdered on the streets of Amsterdam by a Muslim incensed by his anti-Islamic films. Many Muslims, they reminded Bluitgen, considered it blasphemous to portray Muhammad in the flesh. Fresh in their minds, too, was an extraordinary incident the previous December in which a lecturer at the Niebuhr Institute at the University of Copenhagen had been assaulted by five men who objected to his reading of the Qur'an to non-Muslims during a lecture.

The left-wing newspaper *Politiken* ran a story about Bluitgen's fruitless search, under the headline '*Dyb angst for kritik af islam*' ('Profound Anxiety about Criticism of Islam'). In response, Flemming Rose, the culture editor of *Politiken*'s right-wing rival *Jyllands-Posten*, asked the nation's most renowned cartoonists to draw pictures of Muhammad. Rose said he wanted to see 'how deep this self-censorship lies in the Danish public'. He approached forty cartoonists, twelve of whom accepted the challenge. Their caricatures were published in *Jyllands-Posten* on 30 September 2005, under the headline 'Muhammeds ansigt' ('The Face of Muhammad'). The most controversial of the cartoons showed the Prophet wearing a turban in the form of a bomb. In another, dumbfounded suicide bombers are turned away from the gates of paradise with the words, 'Stop. Stop. We have run out of virgins.' 'The modern secular society', Rose wrote in a commentary to the cartoons, 'is rejected by some Muslims. They demand a special position, insisting on special consideration of their own religious feelings. It is incompatible with contemporary democracy and freedom of speech, where you must be ready to put up with insults, mockery and ridicule.' That is why, he added, '*Jyllands-Posten* has invited members of the Danish editorial cartoonists union to draw Muhammad as they see him.'

And so began the infamous Danish cartoons controversy. Except that it didn't – at least not straight away. The publication of the cartoons caused no immediate ructions, not even in Denmark. About a week later, not having created the furor they had hoped for, journalists contacted a number of imams for their responses. The cartoons had simply not registered with Muslim leaders; but once their attention had been drawn to them, Islamists quickly recognized the opportunity provided not just by the caricatures themselves but also by the sensitivity of Danish journalists and politicians to their publication.

Among the first to be contacted was Ahmad Abu Laban, infamous for his controversial views on Osama bin Laden (whom he called a 'businessman and freedom fighter') and 9/11 ('I mourn dry tears for the victims' was Laban's response). Described by the Danish press as a 'spiritual leader', he was in fact a mechanical engineer by trade, and an Islamist by inclination. Having been expelled from both Egypt and the United Arab Emirates because of his radical views, he had sought refuge in Denmark in 1984. There he became leader of the Islamic Society of Denmark, an organization closely linked to the Muslim Brotherhood. It had a novel way of swelling its importance. It declared that all Danish Muslims were members, irrespective of whether or not they had actually prayed on the dotted line. In reality, fewer than a thousand worshippers nationwide attended the Society's Friday prayers.

Abu Laban seized upon the cartoons to transform himself into a spokesman for Denmark's 180,000 Muslims, demanding an apology not just from the newspaper but from the Danish prime minister too, and organizing a demonstration outside the offices of *Jyllands-Posten*. Yet however hard the imams pushed, they could not provoke major outrage either in Denmark or abroad. Three days after the Copenhagen demonstration, the Egyptian newspaper *El Fagr* republished the cartoons. They were accompanied by a critical commentary, but the newspaper made no attempt to blank out Muhammad's face. (When the British liberal magazine *Prospect* republished one of the cartoons to illustrate an essay

I had written about the affair, the Prophet's face was left blank so as not to cause offence.) Neither the Egyptian government nor the country's religious authorities raised any objections to *El Fagr*'s full-frontal photos.

It was not just Abu Laban who recognized the political virtues of the cartoon controversy. Muslim leaders across the world eyed up the prospect of a new Rushdie affair which would allow them to don the armour of defender of the faith at home and to gain political leverage abroad. There was to be no fatwa this time. Some of the cartoonists had to go into hiding after receiving death threats. Jamaat-e-Islami in Pakistan offered a bounty of 50,000 Danish crowns (around $4000) for their murder. In India, Haji Yaqoob Querishi, a minister in the Uttar Pradesh state government, offered in February 2006 a reward of Rs. 51 crore (roughly US$1.1 million) to anyone who beheaded the cartoonists. In February 2008 two Tunisians and a Danish citizen of Moroccan descent were arrested by the Danish security services for allegedly plotting to kill Kurt Westergaard, the creator of the most controversial of the cartoons, the one depicting Muhammad with a bomb in his turban.

Despite such incidents, no national government or religious authority followed in the ayatollah's 1989 footsteps. To have done so, they recognized, would have been divisive and disastrous, particularly against the background of the war on terror. They also recognized that a fatwa was unnecessary. Nearly two decades on from *The Satanic Verses*, Western liberals had become much more attuned to Islamist sensitivities and less willing to challenge them. They had, in the post-Rushdie world, effectively internalized the fatwa.

'You would think twice, if you were honest,' said Ramin Gray, the associate director at London's Royal Court Theatre when asked whether he would put on a play critical of Islam. 'You'd have to take the play on its individual merits, but given the time we're in, it's very hard, because you'd worry that if you cause offence then the whole enterprise would become buried in a sea of controversy. It does make you tread carefully.' In June 2007, the theatre cancelled a new adaptation of Aristophanes' *Lysistrata*, set in a Muslim heaven, for fear of causing offence. Another London theatre, the Barbican, carved chunks out of its production of *Tamburlaine the Great* for the same reason, though the producer David Farr later insisted that the cuts were made on artistic grounds rather than as a means of forestalling Muslim anger, while Berlin's Deutsche Oper cancelled a production of Mozart's *Idomeneo* in 2006 because of its depiction of Muhammad.

That same year, London's Whitechapel Art Gallery removed life-size nude dolls by the surrealist artist Hans Bellmer from an exhibition, just before its opening, simply so as 'not to shock the [Muslim] population' of the east London neighbourhood, according to curator Agnes de la Beaumelle. The year before, the Tate Gallery had refused to exhibit sculptor John Latham's work 'God Is Great'. Originally made in 1991, it consisted of a six-foot-high piece of plate glass with the Bible, the Talmud and the Qur'an extruding through it. The Tate claimed that it would not be 'appropriate' to exhibit the work in the 'sensitive' climate following the London bombings of July 2005. In 2007 the Gemeentemuseum in The Hague removed an exhibition of photos by the Iranian artist Sooreh Hera which depicted gay men wearing masks of Muhammad. 'Certain people in our society might perceive it as offensive,' said museum director Wim van Krimpen. *De Volkskrant*, a Dutch left-wing newspaper, praised the museum for its 'great professionalism' in excising the images. Hera herself received death threats. Tim Marlow of London's White Cube art gallery suggests that such self-censorship by artists and museums is now common, though 'very few people have explicitly admitted' it.

It is not just Islam that has generated such censorship. In 2005 the Birmingham Repertory Theatre cancelled a production of *Bezhti*, a play by the young Sikh writer Gurpreet Kaur Bhatti which depicted sexual abuse and murder in a gurdwara, after protests from community activists. In the wake of those protests Ian Jack, then editor of the literary magazine *Granta*, suggested that artistic self-censorship is necessary in a plural society. 'The state has no law forbidding a pictorial representation of the Prophet,' he wrote. 'But I never expect to see such a picture.' An individual might have the abstract right to depict Muhammad, but the price of free speech is too high when compared to the 'immeasurable insult' that the exercise of such a right could cause – even though 'we, the faithless, don't understand the offence'. And that was a year before the cartoon controversy.

All this explains why the publication of the *Jyllands-Posten* cartoons appeared so startling. They seemed a throwback to the pre-Rushdie days, to the days before secular liberals had become sensitized to the dangers of cultural and religious provocation. They caused anguish to Western liberals – and created an opportunity for Muslim leaders to flex their muscles.

2

In the very week in which *El Fagr* republished the cartoons, without official censure, the Egyptian ambassador to Denmark joined nine other Muslim diplomats in requesting a meeting with the Danish prime minister, Anders Fogh Rasmussen, to demand that he distance himself from the caricatures. Rasmussen refused to see the ambassadors, claiming that to do so would infringe the freedom of the press.

At the beginning of December 2005, the Organization of Islamic Conference (OIC) held a summit in Mecca. A group of Danish imams compiled a forty-page dossier about the cartoons to circulate to the delegates. The file consisted of the original twelve cartoons, pictures from another Danish newspaper, *Weekendavisen*, which were 'even more offending' (they were in fact parodies of the pompousness of the *Jyllands-Posten* caricatures), hate mail sent to Danish Muslims, and letters from Muslim organizations explaining the case for censorship. Also in the dossier were three other pictures that had nothing to do with *Jyllands-Posten* but at least one of which came to be reported on the BBC as having been published in the Danish paper. It showed a man with a pig mask, and was widely taken to be an offensive depiction of Muhammad himself. In fact it was a photo taken at a traditional pig-squealing contest in France; there was no connection to Islam. The imams later claimed that it had been sent to Muslims taking part in an online debate about the cartoons and was included as an illustration of the 'Islamophobia' under which Danish Muslims lived. The OIC summit condemned the cartoons and demanded that the United Nations take action against Denmark.

Two weeks later a second delegation of Danish imams toured various Middle Eastern, Near Eastern and North African countries. At the end of January, Saudi Arabia recalled its ambassador from Copenhagen and launched a consumer boycott of Danish goods. In response a swathe of European newspapers – including *France-Soir*, Germany's *Die Welt, Die Zeit, Tagesspiegel* and *Berliner Zietung*, Italy's *La Stampa, El Periodico* in Spain, and the Dutch paper *Volkskrant* – republished the cartoons in 'solidarity' with *Jyllands-Posten*. It was only now – more than four months after the cartoons had first been published, more than four months of effort to stir up a controversy – that the issue became more than a minor diplomatic kerfuffle. The republication of the cartoons sparked off protests in India, Pakistan, Indonesia, Egypt, Libya, Syria, Iran, Nigeria, Palestine, Afghanistan and elsewhere, leaving more than 250 dead, many of them killed when police fired into crowds. At least a hundred died as Muslim and Christian mobs clashed in Nigeria. Danish embassies in Damascus, Beirut and Tehran were torched. The protests were inflamed by surreal accounts of what Denmark was doing to Muslims. In January 2006 Al Jazeera broadcast a speech from the Danish-based leader of the Muslim Brotherhood, Muhammed Fouad al-Barazi, in which he tearfully described Danish plans to burn the Qur'an. The broadcast led to another round of international protests.

Like the Rushdie affair, the controversy over the Danish cartoons was driven not by theology but by politics. The Islamic art historian (and member of the Jordanian royal family) Wijdan Ali has shown that, far from Islam having always forbidden representations of the Prophet, until comparatively recently it was perfectly common for him to be portrayed. The prohibition against such depictions only emerged in the seventeenth century. Even over the past four hundred years, a number of Islamic, especially Shiite, traditions have accepted the pictorial representation of Muhammad. Edinburgh University Library, the Bibliothèque

National in Paris, New York's Metropolitan Museum of Art and the Topkapi Palace Museum in Istanbul all contain dozens of Persian, Ottoman and Afghan manuscripts depicting the Prophet. A seventeenth-century mural on the Iman Zahdah Chah Zaid mosque in Isfahan in Iran shows a veiled figure of Muhammad; through the veil, his facial features are clearly visible.

Even today, few Muslims have a problem in seeing the Prophet's face. The Iranian newspaper *Hamshahri* (which, in response to the *Jyllands-Posten* caricatures, launched a competition for cartoons about the Holocaust) ran, at the very time it was campaigning against the Danish cartoons, a photo of a mural from a contemporary Iranian building that depicted Muhammad on his Night Voyage. When *El Fagr* republished the cartoons, it did not think it necessary to blank out Muhammad's face, and faced no opprobrium for not doing so. The paper might have been critical of *Jyllands-Posten* but it certainly was not obsessed with the idea that the Prophet must remain unseen – and neither were Egypt's religious and political authorities. It took several months of dedicated, and often hysterical, campaigning to generate an international storm.

Whatever the similarities between the storm over *The Satanic Verses* and the furor over the cartoons, there were, however, also fundamental differences. The cartoon controversy showed how much the Rushdie affair itself had transformed the terrain of free speech. There had been much equivocation by politicians and intellectuals over the Rushdie affair, but no one seriously doubted Rushdie's right to publish his novel. There was little equivocation over the Danish cartoons, just widespread acceptance that it had been wrong to publish, and even more wrong to republish. Writers and artists, political leaders insisted, had a responsibility to desist from giving offence and upsetting religious sensibilities.

'I understand your concerns,' Louise Arbour, the UN high commissioner for human rights, told delegates at the OIC summit in Mecca, 'and would like to emphasize that I regret any statement or act that could express a lack of respect for the religion of others.' The European Union expressed 'regret' about the publication of the cartoons. 'These

kinds of drawings can add to the growing Islamophobia in Europe,'
claimed Franco Frattini, EU commissioner for justice, freedom and
security. 'I fully respect freedom of speech, but one should avoid making
statements like this, which only arouses and incites the growing radicalization.' The Council of Europe criticized the Danish government
for invoking the 'freedom of the press' in its refusal to take action
against the 'insulting' cartoons, its secretary general Terry Davis
suggesting that their publication might have been legal but it was
nevertheless immoral. Former US president Bill Clinton condemned
'these totally outrageous cartoons against Islam' and feared that anti-
Semitism had been replaced by anti-Islamic prejudice. The British foreign
secretary Jack Straw praised the British media for not publishing the
cartoons and condemned as 'disrespectful' the decision of some European
newspapers to reprint them. After a Norwegian Christian newspaper
Magazinet republished some of the cartoons, the ministry of foreign
affairs sent a letter to its ambassadors in the Middle East expressing
regret that the paper had not respected Muslims' beliefs.

Religious leaders were equally appalled. Following the lead of the
Vatican, which insisted that freedom of expression did not include the
right to offend religious beliefs, the Catholic bishops of the five Nordic
countries put out a statement deploring the cartoons. 'It seems that
certain opinion makers feel that they are wholly free to say what they
wish without any respect for the understanding and beliefs of other
people,' they declared, adding that 'Our sympathies go out to our Muslim
sisters and brothers.' The Conference of European Rabbis compared the
cartoons to anti-Semitic caricatures and condemned them for 'humili-
ating and disparaging the feelings of Muslims'. 'The right to express and
the right to satire', added CER president and chief rabbi of France Joseph
Sitruk, 'do not confer the right to humiliate and to injure.'

The authorities did not simply condemn, they also curtailed. The
Swedish government closed down a website, *Sverigedemokraterna*, after
it posted a number of the cartoons online. Universities – supposedly
arenas for free thought – were particularly harsh. Editors of student
magazines at Clare College, Cambridge, Cardiff University, the University

of Illinois and Canada's Prince Edward Island University were all sacked and disciplined for republishing some of the cartoons. The Cambridge authorities cut off funding from its student paper and its editor was forced to go into hiding.

The response to the Danish cartoons revealed how far the landscape of free speech had been remade. Once free speech had been seen as an inherent good, the fullest extension of which was a necessary condition for the elucidation of truth, the expression of moral autonomy, the maintenance of social progress and the development of other liberties. Restrictions on free speech had been viewed as the exception rather than the norm, to be wielded carefully, and only in those cases where speech might cause direct harm. In the post-Rushdie world speech became seen as inherently a problem, because it could offend as well as harm, and speech that offended could be as socially damaging as speech that harmed. Speech, therefore, had to be restrained by custom, especially in a diverse society, with a variety of deeply held views and beliefs, and censorship (and self-censorship) had to become the norm. 'Self-censorship', in the words of Muslim philosopher Shabbir Akhtar, 'is a meaningful demand in a world of varied and passionately held convictions. What Rushdie publishes about Islam is not just his business. It is everyone's – not least every Muslim's – business.' Or, as the British Foreign Office declared in a message about the OIC summit in Mecca, 'The whole international community stands with them in their staunch rejection of those who distort the noble faith of Islam. We join them in celebrating the values of Islamic civilization. Their values are our values.'

3

'I was going to begin this piece with a quote from *The Satanic Verses* in which Salman Rushdie satirizes the divine origins of the Qur'an. It was felt, however, that this would be too provocative and insensitive.' So began an essay I wrote for the *Independent* in 1994. The newspaper had asked me to write an article about the eighteenth-century English revolutionary Tom Paine. It was the 200th anniversary of his masterpiece, *The Age of Reason*, a book that was, as I observed, 'to become *The Satanic Verses* of its day'. Paine said of his book that it was a 'march through Christianity with an axe'. Just as his previous major works, *Common Sense* and *The Rights of Man* – a defence of American independence and of the French revolution, respectively – laid the axe of reason to the tree of feudal despotism and monarchical corruption, so *The Age of Reason* laid it to the other prop of national superstition and imposture, the established church. 'All national institutions of churches,' wrote Paine, 'whether Jewish, Christian or Turkish, appear to be no more than human inventions, set up to terrify and enslave mankind, and monopolize power and profit.'

Few authors have so punctured the pretensions of organized religion or so savaged the claims of divine revelation as Paine. Fewer still have faced such ridicule and vilification for doing so. In England *The Age of Reason* was suppressed for decades and successive publishers imprisoned for blasphemy. Anyone who distributed, read or discussed the book faced prosecution. Some were arrested for simply displaying the portrait of the author. In America, where hitherto Paine had been feted as a hero for his unwavering support for independence, newspapers denounced him as a 'lying, drunken, brutal infidel', 'a lily-livered sinical [*sic*] rogue' and 'a demihuman archbeast'. A century after Paine's death in 1809, the US president Theodore Roosevelt could still describe him as a 'filthy little atheist'. Paine, as I observed in my essay, would have approved of Rushdie. And he would have recognized the character of the campaign against him. It seemed natural therefore to link *The Age of Reason* and *The Satanic Verses*.

The *Independent* did not agree. There was consternation in its editorial offices when I filed my piece. Eventually one of the editors phoned me to say that I couldn't use the quote from *The Satanic Verses* because it was deemed too offensive and insensitive. No amount of logic or reasoning could persuade her otherwise. The irony of having been commissioned to write an essay on Tom Paine, the greatest freethinker of his age, and then being banned from quoting from a freely available book, seemed to escape the *Independent* editors. It was, as I observed then, 'a demonstration of the continuing relevance of Tom Paine to contemporary political discussions'.

These days the idea that we should refrain from giving offence to other cultures seems as incontestable as Rushdie's ability to attract controversy. Back in 1994 it was still a novel concept. The Rushdie affair was the watershed. Rushdie's critics lost the battle in the sense that they never managed to stop the publication of *The Satanic Verses*. But they won the war by pounding into the liberal consciousness the belief that to give offence was a morally despicable act.

'There is all the difference in the world', Shabbir Akhtar suggested about *The Satanic Verses*, between 'sound historical criticism that is legitimate and ought to be taken seriously and scurrilous imaginative writing which should be resolutely rejected and withdrawn from public circulation'. Akhtar was a Cambridge-trained philosopher who became a spokesman for the Bradford Council of Mosques at the height of the controversy over the burning of the book. The real debate, Akhtar declared, was not about 'freedom of speech versus censorship', but about 'legitimate criticism versus obscenity and slander'. While 'freedoms of belief, expression, conscience and dissent are rightly valued in a liberal democratic society', it was nevertheless 'immoral to defend in the name of these freedoms, wanton attacks on established religious (and indeed humanistic) traditions'. *The Satanic Verses*, Akhtar insisted, was just such a wanton attack. For many Western critics, the novel was a strikingly new literary exploration of race and religion in the postmodern world. For many Muslims it was part of the ancient tradition of Orientalism – the Western traducing of Islam. 'The parody of Muhammad and the Muslim tradition in *The Satanic Verses*', Akhtar observed, 'has clear echoes of the worst brand of Orientalist sentiment for which the term "prejudice" is decidedly lenient.' The novel was nothing more than an 'inferior piece of hate literature'.

Not just the novel, but the Western response to Muslim anger, too, was part of an ancient tradition. Rana Kabbani was a Syrian-born novelist who had come to Britain as a child and for whom Islam had left but the faintest of brush-strokes on her soul. The Rushdie affair changed all that. The controversy, Kabbani wrote, 'brought home to me the immense, perhaps unbridgeable, gulf between the world I belong to and the West', a gulf that had existed since the seventh century, when 'Islam emerged as a political and ideological power able to challenge Christendom'. 'Were Westerners to admit it,' she suggested, 'they would no doubt recognize that their own attitudes to Muslims are profoundly marked by half-conscious folk memories of struggle stretching back over the centuries.'

Many secular liberals picked up on this theme, too. The Rushdie affair, the writer Richard Webster suggested in his book on *A Brief History of Blasphemy*, was 'not an isolated skirmish between Islam and the West', but the 'latest battle in a long history of religious and cultural tension which goes back to the seventh century, when Islam first appeared as a religion with the power to challenge Christendom'. The motifs in *The Satanic Verses* 'belong to the ancient tradition of religiously inspired contempt for Islam'. Unsurprisingly, 'What Muslims see in Rushdie's fictional adaptations of ancient stereotypes is not simply hatred but the long, terrible triumphalist hatred which the West has had for Islam almost since its beginning.'

Free speech, such critics observed, was not an absolute. Britain, like most nations, restricted freedom of expression in all manner of ways. Slander, libel, national security, pornography, incitement to racial hatred – all these were routinely used as reasons to curtail speech. Each one demonstrated the willingness of Western intellectuals and politicians – including those staunchly defending Rushdie – to compromise. It is true that many cases of attempted censorship were controversial. The government's attempts in the mid-eighties to ban Peter Wright's *Spycatcher* on grounds of national security, for instance, and the conviction in 1977 of *Gay News* for publishing James Kirkup's blasphemous poem about Jesus Christ, were both bitterly contested. But the very fact of such contestation showed that there was nothing sacred about free speech. Even the staunchest advocate of free expression accepted that the line had to be drawn somewhere. The debate was not about whether free speech was absolute, but where the limits should begin. If speech had to be used responsibly so as to ensure that it did not promote blasphemy against the Christian God or hatred against blacks or Asians, was it unreasonable, asked opponents of *The Satanic Verses*, for Muslims to demand that it should not be used irresponsibly to slander the Prophet Muhammad or to outrage the Muslim community? In the post-Rushdie era, many liberals have felt increasingly compelled to answer, 'No.'

'I respect the right of freedom of speech,' UN secretary general Kofi Annan said of the Danish cartoon controversy, but such a right 'entails responsibility and judgement'. 'Freedom of expression confers rights, it is true,' said Philippe Douste-Blazy, the French foreign minister, 'but it also imposes the duty of responsibility on those who are speaking out.' For the then British foreign secretary Jack Straw, freedom of speech was fine, but not if it led to an 'open season' on religious taboos. 'I believe in free speech. But . . .' has become the rallying cry in the post-Rushdie era.

There is nothing new in the insistence that free speech has to be used responsibly. 'The most stringent protection of free speech would not protect a man falsely shouting fire in a theater and causing a panic,' US judge Oliver Wendell Holmes famously observed in a 1919 court case. What has changed is the perception of what it means to be responsible. We live in a plural world, so the argument runs, in which there are deep-seated conflicts between cultures embodying different values, many of which are incommensurate but all of which are valid in their own context. The controversy over *The Satanic Verses* was one such conflict. For diverse societies to function and to be fair, we need to show respect for other peoples, cultures and viewpoints. We can only do so by being intolerant of people whose views give offence or who transgress firmly entrenched moral boundaries. 'If people are to occupy the same political space without conflict,' the sociologist Tariq Modood suggests, 'they mutually have to limit the extent to which they subject each others' fundamental beliefs to criticism.'

From the Enlightenment onwards, freedom of expression had come to be seen not just as an important liberty, but as the very foundation of liberty. 'He who destroys a good book destroys reason itself,' as John Milton put it in *Areopagitica*, his famous 'speech for the liberty of unlicenc'd printing'. 'Give me the liberty to know, to utter, and to argue freely according to conscience, above all liberties.' he added. All progressive political strands that grew out of the Enlightenment, from liberalism to Marxism, were wedded to the principle of free speech.

No longer. Today, in liberal eyes, free speech is as likely to be seen as a threat to liberty as its shield. By its very nature, many argue, freedom of expression can damage basic freedoms. Hate speech undermines the freedom to live free from fear. The giving of offence diminishes the freedom to have one's beliefs and values recognized and respected. In a modern pluralist society, therefore, the cost of free speech – truly free speech – is too great. One of the ironies of living in a plural society, it seems, is that the preservation of diversity requires us to leave less room for a diversity of views.

4

In one sense, the distaste for giving offence, and the desire to curb the speech of all those who do so, is newly sprung from the perceived needs of a multicultural society. In another sense, it is an emotion that reaches back into history. The argument against offensive speech is the modern secularized version of the old idea of blasphemy, reinventing the sacred for a godless age.

Until the abolition of the offence in 2008, blasphemy was committed in British law if there was published 'any writing concerning God or Christ, the Christian religion, the Bible, or some sacred subject using words which are scurrilous, abusive or offensive, and which tend to vilify the Christian religion'. The origins of the law go back a millennium. After the Norman Conquest of 1066 two orders of courts were established. Church courts decided all ecclesiastical cases, under the guidance of canon law, which legislated on moral offences. The civil or king's courts were concerned with offences against the person or property. In 1401 King Henry IV's statute *De heretico comburendo* empowered bishops to arrest and imprison suspected heretics, including 'all preachers of heresy, all school masters infected with heresy and all owners and writers of heretical books'. If a heretic refused to abjure, or if he later relapsed, he could be 'handed over to the civil officers, to be taken to a high place before the people and there to be burnt, so that their punishment might strike fear into the hearts of others'.

Despite the concern with God and Christianity, the outlawing of blasphemy was less about defending the dignity of the divine than of protecting the sanctity of the state. In 1676 John Taylor was convicted of blasphemy for saying that Jesus Christ was a 'bastard' and a 'whoremaker' and that religion was a 'cheat'. 'That such kind of wicked and blasphemous words were not only an offence against God and religion,' observed the Lord Chief Justice, Sir Matthew Hale, in front of whom Taylor was tried, 'but a crime against the laws, States and Government; and therefore punishable in this court; that to say religion is a cheat, is to dissolve all those obligations whereby civil societies are preserved; and Christianity being parcel of the laws of England, therefore to reproach the Christian religion is to speak in subversion of the law.' Any challenge to Christian doctrine was, in other words, also a challenge to the secular social order. The heresy that troubled Lord Chief Justice Hale was the kind of heresy that promoted 'subversion of the law', the kind of dissent that might unstitch civil society. The outlawing of blasphemy was therefore a necessary defence of traditional political authority.

Four hundred years after Taylor's conviction, Lord Denning, perhaps Britain's most important judge of the twentieth century, made, in 1949, much the same point about the relationship between blasphemy and social disorder, though he drew the opposite conclusion about the necessity of the law. Historically, he observed, 'The reason for this law was because it was thought that a denial of Christianity was liable to shake the fabric of society, which was itself founded on Christian religion.' But, Denning added, 'There is no such danger in society now and the offence of blasphemy is a dead letter.'

Not only had Christianity become unwoven from the nation's social fabric, but over the next half-century other faiths and cultures wove themselves in. The multicultural transformation of Britain made even less plausible the traditional arguments for the blasphemy law. In 1985, three years before the Rushdie affair, the Law Commission, an independent statutory body charged with reviewing the law and recommending changes, published a report on blasphemy entitled *Offences against Religion and Public Worship*. 'In the circumstances now prevailing in this country,' the Commission argued, 'the limitation of protection to Christianity and, it would seem, the tenets of the Church of England, could not be justified.' It should be abolished 'without replacement'.

But if the reweaving of Britain's social fabric provided an argument for the abolition of the blasphemy law, it also provided a reason, in some people's minds, for its refashioning into a new offence that embraced non-Christian faiths and cultures. 'A significant number of lawyers, clergymen and laymen', wrote Richard Webster in *A Brief History of Blasphemy*, a book that came out a year after the *Satanic Verses* controversy and was highly critical of Rushdie and his supporters, 'have begun to take the view that some protection of people's religious feelings is necessary not primarily for religious or spiritual reasons but in the interests of social harmony.' One such figure was Lord Scarman. Two years before he wrote his famous report on the Brixton riots, he was one of the Law Lords who presided over the last great blasphemy trial in Britain. In 1977 Mary Whitehouse, founder of the pro-censorship National Viewers' and Listeners' Association, and a doughty defender of 'public morality', had brought a private prosecution for blasphemous libel against the newspaper *Gay News*. It had published a poem by James Kirkup called 'The Love that Dares to Speak its Name', about the love of a centurion for Jesus Christ at the crucifixion. Whitehouse won the case and *Gay News* appealed against the conviction.

In 1979 the case finally came to the House of Lords, the highest appeal court in Britain. The Law Lords, one of whom was Lord Scarman, upheld the original verdict. 'I do not subscribe to the view that the common law offence of blasphemous libel serves no useful purpose in the modern law,' Scarman wrote in his judgement. But such a law must be extended 'to protect the religious beliefs and feelings of non-Christians'. Blasphemy 'belongs to a group of criminal offences designed to safeguard the internal tranquillity of the kingdom. In an increasingly plural society such as that of modern Britain it is necessary not only to respect the differing religious beliefs, feelings and practices of all but also to protect them from scurrility, ridicule and contempt.'

In 1985 the Law Commission looked into this and rejected such an extension, arguing that the deficiencies of the law 'are so serious and so fundamental that . . . no measure short of abolition would be adequate to deal with these deficiencies'. The Commission dismissed the idea that religion should have special protection, observing that 'Reverence for God . . . does not differ fundamentally in character from reverence accorded to any person against whom those according respect are unwilling to entertain grounds of criticism.' Anticipating the arguments of Rushdie's critics that there is a difference between legitimate criticism and unacceptable abuse, the Law Commission pointed out that 'one person's incisive comment (and indeed seemingly innocuous comment) may be another's "blasphemy" and to forbid the use of the strongest language in relation, for example, to practices which some may rightly regard as not in the best interests of society as a whole would, it seems to us, be altogether unacceptable'. In other words, the way of saying something is part of what is said. To say that you must write differently is in practice to say that you must write about different things.

The Law Commission inquiry was, however, far from united in its view. Two of the five members appended a Note of Dissent to the majority report. The dissenters were particularly influenced by an outside working party that had insisted that some legal constraints were necessary for the protection of social harmony. 'If scurrilous attacks on religious beliefs go unpunished by law,' the working party suggested, 'they could embitter strongly held feelings within substantial groups of people, could destroy working relationships between different groups, and where religion and race are intimately bound together could deepen the tensions that already are a disturbing feature in some parts of this country.' The Note of Dissent proposed the replacement of blasphemy by a new offence that recognized 'the duty on our citizens, in our society of different races and people of different faiths and of no faith, not purposely to insult or outrage the religious feelings of others'.

In the end both the majority and minority views came to fruition. The blasphemy law was finally repealed in 2008. But it had already been replaced by a number of laws that secularized the offence of blasphemy. Two years before the blasphemy law was abolished, parliament had passed the Racial and Religious Hatred Act, which made it an offence to incite hatred against a person on the grounds of their religion. The aim was to extend to Muslims, and other faith groups, the same protection that racial groups, including Sikhs and Jews, possessed under Britain's various Race Relations Acts. In fact, it was already an offence to perpetrate hate speech. In 1998 the Public Order Act had been amended to make it an offence to 'display any writing, sign or other visible representation which is threatening, abusive or insulting, within the hearing or sight of a person likely to be caused harassment, alarm or distress'.

Such hate speech laws are now widespread. France, Germany, Canada, New Zealand, Ireland, Sweden, Norway, Brazil and South Africa are among the many nations that ban, in one way or other, and in one context or other, speech that is offensive or incites hatred. Some of these bans are very wide-ranging. Sweden defines hate speech as statements that threaten or 'express disrespect'. Canada prohibits the incitement of hatred against any 'identifiable group'. In Australia, the state of Victoria prohibits speech 'that incites hatred against or serious contempt for, or involves revulsion or severe ridicule of another on the grounds of his race or religious beliefs'. Israel bans speech that 'hurts religious feelings'. In Holland it is a criminal offence deliberately to insult a particular group. Germany bans speech that 'violates the dignity of or maliciously degrades or defames' a group. In each case the law defines hate speech in a different way. But what is common is the use of the law to expand the boundaries of hate speech.

What is being created through such laws is a new secular notion of the sacred. The French sociologist Émile Durkheim pointed out that the most significant aspect of a religion was not the worshipping of a deity but the carving out of a sacred sphere, a social space that was set apart and protected from being defiled. Traditionally, the sacred was a means by which to ensure that certain institutions, beliefs and practices could not be publicly challenged. Blasphemy laws were simply the most visible of such means. In today's more secular age, it is culture and identity, rather than simply religion and God, that the law seeks to protect from public assault. Even laws that ostensibly protect faith – such as Britain's Racial and Religious Hatred Act – are framed in terms of protecting a community's culture and identity. In today's world, identity is God, in more ways than one.

5

The main offices of *Jyllands-Posten* are in Aarhus, Denmark's principal port, situated on the Jutland peninsula. The town is also home to one of Denmark's most radical mosques, the Grimhøjve. The mosque is run by a Salafist organization called Equality and Brotherhood, and its main preacher – until he left for Libya in 2007, 'disgusted', he said, by the consequences of democracy – was Raed Hlayhel, an Islamist who, according to a *Jyllands-Posten* transcript of one of his sermons, believed that 'women can be Satan's instruments against men' and must be covered from head to toe. Even more than Abu Laban, Hlayhel was the man who directed the campaign against the cartoons. He helped organize the Copenhagen demonstration on 14 October, made contact with Middle Eastern embassies, and headed the delegation of Danish imams to Arab countries in December. He was, with Laban, the public face not just of the anti-cartoons campaign but also, for many Danes, of Islam itself.

Aarhus is also home to a very different kind of Muslim leader. Bünyamin Simsek is a city councillor who helped create a network of

Muslims in opposition to the cartoon protests. Simsek is religious – he attends mosque, does not drink or eat pork, and fasts at Ramadan. But he is also secular. In his front room is a photo of Kemal Atatürk, the secular founder of Turkey. 'There is', Simsek says, 'a large group of Muslims in this city who want to live in a secular society and adhere to the principle that religion is an issue between them and God and not something that should involve society.'

Simsek was born in 1970 in Kizilcakisla, a small Anatolian village in the heart of Turkey, a cluster of houses and dirt roads gathered around the mosque. His father, Ali, trained as a Muslim cleric and often preached in the mosque. But the preaching did not pay the bills. So in 1972 Ali emigrated to Denmark to work in a small timber factory in the town of Aarhus. He spoke no Danish – he still does not – and as a 'guest worker' expected to stay for a few years and then return home. Within a few months, however, he had changed his mind and brought his family to join him.

The Simseks were religious, conservative and deeply attached to their Turkish roots. Every summer the whole family would return to Kizilcakisla. When Bünyamin was seventeen, Ali decided that it was time for an arranged marriage. 'I did not know I could say no,' says Bünyamin. 'I had been brought up to honour my parents and to respect their wishes. What my parents said was law.' Ali chose Sorgul Ceran as Bünyamin's bride, a young woman from Kizilcakisla whose father had been a close friend of Ali's since his school days. She was eight years older than Bünyamin, and had never set foot in Ankara, let alone Aarhus.

The couple were married in Kizilcakisla. A year later she received Danish residency papers and finally joined her husband. The cultural gap between them turned into a chasm. 'My wife wore a veil and that was a problem for me,' Simsek says. 'When you come to somewhere like Denmark, you have to adapt, give up something to get something, but she would not. I was going out with Danish friends, but it was awkward with Sorgul. I felt I could not show her in a veil.'

Bünyamin was not just estranged from his wife, he had also fallen in love with another woman. Fatma Oektem had been born in Aarhus, but her grandfather had emigrated to Denmark from the Simseks' home village of Kizilcakisla. She was religious, but Westernized and emancipated.

When Bünyamin announced that he wanted a divorce from Sorgul, his father disowned him (though the two have since become reconciled), as did many within Aarhus' 3000-strong Turkish community. 'They reacted as they might have back in Kizilcakisla. It was like we were back in the village, not in Aarhus. They were talking about bringing dishonour on the community. Women were shouting at Fatma, "It's because of you that we can't let our husbands out of the house."'

But while the hostility was nasty, they also had support from within the Turkish community. 'Many Muslims here are like us. They attend mosque, but they are also Westernized. They recognize they live in Denmark not Turkey.' Bünyamin and Fatma were eventually married in 1999.

Then came the cartoon controversy. By that time Simsek had joined Venstre, Denmark's main liberal political party, and in 2002 had become a city councillor. Appalled by the way that Hlayhel and Laban had come to be seen as the authentic spokesmen for Muslim concerns, Simsek set up a network of Muslims opposed to the Islamists and helped organize a counter-demonstration to the cartoon protests. 'We wanted to show that not all Danish Muslims are Islamists,' he says. 'In fact very few are. But it is the Islamists like Raed Hlayhel and Abu Laban who get all the hearing.'

Simsek is not an isolated voice. 'I never felt offended by the cartoons,' Naser Khader says. 'But I did feel deeply insulted by the Islamist response to them. I felt astonished that the tradition for religious satire in the Middle East had so disappeared, and that a satirical stance on religion has become the privilege of the West. And I was offended that freedom of speech has become the preserve of the Western world.'

Khader is one of the best-known Muslims in Denmark, an MP and founder of the Demokratiske Muslimer movement, aimed at rallying democratic, secular Muslims. People like Raed Hlayhel and Abu Laban, he says, had been waiting for something like the cartoons. They appeared 'at the right time, and in the right place' to be exploited by Islamists who wanted to foment 'confrontation' which could be milked for 'money and support'.

Khader calls himself Muslim, though, unlike Simsek, he is not religious. The family backgrounds of the two men are, however, strikingly similar. One of five children, Khader was born in Damascus in 1963, the son of a Palestinian father and a Syrian mother. The family moved to Denmark when he was eleven, his father working as an unskilled labourer and never managing to learn Danish. 'Working for eight hours in a factory,' Khader recalls, 'he was too tired to go to school and learn Danish. Back then, as unskilled foreign labour, you didn't have to speak Danish to get work.' Khader himself wanted a different kind of life. After studying economics at Copenhagen University, he entered politics and in 2001 became an MP for the Danish Social Liberal Party. He left the Social Liberals shortly after the cartoon controversy broke out, to form his own Liberal Alliance, which won five seats in the 2007 general elections. 'My old party', he says, 'decided that it was wrong of *Jyllands-Posten* to publish the cartoons and that it should apologize to Muslims. I could not accept that.'

The attitude of the Social Liberals is, Khader believes, typical. Liberals have, in his eyes, 'formed an unholy alliance with Islamists. The prime minister, when he needed to talk to Muslims, talked to Islamists. Just months before the cartoon controversy, the prime minister had invited Abu Laban to a conference on terrorism. People like me kept saying, "They only represent a few people." But nobody listened. The government thought if they talked to someone who looked like a Muslim, then they were talking to real Muslims. I don't look like what they think a Muslim should look like – I don't have a beard, I wear a suit, I drink – so I'm not a real Muslim. But the majority of Muslims in Denmark are more like me than they are like Abu Laban.'

Khader recalls a conversation he had with Toger Seidenfaden, editor of *Politiken*, the left-wing newspaper that first broke the story of Kåre Bluitgen's difficulty in finding an illustrator, but which was highly critical of the *Jyllands-Posten* caricatures. 'He said to me that the cartoons insulted all Muslims. I said I was not insulted. He said, "But you're not a real Muslim."'

The echoes of the Rushdie affair are, I told him, unmistakable. Twenty years ago, we had the same kinds of debates in Britain. Critics of Rushdie did not speak for the Muslim community any more than Rushdie himself did. Both represented different strands of opinion within Muslim communities. Today the radical, secular clamour, which found an echo in *The Satanic Verses*, has been reduced to a whisper, largely because it has been strangled by multicultural policy. In the 1980s, however, it beat out a loud and distinctive rhythm within the babel of British Islam. Rushdie's critics spoke for some of the most conservative strands. Their campaign against *The Satanic Verses* was not to protect the Muslim communities from unconscionable attack by anti-Muslim bigots, but to protect their own privileged position within those communities from political attack by radical critics, to assert their right to be the true voice of Islam by denying legitimacy to such critics. They succeeded at least in part because secular liberals embraced them as the authentic voice of the Muslim community.

'That's what I'm frightened of here, too,' said Khader. 'The cartoons were not about Muhammad. They were about who should represent Muslims. What I find really offensive is that journalists and politicians see the fundamentalists as the real Muslims.'

The liberal idea of the 'authentic' Muslim, Bünyamin Simsek says, plays into the hands of racists because every Muslim comes to be seen as backward, reactionary and fundamentalist. Simsek used to work as a flight attendant for a Danish charter airline. Passengers would try to guess where he originated. 'They'd say Greece, Italy or Spain – but never Turkey. They think I'm nice, so they don't imagine I could be Turkish. Turkey, for them, is Islam, and Islam is fundamentalism.' When he told them he lived in Aarhus, they simply would not believe it.

Such racism has led many Muslims to reject the integrationist arguments of politicians like Naser Khader. 'A black man could only become integrated when he started behaving like a white man,' Salman Rushdie wrote of Britain's race relations policy in his 1982 television essay 'The New Empire within Britain'. Many Danish Muslims feel the same today about Danish integration policy. To integrate seems to be to give in to racism. Even Bünyamin Simsek betrays an ambivalence. There is, he says, always a sense of 'us' and 'them', which means that he, with his dark skin, can never be fully Danish. While he rejects the arguments of the Islamists, the attitudes of Danes anger him too. 'The Danes say one thing, that they want to integrate us, and do another,' he says. The liberals' authentic Muslim and the racists' backward fundamentalist become one and the same figure, who is always the outsider.

'Every story one chooses to tell', Rushdie suggested in his novel *Shame*, 'is a kind of censorship, it prevents other tales.' The tale that is told about what it is to be a real Muslim helps prevent other tales from within Muslim communities, helps silence other Muslim voices.

6

In a letter to the *Daily Telegraph* a year after the Ayatollah Khomeini's fatwa, the writer Anthony Lejeune suggested that 'There are certain beliefs, and certain symbols of such beliefs (an enemy's flag perhaps), which I personally would wish to treat with respect simply because human beings have loved them and died for them.' The author Richard Webster agreed. 'By insulting the sacred tradition of the Koran and by burning books,' he suggested, 'what both parties in this dispute have shown is a callous disregard for each other's most sacred symbols and most precious feelings.' The final chapter in Webster's book *A Brief History of Blasphemy* is entitled 'On not burning your enemy's flag'.

In the two decades since the Rushdie affair the idea that certain beliefs are so deeply embedded in certain cultures that they should not be disturbed has come to seem almost common sense. It was at the heart of the unease about the Danish cartoons. 'You don't fool around with other people's religions,' Kofi Annan insisted, 'and you have to respect what is sacred to other people.' 'There are taboos in every religion,' Jack Straw pointed out. 'We have to be very careful about showing the proper respect in this situation.'

Respect is unquestionably the grease of civilized life. It would be a dysfunctional society in which no one showed anyone else any respect, or in which manners and politeness were disregarded. But does respect require us not to burn our enemies' flags? Not at all, says the novelist Monica Ali. 'The idea of respect that liberals in particular promote today takes us down a dangerous road,' she argues. 'It's an idea of respect that jettisons the possibility of moral and political debate and focuses entirely on questions of feeling. A book or an image or an argument comes to be judged not on its moral or political worth but on how it makes someone feel.'

In 2003 Ali's debut novel, *Brick Lane*, was at the heart of a fierce controversy over 'respect'. It is a graceful, luminous story about Nazneen, an eighteen-year-old Bangladeshi woman who finds herself in an arranged marriage to Chanu, an obese forty-year-old man she has never met. Marriage takes her to a small flat on Brick Lane, the heart of east London's Bangladeshi community. She sees in London only 'piles of people loaded on top of the other, a vast dump of people rotting away under a mean strip of sky'. Unable to speak English, and confined to the flat, the highlight of her day is cutting her husband's corns. 'What could not be changed must be borne,' Nazneen believes. 'And since nothing could be changed, everything had to be borne.' Slowly, though, Nazneen comes to realize that 'she could not wait for the future to be revealed but had to make it for herself'. She becomes enraptured by ice-skating, after glimpsing it on TV, begins to find a voice at local community meetings and is drawn into an affair with Karim, a young, British-born Bangladeshi who himself transforms from street trader to Islamic zealot. When Chanu decides to return home to Bangladesh, Nazneen refuses to follow him, preferring to stay in Brick Lane with her two daughters, Shahana and Bibi. At the end of the novel, Nazneen's friend Razia takes her to an ice rink. 'But you can't skate in a sari,' Nazneen protests. 'This is England,' Razia replies. 'You can do whatever you want.'

Even before the novel was published, the literary magazine *Granta* had nominated Ali for its list of the twenty best young British novelists. *Brick Lane* was shortlisted for both the Booker Prize and the *Guardian* First Book Prize. But some within the Bangladeshi community looked very differently on Ali's portrayal of immigrant life. The Greater Sylhet Welfare and Development Council, a nationwide community organization, sent an eighteen-page letter to her publishers. 'We have serious objections to most of the content of this book which is a despicable insult to Bangladeshis at home and abroad,' it declared. 'This has been an awful slight on us and people feel very strongly about it.'

In 2006 Ruby Films announced that it was adapting the novel for the screen. Its attempt to film in Brick Lane itself met with outrage and protest. 'Our community is offended by the lies and slander in the book,' said Abdus Salique, a local businessman and organizer of the campaign against both book and film. The owner of a sweet shop and restaurant, he is also the lead singer in a Bangladeshi band called 'Dishan'. He once wrote a song called 'Trade Union' to help the local trade council recruit more Asian members, has many Labour Party friends and says he has a 'leftish ideology'. 'I have been here nearly forty years,' he said. 'When I first lived here the National Front used to come and attack us. But we fought back. We are proud to live here and we don't want Monica Ali to say despicable things about us.'

What despicable things? I asked him. 'She says we are dirty, we have lice, we are uncivilized, we are like monkeys.' No, she doesn't, I said. It is Chanu, Nazneen's husband, who says of Sylhetis that 'Most of them have jumped ship. That's how they come. They have menial jobs on the ship, doing donkey work, or they stow away like little rats in the hold.' He adds that 'to a white person, we are all the same: dirty little monkeys all in the same monkey clan. But these people are peasants. Uneducated. Illiterate. Close-minded. Without ambition.' 'I don't look down on them,' Chanu says of his Sylheti neighbours, 'but what can you do? If a man has only ever driven a rickshaw and never in his life held a book in his hand, then what can you expect from him?' Pompous and prejudiced, Chanu cuts a sad figure in *Brick Lane*, a man whose self-regarding narrow-mindedness obstructs his own plans for betterment. He dreams of 'going home a Big Man' but comes to realize that he has 'been waiting on the wrong side of the road for a bus that was already full'. Chanu's views reveal more about himself than it does about Sylhetis. It is out of the shadow of his prejudices that Nazneen herself has to emerge.

I had brought a copy of *Brick Lane* with me when I talked to Abdus Salique about Chanu, Nazneen, ice-skating and migrant dreams of freedom. But there was nothing I could say to persuade him. Like Sher Azam's unshakeable conviction that *The Satanic Verses* was part of a world-wide conspiracy against Islam, and Iqbal Sacranie's insistence that 90–95 percent of those stopped and searched under Britain's terror laws were Muslim, neither fact nor reason could sway Salique from his belief that *Brick Lane* insulted Sylhetis. There seemed to be more than a touch of Chanu about him.

In July 2006, around a hundred people took part in a protest march through Brick Lane. The organizers had promised to burn a copy of the novel, in imitation of the anti-Rushdie protests. The book-burning never happened, the marchers confining themselves to shouting 'Community, community, Bangladeshi community' and 'Monica's book, full of lies'. Nevertheless, the threats were sufficient for Ruby Films to abandon its plans to film in Brick Lane.

The whole campaign, says Ali, 'was a phoney war played out for the headlines'. Shortly after the novel was published the *Guardian* printed an article under the banner 'Brickbats fly as community brands novel "despicable"'. 'The community branded nothing,' Ali responds. 'It was just one man. But it was just before the *Guardian* book prize, and it was good publicity to generate some controversy.'

The campaign against the film was equally phoney. 'The protest march went through Brick Lane, and it would have been very easy to join the demo if people really felt angry. But very few did. It was mainly elderly men, and many had been bussed down from Bradford. The organizers suggested that they might burn the book. They didn't, of course, but it was a dog-whistle issue for the press. It got the headlines. There were more press than protestors on the day. There were a hundred people on that march. But a thousand people queued up to be extras on the film.'

Many Bangladeshis were sympathetic to Ali. Johann Hari, a columnist for the *Independent*, who lives in the area, talked to locals. Abdul Quayam, co-owner of Taj Stores, the oldest Bengali shop in Brick Lane, dismissed Abdus Salique as 'a big-mouth who wants publicity' adding that 'It is uneducated people like this who stop the progress of our community.' Restaurant owner Amzal Hussein said he would be 'very happy for this film to be made in my restaurant'. After the book was published, Ali had given readings in the East End. There were, she says, 'lots of youngsters, and many women, who came along. They did not complain about the book insulting them. They were interested in talking about writing. They realized it was difficult to express the ideas in the book, and they were fascinated in how you go about expressing those ideas.'

Many liberals, on the other hand, were sympathetic to the protestors. Germaine Greer claimed that 'the community has the moral right to keep the film-makers out'. She chided Ali for not concerning herself 'with the possibility that her plot might seem outlandish to the people who created the particular culture of Brick Lane'. And she compared Ali to old-fashioned novelists of the British Empire. Ali's 'approach to her Bengali characters', Greer suggested, was akin to 'Paul Scott's treatment of his Indian characters in the *Raj Quartet*'.

The *Guardian* argued in a leader that while Bangladeshis 'cannot have the right of veto over how they are portrayed', nevertheless their concerns were not 'irrelevant'. Ali, it claimed, showed 'little subtlety when she dismisses those offended by her book'. She needed to demonstrate 'a greater sense of responsibility' towards the community she was portraying and to treat her subjects 'with greater care'.

Ali gives such criticism short shrift. Liberals, she says, 'begin with sympathy for the underdog. They want to defend minority communities because they are beleaguered communities. But what they end up doing is listening to the loudest voices in those communities and ignoring the diversity.' It is striking, she points out, how, in the name of respect for minorities, minority voices themselves get silenced – Salman Rushdie, Gurpreet Kaur Bhatti (author of *Bezhti*) and Ali herself. But such voices are, for many critics, inauthentic and not truly expressive of minority experience. Ali's own story, Germaine Greer suggested, revealed why she could not represent the people of Brick Lane.

Ali was born in Dhaka, to an English mother, Joyce, and a Bangladeshi father, Hatem. The two had met in the mid-sixties at a dance in Bolton, where Joyce lived and Hatem was a student. When Hatem returned to what was then East Pakistan at the end of the sixties, to take up a post as inspector of technical colleges, Joyce followed him, which must have been a very brave move for a young white woman at that time. The two got married, much to the dismay of Hatem's family, which had already arranged a bride for him. Two children followed, including Monica. Then came the civil war – the bloody struggle in 1971 between East and West Pakistan, at the end of which East Pakistan declared independence and renamed itself Bangladesh.

Joyce and Hatem fled the fighting and returned to Bolton. 'It was a northern mill town,' Ali recalls with a shrug. 'England was very different then. Racism was in the air.' Initially estranged, Joyce's parents later became reconciled to her marriage. Nevertheless, Ali says, she found herself 'on the far side of two cultures', always 'having to work to fit in. When I was at a white friend's house I had to do things one way, and with Bangladeshi friends another way.' When I asked her how she saw herself, she dismissed the idea that she should view herself through any particular lens. She has never felt herself to be Asian or Bangladeshi, white or black. 'Perhaps it is the sensibility you need to be a writer,' she says. 'You don't fit into any category. You're always slightly on the outside. It gives you a different perspective.'

For Ali's critics, however, not fitting in is a sign of her inauthenticity. Germaine Greer dismissed Ali's claim that she was at the far side of two cultures. She is, in fact, Greer wrote, 'on the near side of British culture, not far from the middle. She writes in English and her point of view is, whether she allows herself to impersonate a village Bangladeshi woman or not, British. She has forgotten her Bengali, which she would not have done if she had wanted to remember it.' 'The fact that Ali's father is Bangladeshi was enough to give her authority in the eyes of the non-Asian British,' Greer sneered, 'but not in the eyes of British Bangladeshis.' Ali, the *Guardian* wrote, is 'a mixed-race Oxford graduate whose main characters were not from Sylhet (the original home of nearly all Brick Lane residents) but a completely different region: Mymensingh. This is a bit like a story about geordies being treated as if it were about cockneys.'

Such criticism, Ali suggests, says more about the current obsession with cultural authenticity than about her own sense of being. The liberal idea of respect, she points out, is not just selective, but highly patronizing. 'It is really a kind of moral superiority. What liberals mean when they talk about respect is that they can handle complex fiction, ambiguity, criticism. But other people can't, especially people in minority communities, because they are too sensitive.' And because Ali, like Rushdie, is comfortable in the world of complexity and ambiguity, she cannot be an authentic minority voice.

Ali challenges not just contemporary notions of authenticity but also the belief which has gained ground in the post-Rushdie world that in a plural society there is greater need for restraint and censorship, and that people, in Tariq Modood's words, 'mutually have to limit the extent to which they subject each other's fundamental beliefs to criticism'. Not true, suggests Ali. Because religious, cultural and ideological clashes are unavoidable in a plural world, not just between minority communities and mainstream society but within minority communities too, so it is better to deal openly with those clashes than simply to suppress them in the name of cultural or religious 'respect'. The giving and accepting of offence is a natural part of living in a plural world. If we want the pleasures of pluralism, we have to be grown-up enough to accept the pain too.

Ali goes further. The giving of offence is not just inevitable. It may also be important. Women, she points out, are often the ones to pay the price for prohibitions against giving offence. 'I suspect that what the protestors against *Brick Lane*, who were mainly men, really objected to', she says, 'was the portrayal of Nazneen having an affair, and of her sexual and social awakening.' It is certainly what Abdus Salique objected to. 'Our women mostly respect their husbands and respect their tradition. That is right. But Monica Ali says Bangladeshi women should behave like white women. That is not right.'

Rahila Gupta of the Southall Black Sisters agrees that religious and cultural taboos often conspire to maintain women's second-class status. 'A "cultural" practice is difficult enough to challenge,' she points out, 'but one which has been given the dubious honour of being ratified by a holy book, open as that may be to interpretation, is even harder to resist. Our choices are limited by our ascribed roles: as guardians of sexual morality; transmitters of cultural values to the next generation; and vessels bearing the honour of the community.'

Southall Black Sisters is a feminist version of the Asian Youth Movement – and one that, unlike the AYM, has managed to survive for the past thirty years. It was born in 1979 in the wake of the murder of Gurdip Singh Chaggar and at the height of radical ferment on Britain's streets. Its very title evokes a different age, one in which 'black' was not an ethnic label but a political badge. Southall was a largely Asian area of London, and the Sisters, too, were largely Asian. But they were – and remain – also defiantly black.

For thirty years SBS has been combating both racism and discrimination against women. It campaigns against domestic abuse, forced marriage and violence. But it has taken an equally strong line against religious fundamentalism, multiculturalism and restrictions on free speech. On 9 March 1989 – International Women's Day – SBS helped organize a meeting at the Dominion Theatre in Southall, the symbolic heart of the local black and Asian communities, in defence of Salman Rushdie. It was less than a month after the fatwa. 'As a group of women of many religions and none,' the meeting declared, 'we would like to express our solidarity with Salman Rushdie. Women's voices have been largely silent in the debate where battle lines have been drawn between liberalism and fundamentalism. Often it has been assumed that the views of local community leaders are our views, and their demands are our demands. We reject this absolutely.' It was out of this meeting that a new organization called Women Against Fundamentalism (WAF) emerged. On 29 May 1989, as twenty thousand anti-Rushdie protestors took to the streets of London, marching from Parliament Square to Hyde Park, WAF organized a counter-demonstration in support of Rushdie.

Voices such as Gupta's and the Southall Black Sisters, Ali says, are all too rarely heard today. The liberal consensus in defence of Enlightenment values and freedom of expression has 'broken down'. In the past, liberals recognized the importance of free speech to the overcoming of social iniquities. The nineteenth-century liberal philosopher John Stuart Mill's book *On Liberty* is often regarded as the bible of classical liberal thinking. Mill, Ali points out, 'saw offence not as doing harm but as doing good', because it was 'necessary for social progress'. Organizations such as the Southall Black Sisters continue to do so. But too many liberals now perceive 'a clash between freedom of expression and the defence of minority communities'.

The SBS has not only supported writers such as Rushdie, Kaur Bhatti and Ali, but has also strenuously opposed the British government's attempts to introduce a law banning 'incitement to religious hatred'. The Racial and Religious Hatred Act finally entered the statute books in 2006. 'People of all backgrounds and faiths have a right to live free from hatred, racism and extremism,' Home Office minister Paul Goggins claimed in defending the necessity for such legislation. But, Rahila Gupta responded, 'if the government expects the law to have a deterrent effect, then we must ask whose voices will be silenced in the process. Not merely those of the artistic community, but also the more vulnerable groups within religious communities, like women, who may find the newly strengthened group rights weaken their own position.' The law, she suggests, can only help 'strengthen the voices of religious intolerance and choke off women's right to dissent'. And that 'is too high a price to pay to appease an alienated community'.

7

In *The Satanic Verses*, Salman, the scribe who commits to paper God's revelations that Mahound received from the Archangel Gibreel, begins to 'notice how useful and well-timed the angel's revelations tended to be, so that when the faithful were disputing Mahound's views on any subject, from the possibility of space travel to the permanence of Hell, the angel would turn up with an answer, and he always supported Mahound, stating beyond a shadow of a doubt that it was impossible that a man should ever walk upon the moon, and being equally positive of the transient nature of damnation'. It would be one thing, Salman thinks, 'if Mahound took up his positions after receiving the revelation from Gibreel; but no, he just laid down the law and the angel would confirm it afterwards'. There are few passages in the novel that Muslim critics of Rushdie find more offensive, and it is not hard to see why: not because it excoriates God's words, but because it X-rays human power. For the powerful and the corrupt, Rushdie suggests, the word of God provides an impregnable cloak with which to surround their earthly rule. Those who wish to challenge earthly power inevitably have to blaspheme and give offence.

The irony of the campaign against *The Satanic Verses* is that Islam itself is a testament to the necessity for giving offence. The creation of the faith in the seventh century was shocking and viscerally offensive to the adherents of the pagan religion out of which it grew, and equally so to the two other monotheistic religions of the age, Judaism and Christianity. Without treating with disrespect the beliefs that human beings loved and for which they were willing to die, without being willing to burn its enemies' flags, Islam would never have been born. Had seventh-century incarnations of Shabbir Akhtar or Ziauddin Sardar had their way, the twenty-first-century versions may still have been fulminating against offensive speech, but it certainly would not have been Islam that was being offended.

The creation of Islam illustrates the way in which every great social, political and religious change has had to be carved out of history in the face of fierce opposition from entrenched authority, to which such change appears scurrilous, abusive and offensive. Those in power have always declared certain beliefs and practices to be sacred and therefore beyond challenge.

'Islamic doctrine', Shabbir Akhtar has insisted, 'wisely discourages inappropriate kinds of curiosity; and orthodoxy encourages "safe" thoughts. Muslims generally refuse to countenance any subtlety of mind or will that might undermine Islam.' Historically this is false; without the inappropriate curiosity of Islamic thinkers such as Ibn Sina (better known in Europe as Avicenna) and Ibn Rushd, science, philosophy and medicine would have been that much poorer and the births of the Renaissance, the Enlightenment and the scientific revolution that much more painful. Today, too, there are a number of Islamic thinkers trying to remake the faith for a secular age. Akhtar's comments do illuminate, however, the fear of open-mindedness felt by those with power and their need for certain ideas to be left unsaid. As Leszek Kolakowski, the Polish Catholic philosopher who began life as a Marxist, has observed, 'The sacred order never ceased, implicitly or explicitly, to proclaim "this is how things are, they cannot be otherwise".' It was a means of protecting not the kingdom of heaven but the citadels of earthly power. The sacred, Kolakowski pointed out, 'simply reaffirmed and stabilized the structure of society – its forms and its systems of divisions, and also its injustices, its privileges and its institutionalized instruments of oppression.'

Edmund Burke, the Irish philosopher and the founder of modern conservatism, complained of Thomas Paine that he sought 'to destroy in six or seven days' that which 'all the boasted wisdom of our ancestors has laboured to perfection for six or seven centuries'. To which Paine replied, 'I am contending for the rights of the living and against their being willed away, and controlled, and contracted for, by the manuscript-assumed authority of the dead.' Laws against giving offence protect 'the manuscript-assumed authority of the dead'. Free speech gives voice to 'the rights of the living'.

8

Lincolnshire is flat, rolling country, boring as far as the eye can see. It lies in the east of England, and its dull nothingness makes for great agricultural land. Much of it is fenland, fresh or saltwater wetlands that have been artificially drained and are now protected from floods by drainage banks and pumps. Here grow turnips and barley and Brussels sprouts by the mile. At the heart of the county lies the town of Boston. In the seventeenth century it was a hotbed of religious dissent, and many locals were forced to emigrate to escape persecution. Some of the pilgrims on the *Mayflower* hailed from here, and emigrants from the town have created Bostons across the world, including, most famously, Boston, Massachusetts.

These days Boston is more famous for its immigrants than its emigrants. It is an area that now depends on foreign labour, especially east Europeans, to pick and pack its agricultural produce. And that was why I found myself there in 2005, making a TV documentary about immigration for Channel 4. Called 'Let 'Em All In', it was a polemical piece about open borders. I went to Boston to interview both migrant workers and locals, many of whom were hostile to the newcomers. In the final cut, the director mischievously used 'Duelling Banjos', a tune made famous in the 1972 John Boorman film *Deliverance*, as background music to the Boston scenes. The far-right British National Party was not amused and complained to Ofcom, the broadcasting regulator:

> The use of the music from the soundtrack from the film deliverance was designed to portray the White Anglo-Saxon people those comments during the interview as being idiotic, redneck, inbred yokels as per the film 'Deliverance'. This was both racist and highly offensive to the individuals filmed and the White Anglo-Saxon community itself. [*sic*]

There is something more than a little comical about a white supremacist group so deftly exploiting multicultural neuroses about the giving of offence in order to play the role of the violated victim. But, then, we live in an age in which everything can be turned into a form of identity. From anorexia to zydeco, the philosopher Kwame Anthony

Appiah has observed, there is little we don't talk about as the product of some group's culture. Why should racists not join the club? 'I'm white. I want to preserve my culture and my heritage. And I don't want my dignity and beliefs to be mocked.' The appropriation by racists of the language of diversity raises an interesting question. If we accept with Shabbir Akhtar that 'in a plural democracy, we should all generate respect rather than hatred for opposed yet conscientiously held convictions', if we agree with Anthony Lejeune that deeply embedded cultural symbols should be respected, if we believe with Richard Webster that 'we shouldn't burn our enemy's flag', why should those who believe in white history and white culture, and fear that the symbols and flags of such history and culture are being polluted by immigrants, be excluded from our sympathy and respect?

One answer might be that racism is an obnoxious ideology, and that whites, unlike, say, Muslims, are not a powerless, vulnerable group. But then, many people view Islamism as equally obnoxious; many despise Islam itself. The Dutch politician Geert Wilders, infamous for his anti-Muslim film *Fitna*, has campaigned for a ban on the Qur'an on the grounds that it promotes hatred, bigotry and violence.

As for the idea that whiteness equates with power, the residents of Mixenden in West Yorkshire are unlikely to agree. Mixenden is a typical working-class 'sink' estate on the edge of Halifax, the town that inspired William Blake's vision of dark satanic mills. There is a certain faded Georgian elegance about the town center, a reminder of past glories, but, as in nearby Bradford, the woollen mills have long since closed down. Around 10 percent of the population is of Pakistani origin. But none of them live in Mixenden. Mixenden is very white, very poor and very resentful. Not only have most of its inhabitants lost their jobs, they have also lost their political voice. The institutions that once spoke to their needs, such as trade unions, are as decayed as the mills. The Labour Party, which most people in Mixenden used to support, has long since jettisoned its working-class roots in order to gain influence with voters in 'Middle England'. White and working-class, Mixenden felt left out of Britain's multicultural map.

I had gone to Mixenden, two years before I was in Boston, to make another film, this time about multiculturalism. A local election was taking place and, feeling discarded by Labour, Mixenden voters were turning to the far-right British National Party. On the last day of filming, the BNP's Adrian Marsden was elected as the local councillor. It was the kind of area that twenty years ago I would have treated as 'enemy territory': somewhere you walked around with the hairs standing up on the back of your neck, always expecting to get into a ruck with racists. But Mixenden never felt like that. Sure, there was much talk among locals about sending asylum-seekers back, and much anger directed at the nearby, predominantly Asian, area of St John's which they perceived (wrongly) as creaming off all the resources. There was, however, little racist graffiti on the estate, few BNP posters, just a single cross of St George (the symbol of England which has also become a symbol of the far-right). Never did I feel physically threatened or verbally intimidated, even when I was wandering around by myself. These were people with whom I could – and did – go drinking.

What there was in Mixenden was a sense of being abandoned by mainstream politics and politicians, as a result of which some people had rejected the political process entirely ('Politicians – they're only in it for themselves'). And some had embraced the British National Party, seemingly as the only way of giving voice to their grievances. What set the estate apart was not the intensity of its racism but the depth of its resentment. Other ethnic groups are allowed to promote their identity, so why not the English? Why has the English heritage been abandoned? Why should white identity not be included in the multicultural map? The same questions on every doorstep and in every pub.

Bill Heskey had been a Labour Party activist, and trade union convenor, for nearly thirty years. He had worked first in the mills and then on the railways. He is steeped in working-class history. Among the books in his front room were Tony Benn's *Diaries*, Trotsky's *History of the Russian Revolution*, and a biography of the Red Clydeside MP, James Maxton, by a certain Gordon Brown – then an MP and, a decade later, PM. Why was he supporting the BNP, I asked him in the pub one evening. 'They listen to us,' he said. 'No one else does. And they stand up for the white man. No one else does.' But they are racist, I protested. Many are fascist thugs. 'What's racist about standing up for yourself?' he responded. 'The Labour Party won't stand up for us. I know because I was a party member for thirty years. They'll take our votes, but won't do anything for us. No one will. They all just piss on us.'

The atmosphere and alienation in Mixenden was not that different from that in Beeston, the Leeds suburb from which three of the 7/7 bombers came (and which lies about fifteen miles away), nor was its warped sense of white identity so distant from the ideology of Islamism to which the Mullah Boys were drawn. The anger and frustration that drove people in Mixenden to vote for the BNP mirrored in many ways the fury and rage displayed by Muslim demonstrators on the streets of Bradford and Bolton which had led them to burn a book.

Inayat Bunglawala is a leading figure in the Muslim Council of Britain. He was a first-year computer science student at Queen Mary College in east London in 1989. He had never read the Qur'an as a child, barely attended mosque. Then came the Rushdie affair. 'It felt like we were being urinated upon from a great height,' Bunglawala remembers. 'I kept asking: Why are we being singled out? Why are we being attacked? Why can't anyone see we are under attack? It felt very frustrating because we did not seem to be able to do anything about it.' When Ayatollah Khomeini issued the fatwa, 'I felt a thrill. It was incredibly uplifting. The imam addressed "Proud Muslims" and I felt proud myself. It transformed the power equation. I no longer felt isolated. Muslims were standing up for themselves.'

The two men belong to different worlds. Bill is an unpolished fifty-something, a man who left school at sixteen and whose gruff articulacy comes from the rough and tumble of trade union politics. Bunglawala is suave, besuited and bespectacled, highly educated and thoroughly media-savvy. And yet there are echoes in the way that each describes his sense of alienation. There are echoes even in the language. 'They all just piss on us,' says Bill. 'It felt like we were being urinated upon from a great height,' says Bunglawala. 'What's racist about standing up for yourself?' asks Bill. The fatwa was uplifting, remembers Bunglawala, because 'Muslims were standing up for themselves.'

I would not wish to gloss over the poisonous character of the BNP's beliefs, nor to make a spurious comparison between racism and Islam. But nor would I wish, as many do, simply to dismiss the residents of places like Mixenden as racists and to wave away their sense of identity as less legitimate than that of, say, Bradford Muslims. The rage on the Mixenden estates about the way that immigration had defiled their white heritage is no less authentic than the fury on the Bradford streets about the way Salman Rushdie had blasphemed the Prophet, and their desire to cling to what they perceive as the symbols of their identity is felt no less deeply. If, then, we take at face value the arguments of Rushdie's critics that symbols should be respected and enemy flags not burnt, the people of Mixenden are surely as deserving of respect for their beliefs, symbols and identity as are the Muslims of Bradford. Or, to put it differently: if, as most people would agree, it is acceptable, indeed necessary, to challenge, ridicule and pour scorn on many of the beliefs and symbols of the white residents of Mixenden, why is it not equally acceptable, indeed necessary, to challenge, ridicule and pour scorn on the beliefs and symbols of Muslims in Bradford?

9

Iqbal Sacranie does not like homosexuality. It is immoral and spreads disease. And he said so, as head of the Muslim Council of Britain, in an interview on BBC Radio's *Today* programme in January 2006. 'It is not acceptable,' he told the interviewer. 'Each of our faiths tells us that it is harmful and, I think, if you look into the scientific evidence that has been available in terms of the various forms of other illnesses and diseases that are there, surely it points out that where homosexuality is practised there is a greater concern in that area.' He also described as 'harmful' the idea of civil partnerships between same-sex couples. 'It does not augur well', he said, 'in building the very foundations of society – stability, family relationships. And it is something we would certainly not, in any form, encourage the community to be involved in.'

Scotland Yard's community safety unit, which keeps an eye on hate crime, immediately launched an investigation into Sacranie's comments to see if he could be charged under the 1986 Public Order Act, which forbids the use of 'threatening, abusive or insulting words or behaviour within the hearing or sight of a person likely to be caused harassment, alarm or distress thereby'. Sir Iqbal (as he was by then) was appalled. 'We may not be happy with the views being expressed by others,' he said. 'But the difficulty comes in that at the end of the day we are human beings.' This was the same Iqbal Sacranie who not only tried to suppress *The Satanic Verses* but said of Salman Rushdie, immediately after the fatwa, 'death is too good for him'.

In response to the police investigation, twenty-two imams and Muslim leaders wrote to *The Times*. 'All Britons,' they declared, 'whether they are in favour of homosexuality or not, should be allowed to freely express their views in an atmosphere free of intimidation or bullying. We cannot claim to be a truly free and open society while we are trying to silence dissenting views.' Every one of the twenty-two still wants *The Satanic Verses* banned, the Danish cartoons censored and the Racial and Religious Hatred Act implemented. 'The Muslim community may have had its differences with the Jews, but obviously not enough to prohibit the borrowing of a very Jewish concept,' the historian David Starkey wryly responded. 'Chutzpah is the first word that comes to mind after reading a letter which declares that: "We cannot claim to be a truly free and open society while we are trying to silence dissenting views", signed by a group of people, many of whom have spent the past two years trying to persuade the government to pass the Religious Hatred Bill in order to silence dissenting views on Islam.'

It is not just Muslim leaders who display such chutzpah. Many of those happy to see cartoons lampooning Muhammad draw the line at anything mocking the Holocaust. Gay rights groups want Muslims (and black ragga artists) to be prosecuted for homophobia, but want the right to criticize Muslims as they see fit. Nick Griffin of the British National Party wants to be free to spout racist abuse, but wants Muslim clerics locked up for doing the same.

Not burning your enemy's flag leads, then, not to more respect for different cultures, but to a cacophonous din about why my flag is more deserving of being left unburnt than yours. The argument against free speech quickly degenerates into the claim that 'my speech should be free but yours is too costly'. It becomes, in other words, a means to defend particular sectional interests. 'What we have developed today', Monica Ali points out, 'is a marketplace of outrage. And if you set up a marketplace of outrage you have to expect everyone to enter it. Everyone now wants to say, "My feelings are more hurt than yours."'

That is why even Inayat Bunglawala has had second thoughts not just about his enthusiasm for the fatwa but about the Rushdie campaign itself. 'What I've come to realize', he says, 'is that it would never work to censor books that are offensive. In a plural society the banning of books cannot work.' He mentions Geert Wilders's campaign to ban the Qur'an in Holland. 'He says he finds it offensive. He compares it to *Mein Kampf*. So where do you stop? The logical conclusion is that once you ban one book because it is offensive, everything would end up being banned because someone would find it offensive.'

How sincere this conversion is, I do not know. Bunglawala says he came to recant his previous views in the mid-1990s, after reading Salman Rushdie's essay 'In Good Faith' (which had originally been written a year after the fatwa). Yet, on the eve of 9/11, he was calling Osama bin Laden a 'freedom fighter', and four years later campaigning for the Danish cartoons not to be republished in Britain.

Whatever the truth about Bunglawala's conversion, there is no denying the truth of his words. Once speech is banned because it is offensive or hateful, then there is no stopping. Freedom of speech, wrote Justice Hugo Black of the US Supreme Court in 1961, 'must be accorded to ideas we hate or sooner or later it will be denied to ideas we cherish'. The Supreme Court had upheld the constitutionality of the 1950 Subversive Activities Control Act. Justice Black dissented. 'The same arguments that are used to justify the outlawry of Communist ideas here', he pointed out, 'could be used to justify the outlawry of the ideas of democracy in other countries.'

If you advocate the criminalization of ideas you don't like, you cannot object if ideas that you do like also become outlawed, as they inevitably will. Muslim groups have used Canada's notorious hate speech laws to launch a number of government investigations of writers and publishers they despise, including Ezra Levant, whose *Weekly Journal* republished in 2006 one of the Danish cartoons. Syed Soharwardy, head of the Islamic Supreme Council of Canada, accused Levant of 'defaming me and my family because we follow and are related to Prophet Muhammad'. Two years later, the Canadian Islamic Congress took the magazine *Macleans* to the British Columbia Human Rights Commission for stirring up racial hatred by serializing parts of Mark Steyn's acerbic book *America Alone*, which argues that the rise of Islam undermines the very existence of the West. It demanded that *Macleans* be forced to publish a rebuttal and be made to compensate Muslims for having injured their 'dignity, feelings and self-respect'.

Both Levant and *Macleans* were eventually acquitted. But by then the biter had already been bit. A key advocate of Canada's hate speech laws was Sunera Thobani, professor of women's studies at the University of British Columbia. In October 2001, barely three weeks after 9/11, she gave a talk at a conference in which she described Americans as 'blood-thirsty, vengeful and calling for blood'. The result? The Canadian police launched a hate crime investigation. The investigation was eventually dropped and, unlike Ezra Levant or the publishers of *Macleans* magazine, she never had to appear before a human rights tribunal. Nevertheless, one hate crime investigator pointed out that while 'Normally people think it's a white supremacist or Caucasians promoting race hate against visible minorities . . . We want to get the message out that it's wrong all round.'

In the two decades since the Rushdie affair what has emerged is an auction of victimhood, as every group attempts to outbid all others as the one feeling the most offended. Even Americans now qualify as poor victims needing the warm embrace of hate speech laws. The only winner in all this is the state, which gets to decide who should say what to whom. Rather than building a plural society in which free speech provides the means of engagement and dialogue between different groups, what we are now creating is a sectional society in which restrictions on free speech help the authorities police the fragments.

10

In October 1989 the Muslim Institute helped organize a large meeting on the Rushdie affair at Manchester Town Hall. TV cameras were present. On the platform was the Institute's founder Kalim Siddiqui. The fatwa, he told the audience, was just, and Rushdie had to die. How many of you, he asked, support the death sentence? The majority of the audience raised their hands. How many, Siddiqui asked, would be willing to carry it out? Almost the same number kept their hands up. It was an electrifying moment, caught on camera and replayed on the evening news.

The barrister Francis Benyon phoned Frances D'Souza, chair of the International Committee for the Defence of Salman Rushdie. Siddiqui's comments, and his actions, Benyon suggested, were illegal. Why not pressurize the Director of Public Prosecutions to bring a case of incitement to murder against Siddiqui? Failing that, why not bring a private prosecution against him? A few months earlier, Benyon pointed out, Siddiqui had defended the fatwa and the killing of Rushdie on *Hypothethicals*, a TV programme on moral dilemmas, which that week had been considering the Rushdie case. And on virtually every anti-Rushdie demonstration, some of which Siddiqui had helped organize, the placards and slogans could not have been more unambiguous: 'Kill Rushdie'.

The committee debated the issue. 'I had a view,' D'Souza says, 'which was not an immediately popular one, least of all with Salman.' In her

view, 'Siddiqui's words, although shocking and distasteful, did not constitute incitement since neither he nor his followers were in any position
to carry out the fatwa, nor were they ever likely to be in such a position. They had no weapons, no knowledge of Salman's whereabouts
and no immediate intention of carrying out their threats. Therefore,
using the famous American court ruling on incitement, there was no
"clear and present danger" of Siddiqui's words becoming action.' The
committee took D'Souza's words to heart and no more was said about
the issue.

Eighteen years later, the Metropolitan Police took a very different
view when confronted with a group of Muslim demonstrators protesting
against the Danish cartoons. In October 2007 around three hundred
Muslims gathered outside the Danish embassy in London. Abdul Muhid,
said to be the leader of the demonstration, was filmed by the police
chanting 'Bomb, bomb the UK' and waving a placard with the slogan
'Annihilate those who insult Islam'. Mizanur Rahman called for UK
soldiers to be brought back from Iraq in body bags. 'We want to see
their blood running in the streets of Baghdad', he told the crowd. 'We
want to see the mujahideen shoot down their planes the way we shoot
down birds. We want to see their tanks burn in the way we burn their
flags.' Umran Javed shouted, 'Bomb, bomb Denmark. Bomb, bomb USA.'
Abdul Saleem chanted, '7/7 on its way' and 'Europe, you will pay with
your blood.' ·

The demonstrators were even less in a position to carry out their
threats or to incite others to do so than Kalim Siddiqui had been. There
was no clear and present danger. Nevertheless, Rahman, Javed and Muhid
were all sentenced to six years' imprisonment for 'solicitation of murder',
while Saleem was jailed for four years for incitement to racial hatred.

The contrast between the treatment of the anti-Rushdie protestors
and the anti-cartoon demonstrators is the story of how far attitudes to
free speech have changed over the past twenty years. It is also a morality
tale: be careful what you campaign for. The kind of censorship of offensive thoughts that the anti-Rushdie protestors demanded was the very
kind of censorship of offensive thoughts that imprisoned the anti-

cartoon protestors. Restrictions on speech, the aims of which were supposedly to protect the culture and dignity of minority communities, are now exploited to undermine the civil liberties of those very same communities.

The conviction of the cartoon protestors shows how, over the past two decades, the authorities have used the law both to expand the notion of 'hatred' and to loosen the meaning of 'incitement'. The law is now used to criminalize not just speech that directly leads to harm, but speech that might indirectly cause harm, or which is regarded as morally unacceptable. In 2008 Samina Malik, a shop worker from west London, received a nine-month suspended prison sentence for possessing materials 'likely to be useful to a person committing or preparing an act of terrorism'. She was a twenty-three-year-old fantasist who dreamed of jihad, and combined an intense hatred of Britain with the kind of adulation for Islamic terrorists that teenagers usually reserve for pop stars. She also wrote awful poetry under the moniker of the 'Lyrical Terrorist'. 'Let us make Jihad / Move to the front line / To chop chop head of *kuffar* swine' gives a flavour of her talents. 'It's not as messy or as hard as some may think/ It's all about the flow of the wrist' ran another of her ditties, entitled 'How to Behead'.

Malik was no T.S. Eliot. But neither was she an Osama bin Laden. She was a young woman with some disturbing thoughts in her head. Yet apart from writing doggerel, her only action was to download inflammatory material from freely available websites – some of which I have downloaded myself. Any would-be bomber unable to do so himself is hardly likely to have the wit to carry out a terrorist outrage. The real crime for which Malik was convicted was the thoughts and desires in her unhinged mind. Malik's conviction was later quashed by the Court of Appeal. But the case should never have come to court.

The cartoon protestors and the Lyrical Terrorist are not the only Muslims to be convicted of having bad thoughts. In 2006 the radical preacher Abu Hamza, whose incendiary sermons at Finsbury Park mosque in north London were supposed to have influenced the 7/7 bombers, was sentenced to seven years' imprisonment for incitement to murder and racial hatred. 'The person who hinders Allah's rule,' he preached, 'this man must be eliminated.' His barrister, Edward Fitzgerald QC, claimed that Hamza was simply quoting from the Qur'an, even handing jurors copies of the Holy Book to check for themselves. 'Mr Hamza has said things that most people will find deeply offensive and hateful,' Fitzgerald told the jury. 'But he is not on trial for describing England as a toilet. There is no crime of simply being offensive.' Another 'preacher', Abu Izzadeen, was filmed praising jihad as the 'responsibility of every single Muslim'. 'So we are terrorists,' he said. 'Terrify the enemies of Allah. The Americans and British only understand one language. It's the language of blood.' He was jailed for four and a half years.

Such cases have led to cries of 'Islamophobia'. The British government, many claim, is deliberately targeting Muslims for harbouring unacceptable thoughts. It is true that the war on terror has been used to impose greater restrictions on civil liberties. When the government introduced a new Terrorism Act in 2006, one of its most controversial parts was the section outlawing the 'glorification' of terrorism. Direct, intentional incitement to terrorist acts – whether or not they occur as a result – had been a criminal offence for some time. What was new was the outlawing of 'indirect incitement' – the celebration of, or apology for, acts of terror. The Terrorism Act 2006 is deliberately vague about what constitutes either glorification or terrorism, and does not require demonstration of intention on the part of those charged with an offence.

It would be wrong, though, to pin the blame for such curtailment of free expression simply on the war on terror. The anti-terror laws have exploited a culture of censorship that already existed. The expansion of notions of incitement and hatred began long before 9/11, as did the blurring of the categories between giving offence, fomenting hatred and inciting violence. Some of the fiercest critics of the war on terror have been among the most vocal in arguing for restrictions on free speech, seeking to outlaw, for instance, incitement to racial and religious hatred.

In the debate about *The Satanic Verses*, many suggested that Salman Rushdie was fomenting hatred by using abusive words about Islam.

Shabbir Akhtar called Rushdie's novel 'an inferior piece of hate litera-ture'. The distinguished American academic, and liberal Muslim, Ali Mazrui compared *The Satanic Verses* to *Mein Kampf*. Both books, he wrote, 'are works of alienation and basically divisive in intent and in impact'. Both are 'anti-Semitic but directed at different sections of the Semitic people'. And if, in Mazrui's eyes, the giving of offence was indistin-guishable from the creation of hatred, so, it seemed, was the fomenting of hatred from the inciting of violence. 'A book can be a lethal weapon,' wrote Mazrui. 'A pen writing three provocative paragraphs in London could let loose a flood of dangerous consequences a world away. When is a writer guilty of manslaughter? Could it conceivably be at the moment of writing itself?'

Few would take seriously the comparison of *The Satanic Verses* and *Mein Kampf*, or genuinely entertain the idea that Rushdie might have been guilty of manslaughter. Nevertheless in a more restrained fashion both these ideas have worked their way into British culture and the legal system. The police investigation of Iqbal Sacranie for his comments on homosexuality shows the legal blurring of the ideas of giving offence and fomenting hatred (though it would be hard even to argue that Sacranie was being offensive). Sacranie's is not the only such case. The very idea of hate speech has become a means of rebranding obnoxious political arguments as immoral ones, and hence, rather than of chal-lenging such sentiments politically, of seeking criminal sanctions to outlaw them.

When Mazrui suggests that Rushdie might be guilty of manslaughter because his words inflamed rioters in India, he is obscuring the rela-tionship between words and deeds. Rushdie had no intention of causing violence and the rioters were acting on their convictions, not on Rushdie's words. 'One of the things that the free speech and censor-ship issue raises', the psychoanalyst and writer Adam Phillips observes, 'is can we control the resonances, the interpretations, of our words? And the answer to that is: we can't.'

There is usually, in other words, no direct relationship between words and deeds. How people respond to words depends largely on the individuals themselves. They are responsible for interpreting the words and translating them into actions. Between words and deeds stands a human being, with a mind of his own, an ability to judge between right and wrong and a responsibility to face up to his own actions. It is not the words themselves that cause things to happen, but our estimation of the value and truth of those words. Words have consequences only if we choose to make them consequential. Free speech empowers the speaker. It also empowers the listener, placing a premium on his or her ability to weigh up the arguments and draw their own conclusions.

Most people would accept that there is a distinction between words and deeds and yet in the post-Rushdie world the law often acts as if there is no space between the two. 'Words are deeds,' Aesop wrote in his fable 'Trumpeter Taken Prisoner'. And this is how it appears to the law. Muslim protestors who chant 'Bomb, bomb Denmark' or 'Behead those who insult Islam' may be moronic and offensive. But the idea that they are inciting murder is equally moronic and offensive to our intelligence. People do not respond to words like robots. They think and reason, and act upon their thoughts and reasoning. Bigots are, of course, influenced by bigoted talk. But it is the bigots who must bear responsibility for translating talk into action. In blurring the distinction between speech and action, incitement laws blur the idea of human agency and of moral responsibility.

The convictions of the cartoon protestors, Samina Malik, Abu Hamza, Abu Izzadeen and others are not an expression of Islamophobia. They are an expression of the changing attitudes to words and deeds, a change that those who now cry foul about these convictions did much to bring about. Liberals and anti-racists have long argued that not just harmful actions but bad thoughts and evil ideas too should be a matter for the criminal law. The authorities are now applying that belief not just to racist bigots but to Muslim ones too.

In America, the home of free speech, many influential voices are now calling for the First Amendment to be amended to outlaw the 'hate speech' of radical Islamists. 'A book can be a lethal weapon,' wrote Ali Mazrui about *The Satanic Verses*. 'His weapon was words,' wrote Andrew

McCarthy, senior fellow at the Foundation for the Defence of Democracies and former US federal prosecutor, about a speech by the Islamic cleric Omar Abdel-Rahman. Six weeks before the first bombing of the World Trade Center, in 1993, Rahman had claimed that the Qur'an makes acceptable 'jihad for the sake of Allah, which is to terrorize the enemies of God and our enemies too'. 'With an enemy committed to terrorism,' McCarthy wrote in *Commentary* magazine, 'the advocacy of terrorism – the threats, the words – are not mere dogma, or even calls to "action". They are themselves weapons – weapons of incitement and intimidation, often as effective in achieving their ends as would be firearms and explosives brandished openly.' It is vital, he suggested, to 'criminalize the advocacy of militant Islam and its metier, which is the indiscriminate slaughter of civilians'. It is a call that has been taken up by Newt Gingrich, former Republican speaker of the House of Representatives. He has demanded the rewriting of the First Amendment to 'break up [the terrorists'] capacity to use free speech'.

With the criminalizing of criticism of Islam has come the criminalizing of Islamic dissent. With the ban on incitement to religious hatred has come the ban on the glorification of terrorism. Far from specifically targeting Muslims, the law is taking it upon itself to determine what anyone, Muslim or non-Muslim, can say about others. Many of those who opposed the law against the glorification of terror supported the criminalizing of religious hatred as a protection for a beleaguered minority. Many of those who opposed the religious hatred law as infringing legitimate speech supported constraints on the glorification of terrorism as a necessary measure in the post-9/11 age. We cannot have it both ways. If we invite the state to define the boundaries of acceptable speech, we cannot complain if it is not just speech to which we object that gets curtailed. If the twenty years since the Rushdie affair have taught us anything, it should be that.

CHAPTER SIX

Monsters and myths

What he was rejecting was the portrait of himself and Gibreel as
monstrous. Monstrous indeed: the most absurd of ideas.

Salman Rushdie, *The Satanic Verses*, p.537.

1

It was probably just an eerie coincidence. On the night of 26 September
2008, the London offices of the publishers Gibson Square were firebombed. It was twenty years to the day since the publication of *The
Satanic Verses*.

The police arrested four men almost immediately. Whether the alleged
perpetrators of the attack knew the significance of the date, I do not
know. What seems certain is that Gibson Square was attacked because
it was about to publish *The Jewel of Medina*, a romantic tale about Aisha,
the Prophet Muhammad's youngest wife. Written by an American journalist, Sherry Jones, it had originally been bought by Random House
for a $100,000 advance. But in July 2008 the publishers pulled out of
the deal for fear of sparking another Rushdie affair. It was not an
Islamist, but an American academic, who raised the alarm.

Five months earlier, Random House had sent galley proofs to writers
and scholars, hoping for cover endorsements. One of those on the list
was Denise Spellberg, an associate professor of Islamic history at the
University of Texas. Jones had used Spellberg's book *Politics, Gender and
the Islamic Past*, a study of Aisha's legacy, as a source for her novel.
Spellberg, however, was not impressed, condemning *The Jewel of Medina*
as 'offensive' and as an 'ugly piece of work' which amounted to 'soft-

core porn'. She phoned an editor at Random House, Jane Garrett, to tell her that Jones's novel was 'a declaration of war' and 'a national security issue'. Garrett immediately dispatched an email to Random House executives. 'She thinks there is a very real possibility of major danger for the building and staff and widespread violence,' Garrett wrote. 'Denise says . . . it will be far more controversial than *The Satanic Verses* or the Danish cartoons.' According to Garrett, Spellberg thought that 'the book should be withdrawn ASAP'. It was. Random House immediately pulled the novel.

On the day that the firebombers attacked Gibson Square, Inayat Bunglawala of the Muslim Council of Britain wrote a piece for the *Guardian*'s Comment Is Free blog, ruminating on the twenty years since the publication of *The Satanic Verses*. After acknowledging that he had been 'utterly wrong' in calling for Rushdie's novel 'to be banned or pulped', he suggested that he was not alone in having changed his mind. 'Many Muslims who had once supported the banning/pulping of the book', he claimed, 'have since revised their views and recognized that such actions were quite wrong and completely counterproductive.' He trusted that 'appropriate lessons' had been 'learned from the *Satanic Verses* affair' and that British Muslims would not 'take the bait' proffered by *The Jewel of Medina*.

'Oh boy, what great timing,' Bunglawala ruefully observed about his remarks three days later, following the firebombing. Nevertheless, he maintained, in direct response to my comment that the actions of the firebombers had been given a 'spurious legitimacy by liberals who proclaim it morally unacceptable to give offence', that 'If anyone has given ground in this debate, it is surely those who once believed in banning books because they regarded them as being "offensive".'

Bunglawala himself has certainly given ground. But his personal change of heart should not blind us to the fact that much of the rest of the world has been marching in the opposite direction. In the twenty years since the Rushdie affair, as we saw in the last chapter, the fatwa has become internalized. And nothing could have revealed this better than the differing responses to *The Satanic Verses* and *The Jewel of Medina*.

The books are studies in contrast. One is a complex postmodern account of migration, religion and identity, the other a racy, almost Mills and Boon-ish, historical romance. 'The pain of consummation soon melted away,' Aisha recalls of her wedding night. 'Muhammad was so gentle. I hardly felt the scorpion's sting. To be in his arms, skin to skin, was the bliss I had longed for all my life.'

The Satanic Verses, Rushdie has written, 'is in part a secular man's reckoning with the religious spirit'. It is 'a work of radical dissent and questioning and reimagining', a novel that 'celebrates hybridity, impurity, intermingling, the transformation that comes of new and unexpected combinations of human beings, cultures, ideas, politics, movies, songs'. For Sherry Jones, on the other hand, *The Jewel of Medina* was a means of 'honouring Aisha and all the wives of Muhammad by giving voice to them. They are remarkable women but their roles in the shaping of Islam have so often been ignored by historians. It's a book about being a woman and about women's empowerment. And it's a way of bringing the story of Islam to more people by telling it through the eyes of a young woman.'

The respective publishers' responses to the two books were as distinct as the novels themselves. In 1989 even a fatwa could not stop the continued publication of *The Satanic Verses*. Salman Rushdie was forced into hiding for almost a decade. Translators and publishers were assaulted and even murdered. Yet, apart from its wobble over the paperback edition, Penguin never wavered in its commitment to Rushdie's novel. Nor did many of the other threatened publishers. 'Journalists were constantly asking me, "Will you stop publishing *The Satanic Verses*?"' recalls William Nygaard, the Norwegian publisher shot three times and left for dead outside his Oslo home in 1993. 'I said, "Absolutely not." It was morally important for me as a publisher not to give in. I had to prove that freedom of expression is a basic freedom that could not be stopped by terrorism. Freedom of expression is basic to being a free human being. Without freedom of expression, there can be no dissent, no debate, no democracy.'

Random House was threatened with little more than emails and phone calls from an outraged academic before deciding, in its own words, 'to postpone publication for the safety of the author, employees of Random House, booksellers and anyone else who would be involved in the distribution and sale of the novel'. According to a statement from the publishers, the company had received 'from credible and unrelated sources, cautionary advice not only that the publication of this book might be offensive to some in the Muslim community, but also that it could incite acts of violence by a small, radical segment'.

In fact, what happened was this. Spellberg told Shahed Amanullah, a guest lecturer on one of her courses and editor-in-chief of the popular altmuslim.com website, about *The Jewel of Medina*, claiming that it 'made fun of Muslims and their history'. Amanullah in turn sent an email to an online forum for graduate students in Islamic studies to say that he had 'just got a frantic call from a professor who got an advanced copy of the forthcoming novel *Jewel of Medina* – she said she found it incredibly offensive', and asking if anyone knew any more about the book. Amanullah's email was reposted on Husaini Youths, a website for young Shias. Almost immediately a respondent called Ali Hemami suggested a 'seven-point strategy' for getting an 'apology from . . . the author of the BOOK for writing such stuff'. The strategy involved nothing more sinister than getting 'one volunteer to draft a mail and send to people including us – so that all of us can fwd that mail to as many muslims as possible', another 'volunteer . . . to retreive [*sic*] the copy of this book and read it ASAP and share the details with the group', and finding a 'Couple of volunteers who would read as much material as possible about Holy Prophet's wife Aisha and share the info with the group'. According to Amanullah, Random House executives noticed the post, took fright and moved to spike the book. An email from an outraged academic and a critical post on an online forum – that, it seems, was all it took for Random House to panic.

'If Random House had simply published my book,' Sherry Jones told me, 'I don't think there would have been any trouble. The real problem is not that Muslims are offended, but that people think they will be. It is a veiled form of racism to assume that all Muslims would be offended and that an offended Muslim would be a violent Muslim.'

The firebombing of Gibson Square's offices in London might suggest that at least some offended Muslims are violent Muslims. Yet it is not possible to know whether such an attack would have happened had Random House gone ahead with publication without any fuss. Once Random House had made an issue of the book's offensiveness, then it was inevitable that some Muslims at least would feel offended. There will always be extremists who respond as the Gibson Square firebombers did. There is little that we can do about them. What we can do something about is the broader culture within which such people operate. A culture that robustly defends freedom of expression would provide few resources upon which such extremists could draw. A culture that proclaims it unacceptable to give offence, and in which politicians and intellectuals are terrified at the thought of doing so, provides the firebombers with a spurious moral legitimacy for their actions. Internalizing the fatwa has not just created a new culture of self-censorship, it has also helped generate the very problems to which self-censorship was supposedly a response. The fear of giving offence has simply made it easier to take offence.

Amanullah himself has insisted that *The Jewel of Medina* should not be withdrawn and has pointed out that 'no one has the absolute right not to be offended, nor does anyone have the right to live without the uncomfortable opinions of others'. 'We all need to develop thicker skins, more open minds, and a common understanding of the principles of free speech,' he suggested. By then, however, the damage had already been done.

2

Random House is Salman Rushdie's publisher. 'I am very disappointed to hear that my publishers, Random House, have cancelled another author's novel because of their concerns about possible Islamic reprisals,' he wrote. 'This is censorship by fear and it sets a very bad precedent indeed.'

Nonsense, responded the American academic Stanley Fish, who, in the title of his famous 1993 book, proclaimed that *There Is No Such Thing as Free Speech: And It's a Good Thing Too*. Dismissing Rushdie as 'a self-appointed poster boy for the First Amendment', Fish rejected the charge that the Random House decision amounted to censorship. It is only censorship, he suggested, when 'it is the government that is criminalizing expression' and when 'the restrictions are blanket ones'. Random House was simply making a 'judgment call'.

There is indeed a difference between a government silencing a writer with the threat of imprisonment and a publisher pulling out of a book deal. It is also true that other publishers picked up Jones's novel, including Beaufort in America and Gibson Square in Britain. But Fish missed the point about the changing character of censorship. The Random House decision was not a classic example of state censorship. It was, however, an example of the way that free speech has become more restricted without the need for such overt censorship. The directors of Random House had every right to take the decision they did. But the fact that they took that decision, and their reasons for doing so, say much about how attitudes to free speech have changed over the past twenty years – and about the internalization of the fatwa.

'The way that Random House dropped *The Jewel of Medina* would have been unthinkable in the pre-Rushdie era,' Monica Ali believes. 'And yet the press barely paid attention to it. It is as if everyone is thinking: "It's what you expect." "That's the way it is." "It's fate." People have become resigned to such censorship.'

For Ali, 'What is really dangerous is when you don't know that you've censored yourself.' Does she feel, I wondered, that she censors herself? 'When I write, I try to make sure that the door is closed,' she said. 'I try to keep those pressures out. But it is difficult to know to what extent you've been infected by the debate about offence. It is genuinely difficult to know, because the process of writing is not conscious. Consciously you make sure you don't censor yourself. But unconsciously?' Her voice trailed off.

3

'Nobody', Hanif Kureishi suggests, 'would have the balls today to write *The Satanic Verses*, let alone publish it. Writing is now timid because writers are now terrified.'

Like Rushdie, Kureishi is a writer who came of literary age in the 1980s, exploring the fraught relationship between race, culture, identity and politics in Thatcher's Britain. Where Rushdie had been born in Bombay and his work deeply shaped by the politics and culture of the subcontinent, Kureishi was born in Bromley, in south London, attended the same school as his hero David Bowie (though not at the same time), and his work is infused by the sounds and rhythms of the capital.

The writer Zadie Smith recalls reading as a fifteen-year-old *The Buddha of Suburbia*, Kureishi's semi-autobiographical first novel, published in 1990. 'There was one copy going round our school like contraband,' she says. 'When it was my turn I read it in one sitting in the playground and missed all my classes. It's a very simple pleasure that white readers take absolutely for granted: I'd never read a book about anyone remotely like me before.' Kureishi's characters were not remotely like traditional depictions of Asians either. They were as cocksure, streetwise and sexually charged as Kureishi himself. 'I was a Paki,' he says. 'My family were Pakis. So there were lots of Pakis in my work. There were no representations of Pakistanis in films or novels in those days. At least not Pakistanis I recognized.'

Even more than Rushdie, Kureishi became a talisman to a new generation of Asians who were kicking out not just against racism but also against the conventional image of what an Asian should be. Kureishi's work, the cultural critic Sukhdev Sandhu recalls, transformed the way that both he and his white friends saw what it meant to be Asian. Asians 'had previously been mocked for our deference and timidity. We were too scared to look people in the eye when they spoke to us. We weren't gobby or dissing.' Not so Kureishi's Asians. 'Kureishi's language was a revelation. It was neither meek nor subservient. It wasn't fake posh. Instead it was playful and casually knowing.'

Kureishi hit the mark with *My Beautiful Laundrette*, his 1985 screenplay which told the story of a gay love affair between bored Asian teenager Omar and working-class white lad Johnny, set against the backdrop of racism and recession in eighties Britain. It was shocking, sexy and funny, and quite unlike any other 'ethnic' film. But in detonating all manner of cultural assumptions, it also upset the traditional narratives of immigrant life. Sandhu recalls how his father beat him up after he persuaded his family to watch the film on TV. The teenage Sandhu knew nothing about the film, except that it was about Asians. 'The night it was on TV', he wrote, 'I swept the carpet, prepared snacks – some Nice biscuits and a mug of hot milk each – and sat my parents down.' But the nudity, gay sex, immoral Pakistani businessmen and drug smugglers disguised as mullahs did not go down very well. 'Why are you showing us such filth?' Sandhu's father yelled, his fists flying. 'Just as well we never got to the scene where Omar and Johnny start fucking in the laundrette,' Sandhu wryly observes. 'My father was right to be appalled,' he added. 'The film celebrated precisely those things – irony, youth, family instability, sexual desire – that he most feared. It taught him, though it would take years for the lesson to sink in fully, that he could not control the future. And control – over their wives, their children, their finances, was what Asian immigrants like him coveted.'

It was not just Sandhu's father who took umbrage. Three years before *The Satanic Verses*, Kureishi's screenplay incurred the wrath of Islamists. 'There were demos in New York against it', Kureishi remembers, 'organized by something called the Pakistani Action Group. About a hundred people, all men, all middle-aged, would turn up every Friday to demonstrate outside cinemas shouting "No homosexuals in Pakistan".'

What particularly upset Kureishi's critics was his refusal to play along with the idea that Asian writers had to treat Asian characters with respect and to present them in a good light. 'I am a professional businessman, not a professional Pakistani,' the landlord Nasser tells his white sidekick Johnny in *My Beautiful Laundrette* when Johnny protests that as a non-white Nasser should nòt evict a black tenant. 'It was a new idea of being Asian,' Kureishi says, 'not the traditional notion of victims cowering in the corner. I wanted to show that Asians were not all progressive or nice – so I had an Asian as a vicious Thatcherite.'

But the idea of victimhood not only proved highly seductive, it also helped create strange bedfellows. 'It was the first time that I remember the left and Muslim fundamentalists joining hands,' Kureishi recalls. 'Islamic critics would say, "You're saying we're all homosexuals" and "You shouldn't wash dirty linen in public". And the left would say, "You should be standing up for your community" and "You should not attack minority communities".'

Despite Kureishi's brush with Islamism, he never saw *The Satanic Verses* controversy coming. 'I first read *The Satanic Verses* in proof copy. I didn't notice anything about it that might rouse the fundamentalists. I saw it as a book about psychosis, about newness and change. The eighties was an age of fusion – in music, in food, in literature. *The Satanic Verses* was part of that postmodern fusion.'

Even when the protests began against Rushdie's novel, he did not take them seriously. 'The demos against *My Beautiful Laundrette* had fizzled out after a few months. I thought the same would happen with *The Satanic Verses*.' Kureishi does not even remember the book-burning. 'It didn't register,' he says. 'Only with the fatwa did it become clear how serious and dangerous it was. It seemed mad to imagine that someone could be killed over a book. And I was flabbergasted. How could a community that I identified with turn against a writer who was one of its most articulate voices?'

The fatwa was traumatic for Kureishi, and not just because he was, and remains, a close friend of Rushdie's. 'It changed the direction of my writing. Unlike Salman I had never taken a real interest in Islam. I come from a Muslim family. But they were middle-class – intellectuals, journalists, writers – and very anti-clerical. I was an atheist, like Salman, like many Asians of our generation were. I was interested in race, in identity, in mixture, but never in Islam. The fatwa changed all that. I started researching fundamentalism. I started visiting mosques, talking to Islamists.'

Six years after the fatwa Kureishi produced his first major post-Rushdie work. Set in 1989, *The Black Album* tells the story of Shahid, a lonely, vulnerable student torn between liberalism and fundamentalism – between Deedee, his lecturer and lover, who introduces him to Lacan, sex, Madonna and Prince (the title of the novel is borrowed from a Prince album), and Riaz, for whom all pop music is decadent and who teaches Shahid how to pray, fast and submit. Rushdie celebrated his existence 'in between' cultures. Shahid was terrified that his ignorance of Islam 'would place him in no-man's-land'. At a time when 'everyone was insisting on their identity, coming out as a man, woman, gay, black, Jew – brandishing whichever features they could claim, as if without a tag they wouldn't be human', so 'Shahid, too, wanted to belong to his people. But first he had to know them, their past, and what they hoped for.'

Two years later came 'My Son the Fanatic', a short story, later turned into a film, about the fraught relationship between Parvez, a Bradford taxi driver who dreams of material riches and of 'fitting in' to British culture, and his son, Ali, who turns to Islamic fundamentalism to find a sense of moral order and belonging. 'I love England,' Parvez tells his son. 'They let you do almost anything here.' 'That is the problem,' Ali replies.

The fundamentalists in Kureishi's stories are not first-generation immigrants, bemoaning a world that has been taken from them, like Sukhdev Sandhu's father or the New York protestors against *My Beautiful Laundrette*, but their children, yeaning for an Islam they have never known. It is less a clash of civilizations than a war of generations. The first generation desire material prosperity, the second seek to fill a spiritual void. 'I have a belief,' Shahid's father says in *The Black Album*. 'It's called working until my arse aches.' When Ali confronts Parvez about his drinking in 'My Son the Fanatic', the father explains 'that for years he had worked more than ten hours a day, that he had few enjoyments or hobbies and never went on holiday. Surely it wasn't a crime to have a drink when he wanted one?' Ali insists it is and accuses his father of being 'too implicated in Western civilization'.

'The fundamentalists I met', says Kureishi, 'were educated, integrated, as English as David Beckham. But they thought that England was a cesspit. They had an apocalyptic view of the future. They lived in a parallel universe. They had no idea what life would be like in an Islamic country but they yearned for everything sharia. And they had a kind of Islam that would have disgusted their parents.' Kureishi recalls visiting the house of Farid Kassim, one of the founders of the British branch of Hizb ut-Tahrir. 'Four women brought in the food. They came into the room backwards, bent over, so we could not see their faces. I have never seen that anywhere else.'

The Rushdie affair, Kureishi believes, transformed not just his own work, but also 'the very notion of writing'. The fatwa 'created a climate of terror and fear. Writers had to think about what they were writing in a way they never had to before. Free speech became an issue as it had not been before. Liberals had to take a stand, to defend an ideology they had not really had to think about before.'

How have they borne up to the task? 'The attacks on Rushdie showed that words can be dangerous. They also showed why critical thought is more important than ever, why blasphemy and immorality and insult need protection. But most people, most writers, want to keep their heads down, live a quiet life. They don't want a bomb in the letterbox. They have succumbed to the fear.'

4

'What's been particularly disturbing', says Sherry Jones, 'is the culture of fear that's developed in this country since 2001. The administration has perpetuated the idea that America is under siege from Muslims. It has stoked up fears of another 9/11. We've become so terrified about how we might die that we've stopped thinking about how we should live.'

If the Rushdie affair augured a new sense of fear, 9/11 turned it into a permanent condition of the national psyche, and not just in America. In 1989, the burning book in Bradford provided an intimation of a different kind of social conflict, a clash of civilizations. The burning towers on 9/11 appeared to make that clash concrete in the rubble of Lower Manhattan. The fatwa had sown doubts and fears among Western liberals; the jihad conjured up their most terrible nightmares. 'It has become terrifyingly clear how close the "Barbarians" are, perhaps in reality always have been,' warned the writer (and London-born New Yorker) Sasha Abramsky. He quoted Edward Gibbon's famous lines from *The Decline and Fall of the Roman Empire* on how 'At the hour of midnight the Salarian Gate was silently opened, and the inhabitants were awakened by the tremendous sound of the Gothic trumpet. Eleven hundred and sixty-three years after the foundation of Rome, the Imperial city, that had subdued and civilized so considerable a part of mankind, was delivered to the licentious fury of the tribes of Germany and Scythia.' For Abramsky, the destruction of the World Trade Center revealed how 'a symbol of our age can be destroyed in a moment, much as the fierce greatness of Rome was overrun by hordes lacking science, literature, art, but fuelled by a fanatical hatred of an urban, cosmopolitan, commercial culture and civilization far grander than their own.'

The analogy is telling. Not because of what it tells us about a West besieged by Islamist hordes, but because of the glimpse it provides into the sense of fragility felt by many about Western civilization. 'America today', the former US national security advisor Zbigniew Brzezinski has observed, 'is not the self-confident and determined nation that responded to Pearl Harbor; nor is it the America that heard from its leader, at another moment of crisis, the powerful words "the only thing we have to fear is fear itself"; nor is it the calm America that waged the Cold War with quiet persistence despite the knowledge that a real war could be initiated abruptly within minutes and prompt the death of 100 million Americans within just a few hours. We are now divided, uncertain and potentially very susceptible to panic in the event of another terrorist act in the United States itself.'

In 2003, Brzezinski pointed out, the US Congress had identified 160 sites as potentially important national targets for would-be terrorists. By the end of 2004 the list had grown to 28,360 and by 2005 to 77,769. Two years later the national database of possible targets had some 300,000 items in it, including such events of world significance as the 'Illinois Apple and Pork Festival'. 'America has become insecure and more paranoid,' Brzezinski concluded, as 'the culture of fear' has acquired 'a life of its own'.

Over the past century the world has faced two world wars, a Cold War, Nazism and the Holocaust. There were times when the barbarians did indeed appear not just to be at the gates but to have wrenched those gates right off. The world survived and, indeed, prospered. Despite the post-9/11 sense of millenarian doom, the world is safer today than it has been for the past half-century. War and organized violence have decreased dramatically over the past two decades. According to Ted Robert Gurr and his colleagues at the University of Maryland's Center for International Development and Conflict Management, worldwide violence increased sixfold during the course of the Cold War, peaking just before the collapse of the Soviet Union in 1991. Since then 'the extent of warfare among and within states [has] lessened by nearly half'.

It is true that the nature of violence has changed, becoming less organized and predictable. Standing armies fighting under formal orders have given way to loose networks of fanatical jihadis striking seemingly at random. Yet even here, fears are exaggerated. The bottom line about Islamic terrorism, as Fareed Zakaria, editor of Newsweek International, has put it, is that 'in the six years since 9/11, al-Qaeda Central . . . has been unable to launch a major attack anywhere'. Al-Qaeda, he mocks, 'was a terrorist organization; it has become a communications company, producing the occasional videotape rather than actual terrorism.' Jihadists, he points out, have had to scatter, make do with smaller targets, and operate on a local level, usually through groups with almost no connection to al-Qaeda Central. In countries where jihadists used to nest – such as Indonesia, Egypt and the Philippines – they have been crushed with brutal ferocity.

On 9/11, the hijacked planes tore into the fabric, not simply of the World Trade Center and the Pentagon, but also of the self-assurance of Western societies. Into that gaping hole flew a whole bestiary of demons. 'If a flight full of commuters can be turned into a missile of war,' observed the *New York Times*, 'then everything is dangerous.' It is as much this erosion of self-belief, as the reality of the threat facing the West, from which the culture of fear has emerged.

That is what connects the burning book in Bradford to the burning towers in Manhattan: not just the wrath of Islam but also the insecurities of the West. Islam, as Olivier Roy has put it, 'is not the cause of the crisis' in the West; it is rather 'a mirror in which the West projects its own identity crisis'.

The response to the jihad has echoed the response to the fatwa. Just as many reacted to the Rushdie affair by reassessing their commitment to traditional liberal values and insisting, in the name of multiculturalism, that Islamist sentiments had to be appeased, so many responded to 9/11 with unease and self-loathing. In an infamous piece for the *London Review of Books*, the Cambridge classicist and historian Mary Beard wrote of 'the feeling that, however tactfully you dress it up, the United States had it coming'. 9/11, she suggested, was the wages of sin for the West's 'refusal to listen to what the "terrorists" had to say', adding that 'World bullies, even if their hearts are in the right place, will in the end pay the price.' An editorial in the left-wing British magazine *New Statesman* claimed that the people in the Twin Towers were not 'as innocent and as undeserving of terror as Vietnamese or Iraqi peasants', because, while 'such large-scale carnage is beyond justification', nevertheless 'Americans, unlike Iraqis and many others in poor countries, at least have the privileges of democracy and freedom that allow them to vote and speak in favour of a different order.' The novelist Eva Figes, a Jewish anti-Zionist, suggested that 'On 11 September 2001 the Muslim world finally struck back' to ease the humiliation heaped upon it by the creation of the state of Israel.

Others responded to 9/11, as many had done to the book-burning, by resurrecting the 'clash of civilizations' argument. The American philosopher and liberal secularist Sam Harris believes that the West is at war not with terrorism, nor even with Islamic terrorism, but with 'Islam itself', with 'the vision of life that is prescribed to all Muslims in the Koran'. The distinction between moderate and fundamentalist Muslims is irrelevant because 'most Muslims appear to be "fundamentalist" in the Western sense of the word'. 'Is Islam compatible with a civil society?' asked Harris. 'Is it possible to believe what you must believe to be a good Muslim, to have military and economic power, and to not pose an unconscionable threat to the civil societies of others? I believe that the answer to this question is no.'

The clash of civilizations argument is often presented as a defence of Enlightenment values. September 11, Martin Amis has written, was 'a day of de-Enlightenment'. As much as Iraq or Afghanistan, the Enlightenment has become a key battleground in the war on terror. For Amis and Harris, the war on terror represents a desperate defence of liberal democratic traditions, the scientific worldview and a secular, rationalist culture, in the face of a theocratic assault that seeks to destroy democracy and rights, especially women's rights. Yet, in the hands of the clash of civilization warriors, the Enlightenment has become less a set of values than a myth by which to define the West. Like the caliphate is for Islamists, the Enlightenment has become a loss to be yearned for, a tradition to be revered.

'One of the main claims of Enlightenment philosophy', the writer Ian Buruma observes in *Murder in Amsterdam*, his meditation on the significance of the killing of Dutch film-maker Theo van Gogh by a Moroccan Islamist, 'is that its ideas based on reason are by definition universal. But the Enlightenment has a particular appeal to some . . . because its values are not just universal, but more importantly "ours", that is European, Western values.' In just this vein, the writer Harry Cummins has drawn on the philosopher Jean-Jacques Rousseau to suggest that 'institutions created by and for one population break down if exposed to human groups that behave in a different way'. That is why 'excluding Muslim suspects from Western rights (say at Guantanamo Bay) does not per se compromise Western standards of legality. Western legalism and liberalism were formulated in a different world, and experience has proved (especially in Britain) that attempts to integrate minority cultures into our rights-based system create clashes.'

Democracy, equality, the rule of law: these are not universal values but 'ours'. Not only are they ours in the sense that they are the historic property of the West, they are also ours in the sense that non-Westerners do not deserve, indeed would culturally resist, having these values extended to them. The enemy is not Muslims as such, Sam Harris insists, but Islam is such an alien force that different rules must apply to the way that Muslims are treated. Harris has made a liberal case for torture, arguing that 'if we are willing to drop bombs or even risk that pistol rounds might go astray, we should be willing to torture a certain class of criminal suspect and military prisoners'. Since most terrorists are Muslims, so there is, he argues, a need for ethnic profiling and discriminatory policing. And he believes that 'some propositions are so dangerous that it may even be ethical to kill people for believing them'. Martin Amis has wondered aloud about collective punishment for Muslims to ensure that the whole 'community will have to suffer until it gets its house in order'. Once the Enlightenment becomes a weapon in the clash of civilizations rather than in the battle to define the values and attitudes necessary to advance political rights and social justice, once it becomes a measure as much of tribal attachment as of progressive politics, then everything from torture to collective punishment becomes permissible, and the pursuit of Enlightenment itself becomes a source of de-Enlightenment.

'For are they not conjoined opposites, these two, each man the other's shadow?' asks Salman Rushdie in *The Satanic Verses* about his two protagonists, Saladin Chamcha and Gibreel Farishta. One might ask the same question about the multiculturalist argument and the clash of civilization thesis. These two responses to both fatwa and jihad appear as conjoined opposites, each as the other's shadow, two different expressions of the same anxieties about Enlightenment values. One celebrates a lack of faith in the Enlightenment by giving up on the idea of universal values, suggesting instead that we should accept that every

society is a collection of disparate communities and that every community should be encouraged to express its own identity, explore its own
history, formulate its own values, pursue its own lifestyles.
The other turns belief in the Enlightenment into a tribal affair:
Enlightenment values are good because they are ours, and we should
militantly defend our values and lifestyles, even to the extent of denying
such values and lifestyles to others. Or, as Rushdie says about Saladin
and Gibreel, 'One seeking to transform into the foreignness he admires,
the other seeking contemptuously to transform.'

An assertive, self-confident society that possessed moral clarity about
its beliefs would have little trouble dealing with the claims of fundamentalists, and indeed with the acts of terrorists. Terror is an expression
not of the strength but of the impotence of Islamism; unable to win for
itself a mass following, jihadists have been forced to turn to violence to
gain the attention they could not win through political means. But the
uncertainties and insecurities of Western societies about the worth of
basic liberal values, the descent into tribal politics even by those who
declare an attachment to Enlightenment universalist ideas, and the
emergence of fear as a dominant sentiment, have made Islamists appear
more potent than they are. 'Vulnerability is never the best proof of
strength', as Shabbir Akhtar put it in *Be Careful with Muhammad!*, mocking
the doubts of Western liberals. From fatwa to jihad, politicians and intellectuals have not only exaggerated the threat facing Western societies,
but have also lacked the moral and political resources to respond to it.

5

Angels and devils. Myths and monsters. These are at the heart of *The
Satanic Verses*. The struggle of Saladin Chamcha and Gibreel Farishta,
with themselves and with each other, is a struggle of the human imagination against the constraints placed upon it. One is a devil, the other
an angel, yet they continually betray their own natures. When Saladin
is arrested, Gibreel, the angel, refuses to help him. When the two meet

up again in riot-torn east London, Gibreel appears as Azraeel, the most terrible of angels, wreaking fire and destruction. But even as he is hunted down by Gibreel, the demonic Saladin risks his life to save a family trapped in a burning house.

What Rushdie wants us to see is that the distinction between devil and angel lies less in their inner selves than in the roles that humans ascribe to them. If religion creates the divine and the Satanic in the image of man, secular society equally makes men in the image of devils and angels. Both religious faiths and secular societies deploy their angels and demons to justify their otherwise unjustifiable actions, to create boundaries that cannot be transgressed.

'Angels and devils – who needed them?' Rushdie asks in *The Satanic Verses*. The answer seems to be those who wish to subdue the human spirit. Gibreel, 'in spite of born-again slogans, new beginnings, meta-morphoses, has wished to remain, to a large extent, *continuous* – that is joined to and arising from the past'. Saladin, on the other hand, has shown a '*willing* reinvention', a '*preferred* revolt against history'. Angels, in other words, mean constancy, while devils rock the boat. Angels are used to maintain tradition, while those who bring about unacceptable change – secularists to a religious faith, immigrants in a secular society – are demonized.

But change and transformation, Rushdie insists, are what make us human. Human beings, he observed in his essay 'In Good Faith', 'under-stand themselves and shape their futures by arguing and challenging and questioning and saying the unsayable; not by bowing the knee, whether to gods or to men'. *The Satanic Verses*, he has said, is a 'work of radical dissent'. What does it dissent from? 'From the end of debate, of dispute, of dissent,' Rushdie answers. Rushdie's sympathy is clearly with the devil.

Not just in *The Satanic Verses*, but in the Rushdie affair, too, angels and devils have been conjured up, myths and monsters created. For at the heart of the controversy, as much as of the novel, there has been a struggle over what boundaries may be transgressed, whether the unsayable can be said, and how to dissent from the end of dissent.

There is a scene in *The Satanic Verses* in which Saladin Chamcha finds himself in an immigration detention center. All the inmates have been turned into monsters – water buffaloes, snakes, manticores. 'How could they do it?' Saladin wants to know. 'They describe us,' comes the reply, 'that's all. They have the power of description and we succumb to the pictures they construct.'

Rushdie was portraying the way that racism demonizes its victims. He could equally have been describing the way that the response to the Rushdie affair has created its own monsters. The Rushdie affair is shrouded by myths – that the hostility to *The Satanic Verses* was driven by theology, that all Muslims were offended by the novel, that Islam is incompatible with Western democracy, that in a plural society speech must necessarily be less free. In describing the controversy in this way, by ignoring the political heart of the Rushdie affair, the diverse character of Muslim communities and of the Muslim response to *The Satanic Verses*, and the importance of free speech to minority groups, and by abandoning their attachment to Enlightenment universalist values, liberals have not just created a particular picture of the Rushdie affair, they have also ensured that Western societies have succumbed to the picture they have constructed. They have helped build a culture of grievance in which being offended has become a badge of identity, cleared a space for radical Islamists to flourish, and made secular and progressive arguments less sayable, particularly within Muslim communities.

The myths about the Rushdie affair have helped create many of the post-Rushdie monsters. If we want to slay the monsters, we have to bury the myths.

Notes

p.x   Huntington on the clash of civilizations
Huntington, 'The Clash of Civilizations'.

p.xi   *"All over again . . . the West confronts"*
Amis, *The Second Plane*, p.9.

p.xi   Weldon on Islam and Christianity
Sacred Cows, p.6.

p.xi   *'If Britain's resident ayatollahs cannot accept British values and laws'*
Robert Kilroy-Silk, *The Times*, 17 February 1989.

p.xi   *'in retrospect we might have been more cautious'*
Roy Jenkins, *Independent*, 4 March 1989.

p.xii   *'Officially, as it were . . . we were called immigrants'*
Kureishi, *Something to Tell You*, pp.36–7.

p.xiii   *'Politicians . . . have got very good at inventing fictions which they tell us as the truth.'*
Desert Island Discs, BBC Radio 4, 8 September 1988.

p.xiv   *'about God . . . that was not just a secular sneer'*
Scripsi, 'An interview with Salman Rushdie'.

p.xiv   *'a serious attempt to write about religion and revelation'*
Basu, 'Interview with Salman Rushdie'.

p.xiv   *'the book isn't actually about Islam'*
Rushdie, 'Open Letter to PM'.

p.xvi   *'an epic hung about with ragbag scraps of many different cultures'*
Carter, 'Angels in Dirty Places'.

p.xvi   *'inferior piece of hate literature'*, *'falsified historical records'*, *'a calculated attempt to vilify and slander Muhammad'*
Akhtar, *Be Careful with Muhammad!*, pp.49, 6, 7.

p.xvii   *'For years white people have been tolerant. Now their tempers are up.'*
Daily Sketch, 2 September 1958.

p.xix   *'You have to treat people differently to treat them equally'*
Lee Jasper interviewed in Malik, 'Disunited Kingdom'.

p.xxi   'There is a hole inside me where God used to be'
       Marzorati, 'Salman Rushdie: Fiction's Embattled Infidel'.

p.1   'It would be absurd to think that a book can cause riots'
       Basu, 'Interview with Salman Rushdie'.

p.1   'was positive it would cause a lot of trouble'
       Cited in Ruthven, A Satanic Affair, p.85.

p.2   'Thanks for the good review'
       Rushdie, 'Open Letter to PM'.

p.2   'The very title . . . suggestively derogatory'
       Shahabuddin, 'Open Letter to Salman Rushdie'.

p.2   'I do not have to wade through a filthy drain to know what filth is'
       Shahabuddin, 'Open Letter to Salman Rushdie'.

p.4   An Urdu poster displayed in corner-shop windows throughout Britain'
       Lewis, Islamic Britain, p.1.

p.5   'Was the agitation really against the book which has not been read in
       Pakistan'
       Cited in Pipes, The Rushdie Affair, p.20.

p.5   Eyewitnesses described the police repeatedly firing into the crowd
       'Five killed in Pakistan anti-Rushdie Protest Rally', Independent,
       13 February 1989, reprinted in Appignanesi and Maitland (eds.),
       The Rushdie File, p.81.

p.6   'The life of the Prophet Mohammad . . . is the source of Muslim identity'
       Sardar, Desperately Seeking Paradise, p.281.

p.7   The Kayhan Farangi review was first published in Britain in the
       Independent, 21 February 1989; a shortened version was republished
       in Appignanesi and Maitland (eds.), The Rushdie File, pp.23–4.

p.7   'an extension of the Iranian embassy in London'
       Sardar, Desperately Seeking Paradise, p.166.

p.7   'There was little hostility to the novel'
       Interview with Ghayasuddin Siddiqui, 29 May 2008.

pp.7–   'He took Kalim aside'
8   Interview with Ghayasuddin Siddiqui, 29 May 2008.

p.9   'I am very sad it should have happened'
       'Ayatollah sentences author to death', BBC News, 14 February 1989,
       <http://news.bbc.co.uk/onthisday/hi/dates/stories/february/14/newsid_
       2541000/2541149.stm>.

p.9   'Frankly, I wish I had written a more critical book'
       Steve Lohr, 'Rushdie Expresses Regret to Muslims for Book's Effect',

New York Times, 19 February 1989.

p.9   '*By the time I came off the air*'
Crichton and Shapiro, 'An Exclusive Talk with Salman Rushdie'.

p.9   '*It was very important for me to go to that service*'
Crichton and Shapiro, 'An Exclusive Talk with Salman Rushdie'.

p.9   '*It wasn't the funniest joke I ever heard*'
Crichton and Shapiro, 'An Exclusive Talk with Salman Rushdie'.

p.9   '*I remember Salman as a hunted man*'
Interview with Hanif Kureishi, 9 October 2008.

pp.10– Interview with Peter Mayer, 23 November 2008.
15

p.15   '*It was the 11th October*'
Interview with William Nygaard, 5 September 2008.

p.16   *As the Turkish journalist Yalman Onaran put it*
Onaran, 'Burned: An author charged with inciting a crowd to kill him'.

p.17   *According to one story, Ayatollah Khomeini was watching the evening news on TV*
Pipes, *The Rushdie Affair*, p.26.

p.17   *Rafsanjani... condemned the 'shortsightedness' of Iranian foreign policy*
Ehteshami, *After Khomeini*, p.28.

p.18   '*I felt a thrill*'
Interview with Inayat Bunglawala, 4 August 2008.

p.18   '*organized and planned*'
Cited in Marzorati, 'Rushdie in Hiding'.

p.19   *Tehran reportedly contributed about $1m to the organisation of the May demonstration*
Pipes, *The Rushdie Affair*, p.182.

p.19   '*They came in their thousands from Bradford and Dewsbury, Bolton and Macclesfield*'
Ruthven, *A Satanic Affair*, p.1.

p.20   '*constitutionally disorderly . . . It's simply in their make up*'
Cited in *Daily Mirror*, 30 June 1982.

pp.20– '*Four hundred years of conquest and looting*'
1   Rushdie, 'The New Empire within Britain', Channel 4, 6 December 1982; the text is reprinted in *Imaginary Homelands*, pp.129–38.

p.23   '*Terrorists are a bit like you and me*'
'How jihad went freelance', *The Economist*, 31 January 2008.

pp.23– Sageman, 'Understanding Terror Networks'; see also Sageman,

213

4   *Understanding Terror Networks* and *Leaderless Jihad.*

p.24   *'I wasn't too concerned with religious practice'*
Shiraz Maher, presentation to a conference on 'Engaging with
Young Muslim Men at Risk of Exclusion', London, 5 December 2006.

p.25   *'The illusion held by Islamic radicals'*
Roy, *Globalised Islam*, p.20.

p.25   *'found himself spouting rules, rules, rules'*
Rushdie, *The Satanic Verses*, pp.363–4.

p.26   *'is able to deal with all the modern day issues'*
Hizb ut-Tahrir, 'Islam Is Relevant for All Times and Places'.

p.26   *Faith, as the philosopher Charles Taylor observes, has become disembedded
from its historical culture*
Taylor, *A Secular Age*.

p.26   *'me generation'*
Wolfe, 'The Me Decade and the Third Great Awakening', in *Mauve
Gloves and Madmen, Clutter & Vine*.

p.27   Heelas and Woodhead on spirituality
Heelas and Woodhead, *The Spiritual Revolution*; Woodhead and Riis,
'Religion and Emotion'.

p.27   *'religious experience of a new kind'*
Gole, 'Islam, European Public Space, and Civility'.

p.28   *'today is constructed, reinterpreted and carried into public life'*
Gole, 'Islam, European Public Space, and Civility'.

pp.28– Interview with Sher Azman, 4 February 1989.
31

p.30   *'There was huge pressure from the British government'*
Interview with Peter Mayer, 23 November 2008.

p.32   *'in the past two centuries Britain has been in the front line of plots and
treachery'*
Cited in Pipes, *The Rushdie Affair*, p.33.

p.32   Geoffrey Howe on *The Satanic Verses*
Whitney, 'Britain, in Talk Aimed at Iran, Calls Rushdie Book
Offensive'; Press Association, 2 March 1989.

p.32   *'put on record that the British Government well recognizes the hurt and distress'*
Press Association, 17 March 1989.

p.33   *'We have known in our own religion people doing things which are deeply
offensive'*
Cited in Appignanesi and Maitland (eds.), *The Rushdie File*, pp.140–1.

p.33   *'an outstanding villain'*
Cited in Owen, 'A Victory for Literary Freedom', and Wheatcroft, 'Arise Sir Salman'.

p.33   *'deep sympathy with the Muslims over the publication of the book'*
Cited in Pipes, *The Rushdie Affair*, p.35.

p.33   *'more irritated by Mr Rushdie and his band of supporters than it is shocked by the Iranians'*
'If Rushdie is killed', *The Economist*, 25 February 1989.

p.33   *'humiliated, disgraced and shame-faced'*
Cited in Pipes, *The Rushdie Affair*, p.35.

p.33   *'exaggeration'*
Cited in Pipes, *The Rushdie Affair*, p.35.

p.33   *The American government was equally limp*
American Embassy, James Baker and George Bush, Snr. cited in Pipes, *The Rushdie Affair*, p.155.

p.34   *'There have been times in history'*
Cited in Pipes, *The Rushdie Affair*, p.156.

p.34   *'to set forth in full some of our recent thinking'*
<http://www.salaam.co.uk/themeofthemonth/september03_index.php?l=1>.

p.35   *'are unprepared for the massive immigration of brown-skinned peoples'*
Pipes, 'The Muslims are coming!' (Pipes later suggested that he was not expressing his own sentiments but attempting to characterize European views; see http://www.danielpipes.org/article/198).

p.35   *The prime minister and foreign secretary of Britain humiliated themselves'*
Pipes, *The Rushdie Affair*, p.159.

p.36   Parts of Nasreen Sadique's diary were published in Tompson, *Under Siege*.

p.37   *Nasreen wrote to Arthur Lewis, the local Labour MP, asking for help*
Parts of the letters and the replies are reprinted in Tompson, *Under Siege*, pp.5–11.

p.38   *'Barratt only stated more boldly what everybody else had hinted at'*
Tompson, *Under Siege*, p.10.

p.39   *cadets at the national police academy . . . were asked to write essays about immigrants*
Essays quoted in *Policing London*, 4 (November 1982).

p.39   *'There are 15,000 West Indians in this locality'*
Cited in *Caribbean Times*, 28 August 1987.

p.40   Deaths in police custody
        Details in Institute of Race Relations, *Deadly Silence*.

p.40   *'It sometimes seems . . . that the British authorities . . . have chosen instead*
        to import a new Empire, a new community of subject peoples'
        Rushdie, 'The New Empire within Britain', in *Imaginary Homelands*,
        pp.130, 132.

p.41   *'Our village was very small'*
        Cited in Akhtar, *The Biradari*.

p.42   *You could buy a beat-up back-to-back for £45 in those days*
        Murphy, *Tales from Two Cities*, p.10.

p.42   *'Mohammed made his way out of Heathrow'*
        Manzoor, *Greetings from Bury Park*, p.10.

p.43   *'A large coloured community as a noticeable feature of our social life'*
        Cited in Joshi and Carter, 'The Role of Labour in the Creation of a
        Racist Britain'.

p.44   *'Good times, bad times, there is always someone there for you'*
        Akhtar, *The Biradari*.

p.44   *'Everything was alien to us'*
        Interview with Sher Azam, 4 February 1989.

p.44   *'At present . . . there is a void between the first generation'*
        Akhtar, *The Biradari*.

p.45   *'Forty years after arriving in Britain'*
        Akhtar, *The Biradari*.

p.45   *'unwritten law of social conduct revolving around ideas of honour'*
        Maher, 'Campus Radicals'.

p.45   *'they still seemed utterly* foreign'
        Ruthven, *A Satanic Affair*, p.1.

p.46   *'is wearing a loose slate grey suit with a black tie'*
        Manzoor, *Greetings from Bury Park*, pp.11–12.

p.46   *'suffered an almost total lapse of religious observance'*
        Barton, *The Muslims of Bradford*, p.12.

p.46–   *'They did not bring drink home'*
7   Interview with Pervaiz Khan, 20 October 2008.

p.48   *'It was there that we really started thinking that we've got to get our own*
        house in order'
        Cited in Ramamurthy (ed.), *Kala Tara*.

p.48   *'they believed that the economic lot of Indian workers was intimately*
        intertwined with that of British workers'

Hiro, *Black British, White British*, pp.139–40.

p.49 *'They have got to learn to fit in our ways, you know.'*
Wilson, *Finding a Voice*, p.58.

p.49 *'black workers must never for a moment entertain the thought of separate black unions'*
Cited in Counter Information Services, *Racism: Who Profits?*, p.22.

p.50 *'In the 1970s, I was called a black bastard and a Paki'*
Cited in Ramamurthy, 'Secular Identities and the Asian Youth Movements'.

p.51 *'Asian women are the most oppressed section of our community'*
Liberation, April 1981, p.6.

p.51 *'I had grown up in a profoundly secular environment'*
Cited in Ramamurthy, 'Secular Identities and the Asian Youth Movements'.

p.52 *'Most of us were workers and sons of workers'*
Cited in Ramamurthy, 'Secular Identities and the Asian Youth Movements'.

p.52 *'formation of the Asian Youth Movement in Bradford'*
Ramamurthy, 'Secular Identities and the Asian Youth Movements'.

p.52 *'We had to put our own house in order'*
Cited in Ramamurthy, 'Secular Identities and the Asian Youth Movements'.

p.53 *'we might continue to meet the wishes of the community'*
Cited in Glynn, 'Playing the Ethnic Card'.

p.53 *'Some people said, "You are creating a ghetto"'*
Cited in Glynn, 'Playing the Ethnic Card'.

p.53 *A 1982 report on housing allocation in East London*
Spitalfields Housing and Planning Rights Service, *Bengalis and GLC Housing Allocation in E1*.

p.53 *'Somewhere, somehow deliberate decisions must have been taken'*
Spitalfields Housing and Planning Rights Service, *Bengalis and GLC Housing Allocation in E1: An Update Report*.

p.54 *an infamous interview that Margaret Thatcher . . . in which she had warned about British culture being 'swamped' by foreigners*
'TV Interview for Granada *World in Action*', <http://www.margaret-thatcher.org/speeches/displaydocument.asp?docid=103485>.

p.56 *'Measured by any standards . . . this revolt assumed serious insurrectionary proportions'*

Howe, *From Bobby to Babylon*, p.52.

p.56   *'back behind the Tory party'*
'TV Interview for Granada *World in Action*', <http://www.margaret-thatcher.org/speeches/displaydocument.asp?docid=103485>.

p.57   *'transform pleas for more political opportunities for black people'*
Fitzgerald, *Black People and Party Politics in Britain*.

p.57   *'back the good guys'*
Cited in 'A good knight's solution', *Sunday Times*, 10 October 1982.

p.57   *'the creation in Britain of a small but prosperous black middle class'*
'A good knight's solution', *Sunday Times*, 10 October 1982.

p.57   Lord Scarman
The Scarman Report.

p.58   *'make as much direct contact as possible with ethnic minorities'*
House of Commons Home Affairs Committee, *Racial Disadvantage*.

p.58   *'On average, fewer than forty people attended each consultation meeting'*
Tompson, *Under Siege*, p.102.

p.59   Figures for GLC funding
National Council for Voluntary Organizations, *After Abolition*.

p.59   *'a black man could only become integrated when he started behaving like a white one'*
Rushdie, 'The New Empire within Britain', in *Imaginary Homelands*, p.137.

p.60   *'society as a whole seemed unbudgeable . . . separate organizations [acting] on behalf distinct interests'*
Gitlin, *The Twilight of Common Dreams*, p.100.

p.61   *'recognition of those things uniquely ours'*
Cited in Gitlin, *The Twilight of Common Dreams*, p.131.

p.61   *'The demand is not for inclusion within the fold of "universal humankind" on the basis of shared human attributes'*
Kruks, *Retrieving Experience*, p.85.

p.61   *'One belonged to a caucus, cultivated a separate culture'*
Gitlin, *The Twilight of Common Dreams*, p.101.

p.61   *'more than an idea'*
Gitlin, *The Twilight of Common Dreams*, p.100.

p.62   *'to preseving the "traditions and cultures" of the different ethnic minorities'*
Sahgal and Yuval-Davis, 'Introduction' to Sahgal and Yuval-Davis (eds.), *Refusing Holy Orders: Women and Fundamentalism in Britain*, p.21.

p.62   *'both a community of citizens and a community of communities'*

Commission on the Future of Multi-Ethnic Britain, *The Future of Multi-Ethnic Britain*, p.ix.

p.64   Interview with Kirk Dawes, 20 November 2005.

p.64   *'There are not enough of you pussies out there in the street!'*
Vulliamy, 'Rumours of a Riot'.

p.64   *'from being about the so-called rape into something about the exploitation of the black community'*
Interview with Kirk Dawes, 20 November 2005.

p.65   Details of the demonstration outside the Beauty Queen in Vulliamy, 'Rumours of a Riot'.

p.65   *'Gang of 19 Rape Teen'*
The Voice, 24–30 October 2005.

p.67   *'The perceived notion of homogeneity of minority ethnic communities'*
Birmingham City Council, *Joint Report of Head of Equalities and Director of Birmingham Race Action Partnership*, p.4.

p.67   *'new class of "ethnic representatives" [that] entered the town halls'*
Kundnani, 'From Oldham to Bradford'.

pp.67–8   *'What the Labour Party was really interested in'*
Interview with Pervaiz Khan, 20 October 2008.

p.68   *'model of engagement through Umbrella Groups tended to result in competition'*
Smith and Stephenson, 'The Theory and Practice of Group Representation'.

pp.68–9   *'People are forced into a very one-dimensional view of themselves by the way that equality policies work'*
Interview with Joy Warmington, 21 November 2005.

p.70   *'We have a South African situation here'*
Cited in Vulliamy, 'Rumours of a Riot'.

p.71   *'deep racism . . . which is sometimes hidden'*
Cited in Vulliamy, 'Rumours of a Riot'.

p.71   *'But Asians have always had it in for the black man'*
Interview with Anthony Gordon, 22 November 2005

p.72   *'Our children were growing up hating our culture'*
Interview with Sher Azam, 4 February 1989.

p.72   *'we have no direct knowledge of Asian needs and requirements'*
Bradford Metropolitan Council, *Turning Points*, p.49.

p.73   *'They were shit-scared'*
Interview with Ali Hussein, 6 February 1989.

p.74   *'tend to be meek . . . very rarely rock the boat'*

Hussain, *The Islamist*, p.39.

p.75   *'What we wanted from the council'*
Interview with Sher Azam, 4 February 1989.

p.76   *'The prospect of thousands of jobless young Muslims, untamed by Islam'*
Murphy, *Tales from Two Cities*, p.29.

p.76   *'If Mohammed Ajeeb's forecast is proved correct . . . then my forecast is Big Trouble Ahead'*
Murphy, *Tales from Two Cities*, p.27.

p.77–   *'There developed a mutual relationship . . . relative peace on the streets.'*
8   Interview with Ali Hussein, 6 February 1989.

p.77   *'functioned as a nursery for Muslim politicians'*
Lewis, *Islamic Britain*, p.147.

p.79   *'The AYM's symbolic black secular clenched fist split open'*
Interview with Mukhtar Dar, 7 November 2008.

p.80   *'Just as I was about to go . . . I heard the bus explode.'*
Cited in Tom Leonard and Duncan Gardham, 'Bomber Took His Seat on Bus and Blew Himself Up', *Daily Telegraph*, 11 July 2005, <http://www.telegraph.co.uk/news/uknews/1493594/Bomber-took-his-seat-on-bus-and-blew-himself-up.html>.

p.81   *'I came here expecting lots of angry young men'*
Khan, 'Young, British and Muslim'.

p.82   Robert Cardiss on Mohammed Siddique Khan
Cited in Malik, 'My Brother the Bomber' and BBC News, 'Suicide Bombers' "Ordinary" Lives', 18 July 2005, <http://news.bbc.co.uk/go/pr/fr/-/1/hi/uk/4678837.stm>.

p.82   *'He seemed a really kind man'*
Sandra Laville and Dipazier Aslam, 'Mentor to the Young and Vulnerable', *Guardian*, 14 July 2005, <http://www.guardian.co.uk/uk/2005/jul/14/july7.uksecurity5>.

p.83   *'Islam is not just a religion'*
Steyn, *America Alone*, p.62.

p.84   *'the West confronts an irrationalist, agonistic, theocratic/ideocratic system'*
Amis, *The Second Plane*, p.9.

p.84   *'To the non-Muslims of Britain . . . you may wonder what you have done to deserve this'*
BBC News, '7/7 pair "visited al-Qaeda camp"', 8 July 2006, <http://news.bbc.co.uk/1/hi/uk/5161526.stm>.

p.84   *'The principal cause of this violence'*

Ali, 'The Price of Occupation'.

p.84 *'What we are confronting here'*
Fisk, 'The Reality of this Barbaric Bombing'.

p.84 *'The key question . . . is not what the Koran actually says, but what Muslims say the Koran says'*
Roy, *Globalised Islam*, p.10.

p.85 *In the five years following 9/11, 2300 Muslims were arrested in Europe . . . there were just 60 such arrests in the USA*
Sageman, *Leaderless Jihad*, p.90.

p.86 Statistics on Muslim views in Europe and the USA
Pew Research Centre, *American Muslims*.

p.86 *'Fundamentalism and radical violence . . . are more linked with Westernization than a return to the Koran'*
Roy, *Globalised Islam*, p.2.

p.87 *'True Islam . . . lasted only for a brief period after its inception'*
Cited in Ahmed, *Discovering Islam*, p.63.

p.88 *One study found that of 175 Islamic groups identified as fundamentalist . . . only thirty-two were Shiite.*
Dekmejian, *Islamic Revolution*, pp.130–51.

p.89 *'the enemy is not modernity but tradition.'*
Roy, *Islam and Resistance in Afghanistan*, p.3.

p.91 *'After fifteen years in exile, the seventy-eight-year-old Ayatollah Ruhollah Khomeini had come home.'*
The description of Khomeini's return is taken from 'The Khomeini Era Begins', *Time*, 12 February 1979.

p.91 *'It made dreamers of us all.'*
Sardar, *Desperately Seeking Paradise*, p.164.

p.93 *'fated to witness a wave of Islamist revolutions'*
Christopher Ross, 'Political Islam: Myths, Realities, and Policy Implications', speech delivered to the Salzburg Conference of NEA Public Affairs Officers, 21 September 1993; cited in Kramer, 'Islamist Bubbles'.

p.93 *'come to power in states that are beginning to become pluralist'*
National Intelligence Council, *Global Trends 2015*, p.71.

p.94 *'by the end of the twentieth century the Islamist movement had signally failed to retain political power in the Muslim world'*
Keppel, *Jihad*, p.4.

p.94 *For jihadists people are like firecrackers to be lit and tossed away.*

The image comes from Steyn, *America Alone*.

p.94   *'what it is that attracts a minority from a variety of backgrounds'*
Durodie, 'Home-Grown Nihilism'.

p.96   *'Sadat's gamble . . . was to encourage the emergence of an Islamist move-*
ment which he perceived as socially conservative'
Keppel, *Jihad*, p.83.

p.97   *the Israelis encouraged the growth of the Muslim Brotherhood in Gaza*
Abu-Amer, *Islamic Fundamentalism in the West Bank and Gaza*.

p.97   *'Moslem countries will be concerned'*
<http://edition.cnn.com/SPECIALS/cold.war/episodes/20/documents/brez.carter/>.

p.97   *'a deliberate effort by a powerful atheistic government to subjugate an inde-*
pendent Islamic people'
<http://edition.cnn.com/SPECIALS/cold.war/episodes/20/1st.draft/>.

p.97   *'Some of the most important factors behind the contemporary radicalization*
of European Muslim youth'
Kohlman, 'The Afghan-Bosnian Mujahideen Network in Europe'.

p.99   *One of the Mullah Boys' victims was Tyrone Clarke*
'Life sentences for teen killers', *BBC News*, 4 March 2005,
<http://news.bbc.co.uk/1/hi/england/west_yorkshire/4318617.stm>;
Jones, 'Among the Young of Multiethnic Leeds, a Hardening Hatred'.

p.99   *Shehzad Tanweer . . . was reported to have been questioned about Clarke's*
murder
Gilbertson, 'When I Heard Where the Bombers Were From I Felt
Sick'.

p.100   *an American journalist visited Brett Gardens and talked to five white*
teenagers
Jones, 'Among the Young of Multiethnic Leeds, a Hardening Hatred'.

p.101   *'They introduced to a much wider world'*
Interview with Pervaiz Khan, 20 October 2008.

p.102   *Ed Hussain tells of how his attraction to radical Islam led to a battle with*
his pious but traditional father
Hussain, *The Islamist*, pp.45, 46, 73.

p.104   *'When I went to Pakistan . . . I was rejected.'*
Cited in Malik, 'My Brother the Bomber'.

p.105   *'has positively and forcefully forbidden the Muslims to assume the culture*
and mode of life of the non-Muslims'
Maududi, *Towards Understanding Islam*.

p.107   'after an incident in a nightclub, [Sidique Khan] said he turned to religion'
        Report of the Official Account of the Bombings in London on 7th July 2005,
        p.14.

p.107   'bullshit'
        Cited in Malik, 'My Brother the Bomber'.

p.108   'When I said I've been clubbing, I've smoked some weed, he was cool'
        Cited in Burke, 'Omar was a normal British teenager who loved his
        little brother and Man Utd'

p.108   Hizb ut-Tahrir was also happy to accommodate members with a penchant
        for pornography, fast cars, forged documents
        Hussain, The Islamist, pp. 101, 102–3, 114.

p.109   'wasn't the ranting type'
        Gilbertson, 'When I Heard Where the Bombers Were From I Felt
        Sick'.

p.109   'had gained . . . a reputation as being tougher than the toughest gangsters'
        Hussain, The Islamist, pp.32–3.

p.110   'oozed street cred'
        Hussain, The Islamist, p.140.

p.111   'Up to sixteen thousand British Muslims either are actively engaged in or
        support terrorist activity'
        Phillips, Londonistan, p.9.

p.111   'I was thinking about something with ranges and assault courses, like I'd
        seen on TV'
        Cited in Burke, 'Omar was a normal British teenager who loved his
        little brother and Man Utd'.

p.112   'a politics of intentionality and control'
        Devji, Landscapes of the Jihad, p.12.

p.114   'The Balkan crisis truly radicalized many Muslims in Britain'
        Hussain, The Islamist, p.112.

p.114   One study found that fewer than one in five Muslims could name the presi-
        dent of the Palestinian Authority
        Mirza, Senthikumaran and Ja'far, Living Apart Together, p.57.

p.114   'One such film, The Destruction of a Nation, shook my heart.'
        Fielding, 'From a London Public School to the Shadow of the Noose'.

p.114   'zeal and intention to undergo arms training and join the
        mujahideen'
        Cited in Fielding, 'Diary of a Terrorist'.

p.116   'It felt as though Rushdie had plundered everything I hold dear'

Sardar, *Desperately Seeking Paradise*, pp.279, 282.

p.116   *'All religious revival movements of the late twentieth century'*
Roy, *Globalised Islam*, p.31.

p.119   *"is the belief that jihad is a compulsory individual duty (fard al'ayn)*
while traditionally it has always been considered a collective duty (fard
alkifaya)'
Roy, *Globalised Islam*, p.178.

p.120   *Sadiq Khan . . . was one of a number of prominent Muslims who lambasted*
the government
Helene Mulholland, 'We Must Defeat the Ideas of Extremists, Says
Blair', *Guardian*, 4 July 2006.

p.120   *'Government itself cannot go and root out the extremism in these*
communities'
Philippe Naughton, 'Blair says Muslim Majority Must Stand Up to
Extremists', *The Times*, 4 July 2006.

p.121   *'two polls on Muslim attitudes were published'*
The *Times* / Populus poll results are at
<http://www.populuslimited.com/ the-times-itv-news-muslim-77-poll-
050706.html>. See also Wazir, '7/7: One Year on', Midgley, 'Why I'm
scared to go into the Tube now' and Freal and Syel, 'Muslims in
Britain – a story of mutual fear and suspicion'. The NOP/Channel 4
poll results are at <http://www.
imaginate.uk.com/MCC01_SURVEY/Site%20Download.pdf>. See also
Malik, 'What Muslims want'.

p.123   *'the catalyst for the forging of a more confident Islamic identity among*
many British Muslims'
Interview with Inayat Bunglawala, 10 August 2008.

p.124   *'death, perhaps, is a bit too easy for him'*
Cited in Murtagh, 'Rushdie in hiding after Ayatollah's death threat'.

p.124   *'I was truly elated'*
Interview with Inayat Bunglawala, 10 August 2008.

p.124   *'Dr Kalim took the view that campaigning for a ban on* The Satanic
Verses *would be a . . . pointless distraction'*
Institute of Contemporary Islamic Thought, 'Dr Kalim Siddiqui,
1931–1996'.

pp.124– *'The imam's intervention on February . . . will go down in history as one of*
5   *the greatest acts of leadership'*
Crescent International, 1–15 March 1989.

p.125   *'The conflict over Rushdie was never about religion'*
        Interview with Ghayasuddin Siddiqui, 29 May 2008.

p.125   *'could not believe his luck: he was handed a conflict on a platter'*
        Sardar and Davies, *Distorted Imaginations*, p.198.

p.125   *'It was an unfortunate name because it frightened people'*
        Interview with Ghayasuddin Siddiqui, 29 May 2008.

p.126   *'to empower Muslims with their separate and distinctly Islamic institutions'*
        'The Muslim Parliament – A Historical Background', <http://www.
        muslimparliament.org.uk/history.htm>.

p.126   *'to protect, to promote and to represent UK Jewry'*
        <http://www.boardofdeputies.org.uk/page.php/Historical_Background/
        106/2/1>.

p.126   *'has not yet learnt how to approach the British political system'*
        Raza, *Islam in Britain*, p.44.

p.126   *'been a powerful, well-organized lobby like the Jews, Rushdie's outrages*
        would never have got into print'
        Cited in Ruthven, *A Satanic Affair*, p.128.

p.126   *'representative body . . . support and recognize'*
        Abdul Adil, 'A new Muslim body inaugurated', *Muslim News*, 104, 26
        December 1997.

p.127   *'joined at the hip'*
        Bright, *When Progressives Treat with Reactionaries*, p.25.

p.127   *'Mockbul was a straightforward Islamist'*
        Dipesh Gadher, 'Radical Past of Top Whitehall Islamic Aide', *The*
        Times, 30 July 2006.

p.127   *'increasingly unhappy about the activities of Mockbul Ali'*
        Pasquill, 'I had no choice but to leak'.

p.128   *'Within the FCO . . . certain individuals were sceptical about the festival's*
        value and worried that it was not "Islamic" enough.'
        Pasquill, 'I had no choice but to leak'.

p.128   *'If any activities are seen to contradict the teachings of Islam then we will*
        oppose them'
        Cited in Bright, 'Radical Links of Britain's "Moderate" Muslim
        group'.

p.129   *Gay Muslims were refused permission to stage an event*
        BBC, 'Muslims says gays harmful', <http://news.bbc.co.uk/1/hi/uk/
        4579146.stm>.

p.129   *'belong to or have sympathies with . . . the Jamaat-e-Islami in Pakistan'*

Faraz, 'MCB: Dad's Muslim Army', p.21.

p.129   *'the overwhelming number of organizations that the government talks to are influenced by . . . the Jamaat-e-Islami and the Muslim Brotherhood'*
Cited in Bright, *When Progressives Treat with Reactionaries*, p.25.

p.129   *less than 4 percent thought that the MCB represented British Muslims*
Gfk NOP Social Research, *Attitudes to Living in Britain – a Survey of Muslim Opinion.*

p.129   *An NOP poll for... Policy Exchange found only 6 percent of Muslims thought the MCB represented their views*
Mirza, Senthikumaran and Ja'far, *Living Apart Together*, p.80.

p.129   *'Dad's Muslim Army'*
Faraz, 'MCB: Dad's Muslim Army'.

p.130   *'Why should a British citizen who happens to be Muslim have to rely on clerics . . . to communicate with the prime minister of the country?'*
Interview with Amartya Sen, 28 June 2006; parts of this interview were published in Malik, 'Illusions of Identity'.

p.131   *'Over time the Stone's importance had become essentially that of the grievance it evoked'*
O'Hagan, *The Atlantic Ocean*, pp.20–1.

p.131   *'The next time there are gas chambers in Europe . . . there is no doubt concerning who'll be inside them'*
Akhtar, 'Palestine Within Europe?'; see also *Guardian*, 27 February 1989.

p.131   *'Unless something is done urgently Muslims in Britain face the same fate this century as Jews in Europe in the last'*
Cited in 'Anti-Muslim abuse at dangerous high', *Paigaam*, 84 (March 2000).

p.132   *'are subject to attacks reminiscent of the gathering storm of anti-Semitism in the first decades of the last century'*
Salma Yaqoob, 'Muslims Need to Take Part', *Guardian*, 21 December 2006, <http://www.guardian.co.uk/commentisfree/2006/dec/21/comment.secondworldwar>.

p.133   *Some swimming pools have gender-segregated sessions, and even 'Muslim men only' periods*
<http://www.hurryupharry.org/2008/01/20/single-sex-swimming-religious-minorities-and-anti-discrimination/>.

p.133   *'brutal police state'*
Fahad Ansari, 'Britain: Outpost of Tyranny', *IHRC Bulletin* (October 2005).

p.133   *'95–98 percent of those stopped and searched under the anti-terror laws are Muslim'.*
Iqbal Sacranie interviewed in Malik, 'Are Muslims Hated?'

p.133   Statistics on stop and search
Home Office, *Statistics on Race and the Criminal Justice System – 2003*, pp.28–9.

p.134   *'We do not believe that the Asian community is being unreasonably targeted by stops and searches'*
House of Commons Home Affairs Committee, *Terrorism and Community Relations*, pp.3–4.

p.134   *'condone and endorse such targeting of a specific community'*
Fahad Ansari, 'Britain: Outpost of Tyranny', *IHRC Bulletin* (October 2005).

p.134   *'Blacks . . . formed 3 percent of the population but 14 percent of those stopped and searched'*
Home Office, *Statistics on Race and the Criminal Justice System – 2003*, p.27.

pp.134–   *'When you're looking at evidence, hard evidence, it's very difficult to find the*
5   *data and statistics'*
Interview with Chris Allen, 10 October 2004; part of the interview was broadcast in Malik, 'Are Muslims Hated?'; see also Malik, 'The Islamophobia Myth'.

p.135   *'the strong stand taken by political and community leaders . . . saw a swift reduction in such incidents'*
EUMC, *The Impact of 7 July 2005 London Bomb Attacks on Muslim Communities in the EU*, p.3.

p.135   *'Community and political leaders were quick to distance the actions of a few British-Muslim bombers from the Muslim community in general'*
EUMC, *Annual Report 2006*, p.102.

p.135   *'of a significant backlash against the Muslim community . . . appear to be unfounded'*
'CPS racist and religious crime data shows rise in prosecutions', 4 December 2006, <http://www.cps.gov.uk/news/pressreleases/archive/2006/171_06.html>.

p.136   *Europe, 2020. A dark veil is being drawn across a continent*
Scenario from Steyn, *America Alone*; I am indebted to Johann Hari, 'Apolcalypse Now', for this image of Steyn's vision of Europe's future.

p.137   'European races . . . too self-absorbed to breed'
Steyn, *America Alone*, p.107.

p.137   'healthcare, childcare, care for the elderly . . . effectively severed its citizens from humanity's primal instincts, not least the survival instinct'
Steyn, *America Alone*, p.xxxvii.

p.137   'Why did Bosnia collapse in the worst slaughter . . .'
Steyn, *America Alone*, p.5.

p.138   'Mark Steyn believes that demography is destiny . . . and he makes an immensely convincing case'
Hitchens, 'Facing the Islamist Menace'.

p.138   *Martin Amis is another liberal admirer of Steyn's demographic arguments*
Amis, 'The Decline of the West'.

p.138   'a definite urge . . . to say, "The Muslim community will have to suffer until it gets its house in order"'
Martin Amis interviewed by Ginny Dougary in 'The Voice of Experience'.

p.138   'The people who speak most sensibly about the threat that Islam poses to Europe are actually fascists'
Harris, 'It's real, it's scary, it's a cult of death'.

p.138   'the harshness Amis was canvassing was . . . an experiment in the limits of permissible thought'
Hitchens, 'Martin Amis is no racist'.

p.138   *Even Christopher Hitchens . . . found Harris's comment 'alarming'*
Hitchens, 'Facing the Islamist Menace'.

p.139   'The most remarkable thing about the Qur'an is how progressive it is'
Blair, 'A Battle for Global Values'.

p.139   'There is much we can learn from Islam'
Cited in Phillips, *Londonistan*, p.120.

pp.139–   *Lord Phillips . . . told the London Muslim Council that he was willing to see*
40   *sharia law operate in the country*
Christopher Hope and James Kirpkup, 'Muslims in Britain should be able to live under sharia, says top judge', *Daily Telegraph*, 4 July 2008; BBC News, 'Sharia Law "could have UK role"', <http://news.bbc.co.uk/1/hi/uk/7488790.stm>.

p.140   'very unsatisfactory . . . simply to be under the rule of the uniform law of a sovereign state'
Williams, 'Civil and Religious Law in England: A Religious Perspective'.

pp.140– 'In the dark lecture theatre . . . there were sobs at what people were seeing'
1 Hussain, The Islamist, p.74.

p.141 Hizb ut-Tahrir . . . organizing a rally entitled 'Bosnia Today – Brick Lane tomorrow'
Hussain, The Islamist, pp.119–20.

p.143 'how deep this self-censorship lies in the Danish public'
Cited in Jorg Lau, 'Allah und der Humor', Die Zeit, 1 February 2006.

p.145 'You would think twice, if you were honest'
Cited in Whittle, 'Islam: The Silence of the Arts'.

pp.145– Instances of artistic censorship
7 Dalya Alberg, 'Marlowe's Koran-burning Hero is Censored to Avoid Muslim Anger', The Times, 24 November 2005; David Farr, 'Tamburlaine Wasn't Censored', Guardian, 25 November 2005; 'Fury as Berlin Opera Cancels Performance', Spiegel Online, 26 August 2006, <http://www.spiegel.de/international/0,1518,439393,00.html>; 'London Gallery Pulled Art, Fearing Muslim Reaction: Curator', CBC News, 7 October 2006, <http://www.cbc.ca/arts/story/2006/10/07/london-gallery-muslims.html>; 'Tate "Misunderstood" Banned Work', BBC News, 26 September 2005, <http://news.bbc.co.uk/1/hi/entertainment/4281958.stm>; Matthew Campbell, 'Woman Artist Gets Death Threats Over Gay Muslim Photos', The Times, 6 January 2008.

p.146 'Tim Marlow . . . suggested that such self-censorship by artists and museums was now common'
Cited in Bawer, 'An Anatomy of Surrender'.

p.146 'The state has no law forbidding a pictorial representation of the Prophet . . . But I never expect to see such a picture.'
Jack, 'Beyond Belief'.

p.147 a forty-page dossier about the cartoons
The Danish newspaper Politiken has produced a photocopy of the dossier, <http://politiken.dk/media/pdf/5679.PDF>.

p.147 they were in fact parodies of the pompousness of the Jyllands-Posten caricatures
<http://www.dr.dk/Nyheder/Indland/2006/01/04/161736.htm>.

p.147 Also in the dossier were three other pictures that had nothing to do with Jyllands-Posten
Reynolds, 'A Clash of Rights and Responsibilities'; Reynolds, 'Cartoons: Divisions and Inconsistencies'.

p.148 At least a hundred died as Muslim and Christian mobs clashed in Nigeria

Lydia Polgreen, 'Nigeria Counts 100 Deaths Over Danish Caricatures', *New York Times*, 24 February.

p.148   *Al Jazeera broadcast a speech from . . . Muhammed Fouad al-Barazi'*
Anna Reimann, 'Genese des Zorns', *Spiegel Online*, 9 February 2006, <http://www.spiegel.de/politik/ausland/0,1518,400019,00.html>.

p.148   *Wijdan Ali has shown that . . . it was perfectly common for him to be portrayed*
Ali, 'From the Literal to the Spiritual'.

pp.148–   *Even over the past four hundred years, a number of Islamic . . . traditions*
9   *have accepted the pictorial representation of Muhammad*
See the Mohammed Image Archive: <http://www.zombietime.com/ mohammed_image_archive/>.

p.149   *a photo of a mural from a contemporary Iranian building that depicted Muhammad on his Night Voyage*
Hamshahri has removed the photo from its website but details are in the Mohammed Image Archive: <http://www.zombietime.com/ mohammed_image_archive/islamic_mo_full/>

p.149   *'I understand your concerns'*
Ole Damkjaer, 'FN Bekymret Over Profet-Tegninger', *Berlingske Tidende*, 7 December 2005; translated at <http://fjordman.blogspot. com/2005/12/un-is-appeasing-muslims-again.html>; 'Prophet Cartoons Worry UN Commissioner', *Copenhagen Post*, 7 December 2005, <http:// www.cphpost.dk/get/92663.html>.

p.150   *'These kinds of drawings can add to the growing Islamophobia in Europe'*
'EU Commissioner Lashes Out at Mohammad Drawings', *Copenhagen Post*, 23 December 2005, <http://www.cphpost.dk/get/93006.html>.

p.150   *The Council of Europe criticized the Danish government for invoking the 'freedom of the press'*
Simmons (ed.), *The Wikipedia Muhammad Cartoons Debate*, pp.25, 40.

p.150   *Bill Clinton condemned 'these totally outrageous cartoons against Islam'*
Anthony Browne, 'Denmark Faces International Boycott Over Muslim Cartoons', *The Times*, 31 January 2006.

p.150   *Jack Straw... condemned as 'disrespectful' the decision of some European newspapers who reprinted them*
'Muslim Leader Condemns Protestors', *BBC News*, 4 February 2006, <http://news.bbc.co.uk/1/hi/uk/4676524.stm>.

p.150   *the ministry of foreign affairs sent a letter . . . expressing regret that the paper had not respected Muslims' beliefs*
Hasan Cucuk, 'Norway Apologises for Cartoons Insulting Prophet

Mohammad', *Today's Zaman*, 28 January 2006, <http://www.todays
zaman.com/tz-web/detaylar.do?load=detay&link=29124>.

p.150　*the Vatican . . . insisted that freedom of expression did not include the right
to offend religious beliefs*
'Vatican Cardinal Criticizes Cartoons Satirizing Prophet
Mohammed', *Catholic Online*, 2 March 2006, <http://www.catholic.org/
international/international_story.php?id=18582>.

p.150　*'certain opinion makers feel that they are wholly free to say what they wish
without any respect for the understanding and beliefs of other people'*
'The Nordic Bishops' Conference Deplores the Publication of
Cartoon Drawings of the Prophet Mohammed', <http://www.vortex.is/
catholica/mass.html>.

p.150　*The Conference of European Rabbis compared the cartoons to anti-Semitic
caricatures*
Conference of European Rabbis, 'The Right to Satirize is not the
Right to Injure or Humiliate', 5 February 2006, <http://www.cer-
online.org/en/news.asp?AID=35>.

p.150　*The Swedish government closed down a website*
Iver Ekman, 'Controversy Over Cartoons Deals "Nordism" a Powerful
Blow', *International Herald Tribune*, 24 February 2006.

p.151　*Editors of student magazines in Clare College, Cambridge, Cardiff University,
the Univeristy of Illinois and Canada's Prince Edward Island University were
all sacked and disciplined for republishing some of the cartoons*
'Danish Cartoon Printed at Clare', *Varsity*, <http://www.varsity.co.uk/
news/105/1/>; 'Clare Student Out of Hiding', *Varsity*, <http://www.
varsity.co.uk/news/160/1/>; Nick Cohen, 'These Mocking Artists Have
No Principles, *Observer*, 11 March 2007; 'Paper Withdrawn Over
Cartoon Row', *BBC News*, 7 February 2006, <http://news.bbc.co.uk/
1/hi/wales/4689442.stm>; 'Muslim Cartoon Controversies at Harvard
and Illinois', *Inside Higher Ed*, 16 February 2006, <http://www.inside
highered.com/news/2006/02/16/cartoon>; Monica Davey, 'The
Cartoon Controversy Hits Home: The uproar over the Danish
cartoons that satirized Muhammad has come to American college
campuses, pitting free speech against cultural sensitivity', *New York
Times*, 3 April 2006; Richard Foot, 'PEI Student Publication Raided',
The Gazette, 9 February 2006, <http://www.canada.com/montreal
gazette/news/story.html?id=7b7d851d-a9d9-49fd-8963-fbc665baa637
&k=72181>.

p.151   'Self-censorship . . . is a meaningful demand in a world of varied and
         passionately held convictions'
         Akhtar, Be Careful with Muhammad!, p.78.

p.151   'The whole international community stands with them in their staunch rejec-
         tion of those who distort the noble faith of Islam'
         Foreign and Commonwealth Office, 'EU Presidency Supports
         Outcome of the Organization of Islamic Conference in Saudi Arabia',
         <http://ukinusa.fco.gov.uk/en?d=0&i=60058&L1=0&L2=0&a=40586>.

p.151   'I was going to begin this piece with a quote from The Satanic Verses . . .
         It was felt, however, that this would be too provocative and insensitive'
         Malik, 'The Second Age of Unreason'.

p.152   'All national institutions of churches . . . appear to be no more than human
         inventions, set up to terrify and enslave mankind, and monopolize power
         and profit.'
         Paine, The Age of Reason, p.50.

p.152   newspapers denounced him as a 'lying, drunken, brutal infidel', 'a lily-
         livered sinical rogue' and 'a demihuman archbeast'
         Cited in Phillip S. Foner, 'Introduction' to Paine, The Age of Reason,
         p.40.

p.153   'There is all the difference in the world . . . sound historical criticism . . .
         and scurrilous imaginative writing'
         Akhtar, Be Careful with Muhammad!, pp.6, 39, 8, 49.

p.154   'brought home to me the immense, perhaps unbridgeable, gulf between the
         world I belong to and the West'
         Kabbani, Letter to Christendom, pp.1, 3.

p.154   'not an isolated skirmish . . . latest battle in a long history of religious and
         cultural tension'
         Webster, A Brief History of Blasphemy, pp.37, 39, 40.

p.155   Kofi Annan, Philippe Douste-Blazy and Jack Straw
         'Annan Urges Calm in Cartoon Row', BBC News, 4 February 2006,
         <http://news.bbc.co.uk/1/hi/world/europe/4680208.stm>; Reynolds, 'A
         Clash of Rights and Responsibilities'; 'Muslim leader condemns
         protestors', BBC News, 4 February 2006, <http://news.bbc.co.uk/1/hi/
         uk/4676524.stm>.

p.155   'If people are to occupy the same political space without conflict . . . they
         mutually have to limit the extent to which they subject each others'
         fundamental beliefs to criticism.'
         Modood, Multicultural Politics, p.145.

p.156   *'He who destroys a good book destroys reason itself'*
Milton, *Areopagitica*, p.28.

p.156   *'Give me the liberty to know, to utter, and to argue freely according to conscience, above all liberties.'*
Milton, *Areopagitica*, p.54.

p.157   *'all preachers of heresy . . . and all owners and writers of heretical books'*
Cited in International Committee for the Defence of Salman Rushdie and His Publishers, *The Crime of Blasphemy*.

p.157   *'That such kind of wicked and blasphemous words were not only an offence against God and religion . . . but a crime against the laws, States and Government'*
Cited in Stephen, *A History of the Criminal Law of England*, p.470.

p.157   *'There is no such danger in society now and the offence of blasphemy is a dead letter'*
Cited in Law Commission, *Offences against Religion and Public Worship*, p.16.

p.158   *'A significant number of lawyers, clergymen and laymen have begun to take the view'*
Webster, *A Brief History of Blasphemy*, p.66.

pp.158–   *'I do not subscribe to the view that the common law offence of blasphemous*
9   *libel serves no useful purpose in the modern law'*
Cited in Webster, *A Brief History of Blasphemy*, pp.64–5.

p.159   *'are so serious and so fundamental . . . be altogether unacceptable.'*
Law Commission, *Offences against Religion and Public Worship*, p.57.

p.159   *'If scurrilous attacks on religious beliefs go unpunished . . . they could embitter strongly held feelings within substantial groups of people'*
Cited in Webster, *A Brief History of Blasphemy*, p.64.

p.161   *The French sociologist Émile Durkheim pointed out*
Durkheim, *The Elementary Forms of Religious Life*.

p.162   *'There is . . . a large group of Muslims in this city who want to live in a secular society'*
Cited in Hortur Gudmundsson, 'Denmark: Moderate Muslims Oppose Imams', *The Brussels Journal*, 19 January 2006, <http://www.brusselsjournal.com/node/689>.

p.162   *'I did not know I could say no'*
Interview with Bünyamin Simsek, 15 October 2008.

p.163   *'I never felt offended by the cartoons . . . But I did feel deeply insulted by the*

Islamist response to them'
Interview with Naser Khader, 29 September 2008.

p.165 *'A black man could only become integrated when he started behaving like a white man'*
Rushdie, 'The New Empire within Britain', in *Imaginary Homelands*, p.137.

p.166 *'The Danes say one thing, that they want to integrate us, and do another'*
Interview with Bünyamin Simsek, 15 October 2008.

p.166 *'There are certain beliefs, and certain symbols of such beliefs (an enemy's flag perhaps)'*
Cited in Webster, *A Brief History of Blasphemy*, p.134.

p.166 *'By insulting the sacred tradition of the Koran and by burning books'*
Webster, *A Brief History of Blasphemy*, p.134.

p.166 *'You don't fool around with other people's religions'*
Kofi Annan interviewed on Danish TV; see <http://wincoast.com/forum/showthread.php?t=26586>.

p.166 *'There are taboos in every religion'*
Chris Tryhorn, 'Jack Straw praises UK media's "sensitivity" over cartoons', *Guardian*, 3 February 2006.

p.167 *'The idea of respect that liberals in particular promote today takes us down a dangerous road'*
Interview with Monica Ali, 10 October 2008.

p.168 *'We have serious objections to most of the content of this book'*
Matthew Taylor, 'Brickbats fly as community brands novel "despicable"', *Guardian*, 3 December 2003.

p.168 *'Our community is offended by the lies and slander in the book'*
Interview with Abdus Salique, 2 August 2006.

pp.169– *'Johann Hari . . . talked to locals'*
70 Hari, 'What's at stake in the Battle of Brick Lane'.

p.170 *'the community has the moral right to keep the film-makers out'*
Greer, 'Reality bites'.

p.170 *'cannot have the right of veto over how they are portrayed'*
'The Trouble with Brick Lane', *Guardian*, 27 October 2007.

p.171 *'on the near side of British culture, not far from the middle'*
Greer, 'Reality bites'.

pp.171– *'Ali . . . a mixed-race Oxford graduate'*
2 'The Trouble with Brick Lane', *Guardian*, 27 October 2007.

p.172 *'Our women mostly respect their husbands and respect their tradition'*
Interview with Abdus Salique, 2 August 2006.

p.173   'A "cultural" practice is difficult enough to challenge'
Gupta, 'Too High a Price to Pay'.

p.173   'As a group of women of many religions and none . . . we would like to express our solidarity with Salman Rushdie'
Women Against Fundamentalism, 'The Rushdie Affair'.

p.174   'People of all backgrounds and faiths have a right to live free from hatred, racism and extremism'
'Atkinson attacks "draconian" law', BBC News, 20 June 2005, <http://news.bbc.co.uk/1/hi/uk_politics/4112118.stm>.

p.174   'strengthen the voices of religious intolerance'
Gupta, 'Too High a Price to Pay'.

pp.174–5   'notice how useful and well-timed the angel's revelations tended to be'
Rushdie, The Satanic Verses, pp.364–5.

pp.175–6   'Islamic doctrine . . . wisely discourages inappropriate kinds of curiosity'
Akhtar, Be Careful With Muhammad!, pp.103–4.

p.176   'The sacred order never ceased, implicitly or explicitly, to proclaim "this is how things are, they cannot be otherwise".'
Kolakowski, Modernity on Endless Trial, p.70.

p.176   'I am contending for the rights of the living and against their being willed away'
Paine, Rights of Man, p.11.

p.179   'They listen to us . . . No one else does'
Interview with Bill Heskey, 22 January 2003.

p.180   'It felt like we were being urinated upon from a great height'
Interview with Inayat Bunglawala, 4 August 2008.

p.181   'It is not acceptable'
'Muslim head says gays "harmful"', BBC News, 3 January 2006, <http://news.bbc.co.uk/1/hi/uk/4579146.stm>.

p.182   'All Britons . . . should be allowed to freely express their views in an atmosphere free of intimidation or bullying'
'Islam and homosexuals', The Times, Letters, 14 January 2006, <http://www.timesonline.co.uk/tol/comment/letters/article788207.ece>

p.182   'The Muslim community may have had its differences with the Jews'
David Starkey, 'Right to Free speech', The Times, Letters, 16 January 2006,
http://www.timesonline.co.uk/tol/comment/letters/article788854.ece>

p.183   'What we have developed today . . . is a marketplace of outrage'
Interview with Monica Ali, 10 October 2008.

p.183   *'What I've come to realize . . . is that it would never work to censor books that are offensive'*
Interview with Inayat Bunglawala, 4 August 2008.

p.183   *on the eve of 9/11, he was calling Osama bin Laden a 'freedom fighter'*
Martin Bright, 'Muslims Accuse BBC of a Witch-Hunt', *Observer*, 21 August 2005, <http://www.guardian.co.uk/media/2005/aug/21/bbc. religion>. Bunglawala has said that he was talking only about Bin Laden fighting the Soviet troops in Afghanistan: 'Osama was a mujahid. I do not consider him as such now. People change.'

p.183   *'must be accorded to ideas we hate or sooner or later it will be denied to ideas we cherish'*
'Communist Party of the United States v. Subversive Activities Control Board No. 12', 367 U.S. 1 (1961) Black, J. Dissenting Opinion, <http://www.law.cornell.edu/supct/html/historics/USSC_CR_0367_0001 _ZD1.html>.

p.184   *'defaming me and my family because we follow and are related to Prophet Muhammad'*
Cited in Greenwald, 'The Noxious Fruits of Hate Speech Laws'.

p.184   *the Canadian Islamic Congress took the magazine* Macleans *to the British Columbia Human Rights Commission for stirring up racial hatred*
Liptak, 'Unlike Others US Defends Right to Offend in Speech'.

p.184   *'Normally people think it's a white supremacist or Caucasians promoting race hate against visible minorities'*
Bernstein, *You Can't Say That!*, p.71.

p.185   *'Siddiqui's words, although shocking and distasteful, did not constitute incitement'*
Personal communication.

p.186   *the Metropolitan Police took a very different view*
'Four men jailed over cartoon demo', *BBC News*, 18 July 2007, <http://news.bbc.co.uk/1/hi/uk/6904622.stm>.

p.187   The Samina Malik case
Haroon Sidique, '"Lyrical Terrorist" convicted over hate record', *Guardian*, 8 November 2007.

p.187   *Abu Hamza . . . was sentenced to seven years' imprisonment for incitement to murder and racial hatred*
'The preachings of Abu Hamza', *Guardian*, 7 February 2006; Sean O'Neil, '"Offensive" remarks take straight from the Koran, defence says', *The Times*, 20 January 2006.

p.188   *Abu Izzadeen . . . was jailed for four and a half years.*
         Duncan Gardham, 'Muslim preacher Abu Izzadeen guilty of
         inciting terrorism', *Daily Telegraph*, 18 April 2008.

p.188   *Ali Mazrui compared* The Satanic Verses *to Mein Kampf*
         Mazrui, 'The Satanic Verses or a Satanic Novel?'

p.189   *'One of the things that the free speech and censorship issue raises . . . is can*
         we control the resonances, the interpretations, of our words?'
         Adam Phillips with Lisa Appignanesi, 'Free Speech: An Exchange', in
         Appignanesi (ed.) *Free Expression is No Offence*, p.164.

p.191   *'With an enemy committed to terrorism . . . the advocacy of terrorism – the*
         threats, the words – are not mere dogma'
         McCarthy, 'Free Speech for Terrorists?'

p.191   *Newt Gingrich . . . has demanded the rewriting of the First Amendment*
         Gingrich, 'The 1st Amendment is Not a Suicide Pact'.

pp.192– Conversation between Spellberg and Garrett and Garrett's email
    3   cited in Nomani, 'You still can't write about Muhammad'.

p.193   *Inayat Bunglawala . . . ruminating on the twenty years since the publication*
         of The Satanic Verses
         Bunglawala, 'Words can never hurt us'.

p.193   *the firebombers had been given a 'spurious legitimacy by liberals'*
         Malik, 'Self-censor and be damned!'

p.193   *'If anyone has given ground . . . it is surely those who once believed in*
         banning books because they regarded them as being "offensive".'
         Bunglawala, 'The right to offend'.

p.194   *'is in part a secular man's reckoning with the religious spirit'*
         Rushdie, 'In Good Faith', in *Imaginary Homelands*, pp.396, 395, 394.

p.194   *'honouring Aisha and all the wives of Muhammad'*
         Interview with Sherry Jones, 24 September 2008.

p.194   *'Journalists were constantly asking me, "Will you stop publishing* The
         Satanic Verses?"'
         Interview with William Nygaard, 5 September 2008.

p.195   *'to postpone publication for the safety of the author'*
         Random House, 'The Jewel of Medina Statement', <http://www.random
         house.com/rhpg/medinaletter.html>.

p.195   *'a respondent . . . suggested a "seven-point strategy"'*
         <http://www.husainiyouths.com/forum/topics/1979414:Topic:19950>.

p.195   *'If Random House had simply published my book . . . I don't think there*
         would have been any trouble'

Interview with Sherry Jones, 24 September 2008.

p.196 *Amanullah himself has insisted that* The Jewel of Medina *should not be withdrawn*
Amanullah, 'Free Speech is a Two-Way Street'.

p.196 *'I am very disappointed to hear that my publishers'*
Bone, 'Salman Rushdie attacks "censorship by fear" over *The Jewel of Medina*'.

p.197 *Nonsense, responded the American academic Stanley Fish*
Fish, 'Crying Censorship'.

p.197 *'The way that Random House dropped* The Jewel of Medina *would have been unthinkable in the pre-Rushdie era'*
Interview with Monica Ali, 10 October 2008.

p.198 *'Nobody... would have the balls today to write* The Satanic Verses, *let alone publish it'*
Interview with Hanif Kureishi, 9 October 2008.

p.198 *'There was one copy going round our school like contraband'*
Cited in Donadio, 'My Beautiful London'.

p.198 *Kureishi's work . . . Sukhdev Sandhu recalls, transformed the way that both he and his white friends saw what it meant to be Asian*
Sandhu, 'Paradise Syndrome'.

p.201 *'Shahid, too, wanted to belong to his people'*
Kureishi, *The Black Album*, p.76.

p.201 *'I love England'*
Kureishi, 'My Son the Fanatic', in *The Word and the Bomb*, p.70.

p.202 *When Ali confronts Parvez about his drinking in 'My Son the Fanatic'*
Kuresihi, 'My Son the Fanatic', pp.68, 69.

p.202 *'What's been particularly disturbing . . . is the culture of fear that's developed in this country since 2001'*
Interview with Sherry Jones, 24 September 2008.

p.203 *'It has become terrifying clear how close the "Barbarians" are'*
Abramsky, 'Decline and Fall'.

p.203 *'America today . . . is not the self-confident and determined nation that responded to Pearl Harbor'*
Brzezinski, 'Terrorized by "War on Terror"'.

p.204 *'the extent of warfare among and within states [has] lessened by nearly half'*
Gurr and Marshall, *Peace and Conflict 2005*.

p.204 *'in the six years since 9/11, Al Qaeda Central . . . has been unable to launch a major attack anywhere'*

Zakaria, *The Post-American World*, pp.8–9.

p.205   *'If a flight full of commuters can be turned into a missile of war . . . then everything is dangerous'*
New York Times, 'The War Against America'.

p.205   *'is not the cause of the crisis'*
Roy, *Secularism Confronts Islam*, p.xiii.

p.205   *'the feeling that . . . the United States had it coming'*
Mary Beard, '11 September', *London Review of Books*, 4 October 2001.

p.205   *'as innocent and as undeserving of terror as Vietnamese or Iraqi peasants'*
New Statesman, 'In Buildings Thought Indestructible'.

p.205   *'On 11 September 2001 the Muslim world finally struck back'*
Figes, *Journey to Nowhere*.

p.206   *Sam Harris believes that the West is at war . . . with 'Islam itself'*
Harris, *The End of Faith*, pp.109, 110, 151–2.

p.206   *'a day of de-Enlightenment'*
Amis, *The Second Plane*, p.13.

p.206   *'One of the main claims of Enlightenment philosophy'*
Buruma, *Murder in Amsterdam*, p.29.

p.206   *'institutions created by and for one population break down if exposed to human groups that behave in a different way'*
Cummins, 'The fine line between tolerance and political correctness'.

p.207   *'if we are willing to drop bombs'*
Harris, *The End of Faith*, p.197.

p.207   *a need for ethnic profiling and discriminatory policing*
Harris, 'Bombing our Illusions'.

p.207   *'some propositions are so dangerous that it may even be ethical to kill people for believing them'*
Harris, *The End of Faith*, pp.52–3.

p.207   *Martin Amis has wondered aloud about collective punishment for Muslims*
Dougary, 'The Voice of Experience'.

p.207   *'For are they not conjoined opposites, these two, each man the other's shadow?'*
Rushdie, *The Satanic Verses*, p.426.

p.208   *'One seeking to transform into the foreignness he admires, the other seeking contemptuously to transform.'*
Rushdie, *The Satanic Verses*, p.426.

p.208   *'Vulnerability is never the best proof of strength'*

Akhtar, *Be Careful with Muhammad!*, p.102.

p.209   'in spite of born-again slogans, new beginnings, metamorphoses'
Rushdie, *The Satanic Verses*, p.408.

p.209   'understand themselves and shape their futures by arguing and challenging
and questioning and saying the unsayable'
Rushdie, 'In Good Faith', in *Imaginary Homelands*, p.395.

p.209   'work of radical dissent'
Rushdie, 'In Good Faith', in *Imaginary Homelands*, p.395.

p.209   'From the end of debate, of dispute, of dissent'
Rushdie, 'In Good Faith', in *Imaginary Homelands*, p.396.

p.210   There is a scene in The Satanic Verses in which Saladin Chamcha finds
himself in an immigration detention centre
Rushdie, *The Satanic Verses*, p.168.

Bibliography

Abramsky, Sasha, 'Decline and Fall', *Independent*, 29 September 2001.

Abu-Amer, Ziad, *Islamic Fundamentalism in the West Bank and Gaza: Muslim Brotherhood and Islamic Jihad* (Indiana University Press, 1994).

Ahmed, Akbar S., *Discovering Islam: Making Sense of Muslim History and Society* (Routledge, 2002).

Akhtar, Navid, *The Biradari*, BBC Radio 4, 26 August 2003.

Akhtar, Shabbir, *Be Careful with Muhammad!: The Salman Rushdie Affair* (Bellew Publishing, 1989).

Akhtar, Shabbir, 'Palestine Within Europe?', *Muslim News*, 42 (August 1992).

Ali, Monica, *Brick Lane* (Doubleday, 2003).

Ali, Tariq, 'The Price of Occupation', *Guardian*, 8 July 2005.

Ali, Wijdan, 'From the Literal to the Spiritual: The Development of the Prophet Muhammad's Portrayal from 13th-Century Ilkahnid Miniatures to 17th-Century Ottoman Art', in Kiel, Landsman and Theunissen (eds.) *Proceedings of the 11th International Congress of Turkish Art*, <http://www2.let.uu.nl/Solis/anpt/ejos/pdf4/07Ali.pdf>.

Amanullah, Shahed, 'Free Speech is a Two-Way Street', *altmuslim*, 7 August 2008, <http://www.altmuslim.com/a/a/print/2781/>.

Amis, Martin. 'The Decline of the West', *The Times*, 14 April 2007; reprinted in Amis, *The Second Plane*, pp.155–9.

Amis, Martin, *The Second Plane: September 11: 2001–2007* (Jonathan Cape, 2008).

Appignanesi, Lisa (ed.), *Free Expression is No Offence* (Penguin, 2005).

Appignanesi, Lisa, and Maitland, Sara (eds.), *The Rushdie File* (Fourth Estate, 1989).

Barton, S., *The Muslims of Bradford*, Research Paper no. 13 (Centre for the Study of Islam and Christian-Muslim Relations, 1982).

Basu, Shrabani, 'Interview with Salman Rushdie', *Sunday* (India), 18–24 September 1988; reprinted in Appignanesi and Maitland (eds.), *The Rushdie File*, p.40.

Bawer, Bruce, 'An Anatomy of Surrender', *City Journal* (Spring 2008), <http://www.city-journal.org/2008/18_2_cultural_jihadists.html>.

Bernstein, David E., *You Can't Say That!: The Growing Threat to Civil Liberties from Antidiscrimination Laws* (Cato Institute, 2003).

Birmingham City Council, *Joint Report of Head of Equalities and Director of Birmingham Race Action Partnership: Development of Issue-Based Community Action Forums* (Birmingham City Council, 1999).

Blair, Tony, 'A Battle for Global Values', *Foreign Affairs*, January/February 2007, <http://www.foreignaffairs.org/20070101 faessay86106/tony-blair/a-battle-for-global-values.html>.

Bone, James, 'Salman Rushdie attacks "censorship by fear" over *The Jewel of Medina*', *The Times*, 16 August 2008, <http://entertainment. timesonline.co.uk/tol/arts_and_entertainment/books/article4543243 .ece>.

Bradford Heritage Recording Unit, *Here to Stay – Bradford's South Asian Communities* (Bradford Heritage Recording Unit, 1994).

Bradford Metropolitan Council, *Turning Points: A Review of Race Relations in Bradford* (Bradford Metropolitan Council, 1981).

Bright, Martin, 'Radical Links of Britain's "Moderate" Muslim group', *Observer*, 14 August 2005.

Bright, Martin, *When Progressives Treat with Reactionaries: The British State's Flirtation with Radical Islamism* (Policy Exchange, 2006).

Brzezinski, Zbigniew, 'Terrorized by "War on Terror"', *Washington Post*, 25 March 2007, <http://www.washingtonpost.com/wp-dyn/ content/article/2007/03/23/AR2007032301613.html>.

Bunglawala, Inayat, 'The right to offend', *Comment is Free*, 29 September 2008, <http://www.guardian.co.uk/commentisfree/2008/ sep/29/publishing.civilliberties>.

Bunglawala, Inayat, 'Words can never hurt us', *Comment is Free*, 26 September 2008, <http://www.guardian.co.uk/commentisfree/2008/ sep/26/islam.religion>.

Burke, Jason, 'Omar was a normal British teenager who loved his little brother and Man Utd. So why at 24 did he plan to blow up a nightclub in central London?', *Observer*, 20 January 2008.

Buruma, Ian, *Murder in Amsterdam: The Death of Theo van Gogh and the Limits of Tolerance* (Atlantic, 2006).

Carter, Angela, 'Angels in Dirty Places', *Guardian*, 23 September 1988, <http://www.guardian.co.uk/books/1988/sep/23/fiction.angelacarter>.

Commission for Racial Equality, *Free Speech: Report of a Seminar*, Discussions Papers 2 (CRE, 1989).

Commission on the Future of Multi-Ethnic Britain, *The Future of Multi-Ethnic Britain* (Profile Books, 2000).

Cornish, P. (ed.), *Britain and Security* (The Smith Institute, 2007).

Counter Information Services, *Racism: Who Profits?*, CIS Anti-Report, 16 (Counter Information Services, 1976).

Crichton, Sarah, and Shapiro, Laura, 'An Exclusive Talk with Salman Rushdie', *Newsweek*, 12 February 1990; reprinted in Reder (ed.), *Conversations with Salman Rushdie*, pp.123–31.

Cummins, Harry, 'The fine line between tolerance and political correctness', *The Times*, 26 June 2008, <http://business.times online.co.uk/tol/business/law/article4214369.ece>.

Dekmejian, R. Hrair, *Islamic Revolution: Fundamentalism in the Arab World* (Syracuse University Press, 1995).

Devji, Faisal, *Landscapes of the Jihad: Militancy, Morality, Modernity* (Hurst & Co, 2005).

Donadio, Rachel, 'My Beautiful London', *New York Times*, 10 August 2008, <http://www.nytimes.com/2008/08/10/magazine/10kureishi-t.html?n=Top/Reference/Times%20Topics/Subjects/M/Man%20Booker%20Prize>.

Dougary, Ginny, 'The Voice of Experience', *The Times*, 9 September 2006, <http://www.ginnydougary.co.uk/2006/09/17/the-voice-of-experience/>.

Durkheim, Emile, *The Elementary Forms of Religious Life* (Oxford University Press, 2001; first published 1912).

Durodie, Bill, 'Home-Grown Nihilism: The Clash within Civilizations', in Cornish (ed.), *Britain and Security*, pp.117–28.

Economist, 'How jihad went freelance', 31 January 2008.

Ehteshami, Anoushiravan, *After Khomeini: The Iranian Second Republic* (Routledge, 1995).

EUMC, *Annual Report 2006*, <http://eumc.europa.eu/eumc/material/pub/ar06/AR06-P2-EN.pdf>.

EUMC, *The Impact of 7 July 2005 London Bomb Attacks on Muslim Communities in the EU* (EUMC, 2005).

Faraz, Mohammad, 'MCB: Dad's Muslim Army', *Q-News*, 287–8 (April 1998).

Fielding, Nick, 'Diary of a Terrorist: Inside the Mind of a Fanatic', *Sunday Times*, 14 October 2001.

Fielding, Nick, 'From a London Public School to the Shadow of the Noose', *Sunday Times*, 21 April 2002.

Figes, Eva, *Journey to Nowhere* (Granta, 2008).

Fish, Stanley, 'Crying Censorship', *New York Times*, 24 August 2008, <http://fish.blogs.nytimes.com/2008/08/24/crying-censorship/>.

Fisk, Robert 'The Reality of this Barbaric Bombing', *Independent*, 8 July 2005.

Fitzgerald, Marian, *Black People and Party Politics in Britain* (Runnymede Trust, 1987).

Freal, Alexandra, and Syel, Rajeev, 'Muslims in Britain – a story of mutual fear and suspicion', *The Times*, 5 July 2008.

Furedi, Frank, *Therapy Culture: Cultivating Vulnerability in an Uncertain Age* (Routledge, 2003).

Furseth, Inger, and Leer-Salvesen, Paul (eds.), *Religion in Late Modernity: Essays in Honour of Pål Repstad* (Tapir Academic Press, 2007).

GfK NOP Social Research, *Attitudes to Living in Britain – A Survey of Muslim Opinion* (2006), <http://www.imaginate.uk.com/MCC01_SURVEY/Site%20Download.pdf>.

Gilbertson, Martin, 'When I Heard Where the Bombers Were From I Felt Sick', *Guardian*, 24 June 2006, <http://www.guardian.co.uk/uk/2006/jun/24/july7.uksecurity1>.

Gingrich, Newt, 'The 1st Amendment is Not a Suicide Pact: Blocking the Speech That Calls for Our Death', *Human Events*, 12 April 2006, <http://www.humanevents.com/article.php?id=18314>.

Gitlin, Todd, *The Twilight of Common Dreams: Why America is Wracked by Culture Wars* (Henry Holt, 1995).

Glynn, Sarah, 'Playing the Ethnic Card – Politics and Ghettoization in London's East End', paper presented to a conference on 'Ghettoized Perceptions versus Mainstream Constructions of English Muslims: The Future of the Multicultural Built Environment', University of Birmingham, July 2006, archived as part of the Institute of Geography online series, <http://www.era.lib.ed.ac.uk/bitstream/1842/1397/1/sglynn001.pdf>.

Gole, Nilufer, 'Islam, European Public Space, and Civility', *Eurozine*, 3 May 2007.

Greenwald, Glenn, 'The Noxious Fruits of Hate Speech Laws', *Salon*, 13 January 2008, <http://www.salon.com/opinion/greenwald/2008/01/13/hate_speech_laws/>.

Greer, Germaine, 'Reality bites', *Guardian*, 24 July 2006, <http://www.guardian.co.uk/film/2006/jul/24/culture.books>.

Gupta, Rahila, 'Too High a Price to Pay', *Guardian*, 12 March 2005, <http://www.guardian.co.uk/politics/2005/mar/12/gender.religion>.

Gurr, Ted Robert, and Marshall, Monty G., *Peace and Conflict 2005: A Global Survey of Armed Conflicts, Self-Determination Movements and Democracy* (Center for International Development and Conflict Management, 2005).

Hari, Johann, 'Apocalypse Now?', *New Statesman*, 12 March 2007

Hari, Johann, 'What's at stake in the Battle of Brick Lane', *Independent*, 31 July 2006, <http://www.independent.co.uk/opinion/commentators/johann-hari/johann-hari-whats-at-stake-in-the-battle-of-brick-lane-409992.html>.

Harris, Sam, 'Bombing our Illusions', *Huffington Post*, 10 October 2005, <http://www.huffingtonpost.com/sam-harris/bombing-our-illusions_b_8615.html?view=screen>

Harris, Sam, 'It's real, it's scary, it's a cult of death', *Los Angeles Times*, 18 September 2006.

Harris, Sam *The End of Faith: Religion, Terror and the Future of Reason* (Free Press, 2005).

Heelas, Paul, and Woodhead, Linda, *The Spiritual Revolution* (Blackwell, 2005).

Hiro, Dilip, *Black British, White British: A History of Race Relations in Britain* (Grafton, 1991).

Hitchens, Christopher, 'Facing the Islamist Menace', *City Journal* (Winter 2007), <http://www.city-journal.org/html/17_1_urbanities-steyn.html>.

Hitchens, Christopher, 'Martin Amis is no racist', *Guardian*, 21 November 2007.

Hizb ut-Tahrir, 'Islam is Relevant for All Times and Places', <http://www.hizb.org.uk/hizb/resources/islamic-knowledge/islam-is-relevant-for-all-times-and-places.html>.

Home Office, *Statistics on Race and the Criminal Justice System – 2003* (Home Office, 2004).

House of Commons Home Affairs Committee, *Racial Disadvantage* (HMSO, 1981).

House of Commons Home Affairs Committee, *Terrorism and Community Relations* (House of Commons, 2005).

Howe, Darcus, *From Bobby to Babylon: Blacks and the British Police* (Race Today Publications, 1988).

Huntington, Samuel P., 'The Clash of Civilizations', *Foreign Affairs*, 72 (3), 1993.

Hussain, Ed, *The Islamist: Why I Joined Radical Islam in Britain, What I Saw Inside and Why I Left* (Penguin, 2007).

Institute of Contemporary Islamic Thought, 'Dr Kalim Siddiqui, 1931–1996', <http://www.islamicthought.org/ks-bio-p4.html>.

Institute of Race Relations, *Deadly Silence: Black Deaths in Custody* (Institute of Race Relations, 1991).

International Committee for the Defence of Salman Rushdie and His Publishers, *The Crime of Blasphemy* (1989).

Jack, Ian, 'Beyond Belief', *Guardian*, 1 January 2005, <http://www. guardian.co.uk/stage/2005/jan/01/theatre.society>.

Jones, Sherry, *The Jewel of Medina* (Beaufort Books, 2008).

Jones, Tamara, 'Among the Young of Multiethnic Leeds, a Hardening Hatred', *Washington Post*, 20 July 2005.

Joshi, S., and Carter, B., 'The Role of Labour in the Creation of a Racist Britain', *Race and Class*, 25 (3) (1984).

Kabbani, Rana, *Letter to Christendom* (Virago, 1989).

Keppel, Gilles, *Jihad: The Trail of Political Islam* (I.B. Taurus, 2006; first published 2000).

Khan, Urmee, 'Young, British and Muslim: One Woman's Journey to the Home of the 7/7 Bombers', *Observer*, 18 June 2006.

Kiel, M., Landsman, N., and Theunissen, H. (eds.), *Proceedings of the 11th International Congress of Turkish Art, Utrecht, EJOS* (Electronic Journal of Oriental Studies), 4 (2001).

Kohlman, Evan F., 'The Afghan-Bosnian Mujahideen Network in Europe', paper presented to a conference in Stockholm organized by the Swedish Emergency Management Agency, <http://www.fhs. se/upload/Forskning/centrumbildningar/cats/kohlmann-abm-network-europe.pdf>.

Kolakowski, Leszek, *Modernity on Endless Trial* (University of Chicago Press, 1990).

Kramer, Martin, 'Islamist Bubbles', *National Interest* (Summer 2002), pp. 132–8.

Kruks, Sonia, *Retrieving Experience: Subjectivity and Recognition in Feminist Policy* (Cornell University Press, 2000).

Kundnani, Arun, 'From Oldham to Bradford: The Violence of the Violated', in *The Three Faces of British Racism* (Institute of Race Relations, 2001), <http://www.irr.org.uk/2001/october/ak000003. html>.

Kureishi, Hanif, *Something to Tell You* (Faber & Faber, 2008).

Kureishi, Hanif, *The Black Album* (Faber & Faber, 1995).

Kuresihi, Hanif, *The Word and the Bomb* (Faber & Faber, 2005).

Law Commission, *Offences against Religion and Public Worship* (HMSO, 1985).

Lewis, Philip, *Islamic Britain: Religion, Politics and Identity Among British Muslims: Bradford in the 1990s* (I.B. Taurus, 1994).

Liptak, Adam, 'Unlike Others US Defends Right to Offend in Speech', *New York Times*, 12 June 2008, <http://www.nytimes.com/2008/06/12/us/12hate.html>.

Maher, Shiraz, 'Campus Radicals', *Prospect*, September 2006 (web exclusive), <http://www.prospect-magazine.co.uk/article_details.php?id=7742>.

Malik, Kenan, 'Are Muslims Hated?', Channel 4, 8 January 2005.

Malik, Kenan, 'Disunited Kingdom', Channel 4, 29 October 2003.

Malik, Kenan, 'Illusions of Identity', *Prospect*, August 2006.

Malik, Kenan, 'Self-censor and be damned!', *The Times*, 29 September 2008, <http://www.timesonline.co.uk/tol/comment/columnists/guest_contributors/article4842288.ece>.

Malik, Kenan, 'The Islamophobia Myth', *Prospect*, January 2005.

Malik, Kenan, 'The Second Age of Unreason', *Independent*, 28 January 1994.

Malik, Kenan 'What Muslims want', Channel 4, 7 August 2006, <http://www.channel4.com/news/articles/dispatches/kenan+malik+analysis+of+the+muslim+survey/158240#fold>.

Malik, Shiv, 'My Brother the Bomber', *Prospect*, June 2007.

Manzoor, Sarfraz, *Greetings from Bury Park: Race, Religion, Rock 'n' Roll* (Bloomsbury 2007).

Marzorati, Gerald, 'Rushdie in Hiding', *New York Times*, 4 November 1990.

Marzorati, Gerald, 'Salman Rushdie: Fiction's Embattled Infidel', *New York Times Magazine*, 29 January 1989.

Maududi, Abul A'la, *Towards Understanding Islam* (Kazi Publications, 1992; first published 1932) <http://www.al-islamforall.org/litre/Englitre/Undislam.htm>.

Mazrui, Ali A., 'The Satanic Verses or a Satanic Novel?: Moral Dilemmas of the Rushdie Affair', in Commission for Racial Equality, *Free Speech*, pp.79–103.

McCarthy, Andrew C., 'Free Speech for Terrorists?', *Commentary*, March

2005, <https://www.commentarymagazine.com/viewarticle.cfm/free-speech-for-terrorists—9864?page=1>.

Midgley, Carol, 'Why I'm scared to go into the Tube now', *The Times*, 4 July 2006.

Milton, John, *Areopagitica* (1664); online at <http://files.libertyfund.org/files/103/Milton_1224.pdf>.

Mirza, Munira, Senthikumaran, Abi, and Ja'far, Zein, *Living Apart Together: British Muslims and the Paradox of Multiculturalism* (Policy Exchange, 2007).

Modood, Tariq, *Multicultural Politics: Racism, Ethnicity and Muslims in Britain* (Edinburgh University Press, 2005).

Murphy, Dervla, *Tales from Two Cities: Travel of Another Sort* (John Murray, 1987), p.10.

Murtagh, Peter, 'Rushdie in hiding after Ayatollah's death threat', *Guardian*, 18 February 1989, <http://www.guardian.co.uk/books/1989/feb/18/fiction.salmanrushdie>.

National Council for Voluntary Organizations, *After Abolition: A Report on the Impact of the Abolition of the MCCs and the GLC on the Voluntary Sector* (NCVO, 1986).

National Intelligence Council, *Global Trends 2015: A Dialogue About the Future with Nongovernment Experts* (Central Intelligence Agency, 2000).

New Statesman, 'In Buildings Thought Indestructible', 17 September 2001, <http://www.newstatesman.com/200109170001>.

New York Times, 'The War Against America: An Unfathomable Attack', 12 September 2001, <http://query.nytimes.com/gst/fullpage.html?res=9C07E5DD1238F931A2575AC0A9679C8B63>.

Nomani, Asra Q., 'You still can't write about Muhammad', *Wall Street Journal*, 6 August 2008, <http://online.wsj.com/article/SB121797979078815073.html?mod=opinion_main_commentaries>.

O'Hagan, Andrew, *The Atlantic Ocean: Essays on Britain and America* (Faber, 2008).

Onaran, Yalman, 'Burned: An author charged with inciting a crowd to kill him', *Columbia Journalism Review*, 33 (November/December

1994), <http://findarticles.com/p/articles/mi_qa3613/is_/ai_n8726
563>.

Owen, Ursula, 'A Victory for Literary Freedom', *Independent*, 27 April
1998.

Paine, Thomas, *Rights of Man* (Kessinger Publishing, 1999; first
published 1791).

Paine, Thomas, *The Age of Reason* (Citadel, 1991; first published 1794).

Pasquill, Derek, 'I had no choice but to leak', *New Statesman*, 17
January 2008.

Pew Research Centre, *American Muslims: Middle Class and Mostly
Mainstream* (2007), <http://pewresearch.org/assets/pdf/muslim-
americans.pdf>.

Phillips, Melanie, *Londonistan: How Britain is Creating a Terror State
Within* (Gibson Square, 2006).

Pipes, Daniel, 'The Muslims are coming! The Muslims are coming!',
National Review, 19 November 1990.

Pipes, Daniel, *The Rushdie Affair: The Novel, the Ayatollah and the West*
(Transaction, 1990).

Populus, *Muslim 7/7 Poll* (2006), <http://www.populus.co.uk/the-times-
itv-news-muslim-77-poll-050706.html>.

Ramamurthy, Anandi (ed.), *Kala Tara: A history of the Asian Youth
Movements in the 1970s and 1980s*, <www.tandana.org>.

Ramamurthy, Anandi, 'Secular Identities and the Asian Youth
Movements', paper presented at the 10th International Conference
on Alternative Futures and Popular Protest, Manchester
Metropolitan University, 30 March – 1 April 2005.

Raza, Mohammad S., *Islam in Britain* (Volcano Press, 1991).

Reder, Michael (ed.), *Conversations with Salman Rushdie* (University Press
of Mississippi, 2000).

Report of the Official Account of the Bombings in London on 7th July 2005
(HMSO, 2006), <http://www.homeoffice.gov.uk/documents/7-july-
report?view=Binary>.

Reynolds, Paul, 'A Clash of Rights and Responsibilities', *BBC News*,
<http://news.bbc.co.uk/1/hi/world/south_asia/4686536.stm>.

Reynolds, Paul, 'Cartoons: Divisions and Inconsistencies', *BBC News*, <http://news.bbc.co.uk/1/hi/world/asia-pacific/4708216.stm>.

Roy, Olivier, *Islam and Resistance in Afghanistan* (Cambridge University Press, 1990).

Roy, Olivier, *Globalised Islam: The Search for a New Ummah* (Hurst, 2002).

Roy, Olivier, *Secularism Confronts Islam* (Columbia University Press, 2007).

Rushdie, Salman, 'An Open Letter to PM', cited in Appignanesi and Maitland (eds.), *The Rushdie File*; see also <http://query.nytimes.com/gst/fullpage.html?res=950DE2D81038F934A25751C0A96F948260>.

Rushdie, Salman, *Imaginary Homelands: Essays and Criticism 1981–1991* (Granta), 1991.

Rushdie, Salman, *The Satanic Verses* (Penguin, 1988).

Ruthven, Malise, *A Satanic Affair: Salman Rushdie and the Rage of Islam* (Chatto & Windus, 1990).

Sageman, Marc, *Leaderless Jihad: Terror Networks in the Twenty-First Century* (University of Pennsylvania Press, 2008).

Sageman, Marc, 'Understanding Terror Networks', Foreign Policy Research Insitute e-Notes, 1 November 2004, <http://www.fpri.org/enotes/20041101.middleeast.sageman.understandingterrornetworks.html>.

Sageman, Marc, *Understanding Terror Networks* (University of Pennsylvania Press, 2004).

Sahgal, Gita, and Yuval-Davis, Nira, 'Introduction' to Gita Sahgal and Nira Yuval-Davis (eds.) *Refusing Holy Orders: Women and Fundamentalism in Britain* (Women Living Under Muslim Laws, 1992).

Sandhu, Sukhdev, 'Paradise Syndrome', *London Review of Books*, 18 May 2000, <http://www.lrb.co.uk/v22/n10/sand01_.html>.

Sardar, Ziauddin, *Desperately Seeking Paradise: Journeys of a Sceptical Muslim* (Granta, 2004).

Sardar, Ziauddin, and Wyn Davies, Merryl, *Distorted Imaginations: Lessons from the Rushdie Affair* (Grey Seal Books, 1990).

Scarman, Lord, *The Scarman Report: The Brixton Disorders, 10–12 April, 1981* (Penguin, 1982).

Scripsi, 'An interview with Salman Rushdie', *Scripsi* 3 (2–3) (1985).

Shahabuddin, Syed, 'Open Letter to Salman Rushdie', *Times of India*, 13 October 1988; reprinted in Appignanesi and Maitland (eds.), *The Rushdie File*, pp.45–49.

Simmons, John (ed.), *The Wikipedia Muhammad Cartoons Debate* (Iraq Museum International, 2006), <http://www.baghdadmuseum.org/ wikipedia/wmcd01_060210.pdf>.

Smith, Graham, and Stephenson, Susan, 'The Theory and Practice of Group Representation: Reflections on the Politics of Race Equality in Birmingham', *Public Administration*, 83 (1995), pp.323–43.

Spitalfields Housing and Planning Rights Service, *Bengalis and GLC Housing Allocation in E1* (1982).

Spitalfields Housing and Planning Rights Service, *Bengalis and GLC Housing Allocation in E1: An Update Report* (1984.)

Stephen, James Fitzjames, *A History of the Criminal Law of England* (Routledge, 1996).

Steyn, Mark, *America Alone: The End of the World as We Know It* (Washington: Regnery Publishing, 2006).

Taylor, Charles, *A Secular Age* (Harvard University Press, 2007).

Tompson, Keith, *Under Siege: Racial Violence in Britain Today* (Penguin, 1988).

Various, '11 September', *London Review of Books*, 4 October 2001.

Vulliamy, Ed, 'Rumours of a Riot', *Guardian*, 29 November 2005.

Wazir, Burhan, '7/7: One Year on', *The Times*, 4 July 2006.

Webster, Richard, *A Brief History of Blasphemy: Liberalism, Censorship and 'The Satanic Verses'* (Orwell Press, 1990).

Weldon, Fay, *Sacred Cows* (Chatto & Windus, 1989).

Wheatcroft, Geoffrey, 'Arise Sir Salman', *Slate*, 20 June 2007, <http://www.slate.com/id/2168759/pagenum/all/>.

Whitney, Craig R., 'Britain, in Talk Aimed at Iran, Calls Rushdie Book Offensive', *New York Times*, 3 March 1989.

Whittle, Peter, 'Islam: The Silence of the Arts', *The New Culture Forum*, <http://www.newcultureforum.org.uk/home/?q=node/136>.

Williams, Rowan, 'Civil and Religious Law in England: A Religious

Perspective', foundation lecture at the Royal Courts of Justice, 7 February 2008, <http://www.archbishopofcanterbury.org/1575>.

Wilson, Amrit, *Finding a Voice: Asian Women in Britain* (Virago, 1978).

Wolfe, Tom, *Mauve Gloves and Madmen, Clutter & Vine* (Farrar, Straus & Giroux, 1976).

Women Against Fundamentalism, 'The Rushdie Affair', *WAF Journal*, 1 (1990).

Woodhead, Linda, and Riis, Ole, 'Religion and Emotion', in Furseth and Leer-Salvesen (eds.), *Religion in Late Modernity*, pp.153–69.

Zakaria, Fareed, *The Post-American World* (W.W. Norton & Company, 2008).

Acknowledgements

My thanks to all those whose memories and arguments I have plundered in the course of writing this book, including Monica Ali, Lisa Appignanesi, Sher Azam, Inayat Bunglawala, Mukhtar Dar, Frances D'Souza, Ali Hussein, Sherry Jones, Nasser Khader, Pervaiz Khan, Hanif Kureishi, Peter Mayer, William Nygaard, Ziauddin Sardar, Amartya Sen, Ghayasuddin Siddiqui, Bünyamin Simsek and Joy Warmington. I am particularly grateful to those who were generous with their time despite disagreeing with my views.

The man to whose work I am most in debt is, of course, Salman Rushdie himself. This book is not written, however, with his blessing. He felt he had already talked and written too much about the fatwa and its legacy and did not want to rake over old ground again. I hope, though, that he sees *From Fatwa to Jihad* as more than simply replaying old debates, and that in thinking again about the Rushdie affair it also helps us to rethink some of the most urgent political issues of the day.

Monica Ali, Toby Andrew, Lisa Appignanesi, John Gillott, Jo Glanville, Pervaiz Khan and Hanif Kureishi all read various parts of the manuscript and provided valuable comments. Toby Mundy, at Atlantic Books, has as ever been unstinting in his support and enthusiasm for the project, and sharp in his critical advice.

Finally a special thought for Martin Rynja, of Gibson Square Books. In September 2008 I met him to talk about free speech and *The Satanic Verses*. Within a week his home was firebombed and he was forced into hiding. Why? Because he was about to publish *The Jewel of Medina*, a novel about the Prophet Muhammad's wife Aisha deemed by some to be 'offensive'. His plight is eloquent testimony both to the continuing relevance of the Rushdie affair and to the urgent need for an open debate on the issues it raised – free speech, multiculturalism, radical Islam, the meaning of liberalism, the limits of tolerance. I hope it will not be long before we are able to resume our conversation.

Index

'TSV' indicates *The Satanic Verses*